Children of Wrath

Children
of
Wrath

Political Violence in Northern Ireland

MICHAEL MACDONALD

Polity Press

© Michael MacDonald, 1986

First published 1986 by Polity Press, Cambridge, in association with Basil Blackwell, Oxford.

Editorial Office:
Polity Press, Dales Brewery, Gwydir Street, Cambridge CB1 2LJ, UK.

Basil Blackwell Ltd, 108 Cowley Road, Oxford OX4 1JF, UK.

Basil Blackwell Inc., 432 Park Avenue South, Suite 1503, New York, NY 10016, USA.

British Library Cataloguing in Publication Data

MacDonald, Michael
    Children of wrath: political violence in
    Northern Ireland.
    1. Violence—Northern Ireland—History
    2. Northern Ireland—Politics and government
    I. Title
    322.4'2   DA990.U46

    ISBN 0–7456–0219–3

Library of Congress Cataloging in Publication Data
MacDonald, Michael.
    Children of wrath.

    Originally presented as the author's thesis (doctoral).
    Bibliography: p.
    Includes index.
    1. Northern Ireland—History. 2. Northern Ireland—
Politics and government. 3. Violence—Northern Ireland—
History. I. Title
DA 990.U46M133   1986   941.6   86–8193
ISBN 0–7456–0219–3

Typeset by Cambrian Typesetters, Frimley, Surrey
Printed in Great Britain

Dedicated to the memory of my friend Harry Maines

Contents

Preface

Some conflicts come and go; others endure. The one that has preoccupied Northern Ireland for the past generation is obviously of the intractable variety, so much so that the mere mention of 'Northern Ireland' conjures up images of mindless violence. The conventional wisdom about Northern Ireland, as advanced by British authorities and publicized by the news media, is that a few 'terrorists' have inflicted their fanaticism on the excitable but otherwise moderate people of Northern Ireland. The violence is blamed mainly on the pathologies of the 'men of violence,' though partial responsibility is assigned to the bigotry, obsession with history and general bloody-mindedness of the Northern Irish. Unfortunately this story has been repeated so often that it has become a cliché, saying little and explaining less. True, comparatively few people participate directly in the violence and few prefer war to peace. And true, prejudice is ensconced in Northern Ireland. But it does not follow that the violence is irrational.

The problem with the standard explanations of Northern Ireland's violence is that they fail to explain why an ostensibly small gang of 'gunmen' has been able to capture large communities despite continuing efforts by Britain to repress them. Clearly the 'terrorism' cannot be dismissed as the work of a handful of psychopaths and popular support for it cannot be discounted with facile claims that the Northern Irish 'live in the past.' Such condescension not only implies more extensive backing for 'terrorists' than conventional wisdom wants to admit, but also begs the question of why past divisions exert powerful influence in Northern Ireland today. The 'gunmen' would have passed into oblivion by now were they not sustained by entrenched social and political structures. Unless these structures are identified, 'responsible' opinion condemns violence without examining its causes. In the belief that such condemnations reveal more about the nature of self-righteousness than about Northern Ireland, this

book examines the whys and wherefores of Northern Ireland's
violence. This book is an analysis of the logic of a difficult subject, not
a celebration of sweet reason.

Chapter 1 opens by addressing the central questions of the politics
of Northern Ireland. If Protestants and Catholics are – and have for
some time been – fighting, what are the stakes and why have they been
unable to resolve their differences? Are these really religious communities motivated by religious concerns or are they something
different? The argument developed in the introduction suggests that
religion refers to colonial status as well as confessional preferences.
Catholics are the descendants of the native population, Protestants of
the settlers. When invested with this significance, the political
implications of religion become clear: the conflict that appears to be
about religion is really about the vestiges of colonial privileges which
Protestants retain over Catholics. Thus Northern Ireland's social
order fosters invidious distinctions: Protestants hold one status and
Catholics suffer another.

Chapter 2 explores how and why these privileges evolved, focusing
particularly on the interaction of two conflicts: those of Protestant
versus Catholic and of Protestant versus Britain. It is suggested that
Britain granted Protestants land, power, and status in the hope that
they would help Britain secure control over Ireland. Britain's strategy,
however, inadvertently fostered an extremely contradictory social and
political order in Ireland. Because Protestants received privileges in
exchange for their loyalty to Britain, and because Protestant loyalty
was salient to Britain only in contrast to Catholic disloyalty, Britain
provided Protestants with a powerful incentive to maximize their
value to Britain by denying Catholics social, economic, and political
equality. When in the nineteenth century Britain finally tired of the
costs of this logic, it attempted to include Catholics in the governing of
Ireland, only to be frustrated by Protestants who feared for the
privileges that had come to shape their community. With Britain
unable to reconcile Protestants and Catholics, it partitioned Ireland
and created Northern Ireland.

Chapter 3 addresses the politics of Northern Ireland in its period of
effective autonomy from 1921–69 and pays particular attention to the
ruling Unionist Party. The Unionist Party was comprised of diverse
groups of Protestants, which were integrated into a united party
through the active exclusion of Catholics. Catholics were treated as
adversaries to be controlled, not as constituencies to be represented. In
the face of Protestant unity, Catholics could do little to change

matters: their protests only confirmed the solidarity of Protestants. But the Unionist Party did suffer one hidden weakness; by depending on the disloyalty of Catholics to mediate its internal differences, it was extremely vulnerable to a movement of Catholics which professed loyalty to the state. When Catholics did precisely this in the civil rights movement of the 1960s, the Unionist Party fragmented under the pressure. Events slipped beyond the Party's control and Northern Ireland erupted in violence.

Chapter 4 analyzes the politics of Northern Ireland from the late 1960s through the early 1980s. It suggests that the civil rights advocates undermined Protestant solidarity by pressing for reforms that, while apparently moderate, actually challenged the inequality at the heart of Northern Ireland's politics. When their proposals\provoked Protestant violence, the pattern of Northern Ireland's politics was set for the next 15 years. Protestants were committed to maintaining the vestiges of their privileges, Catholics to overturning them. Between these mutually exclusive demands, Britain oscillated between reform and repression before eventually deciding to cut its losses by minimizing its involvement in Northern Ireland. But Britain's inability to implement either reforms or viable political institutions carries a high cost. It leaves few alternatives to violence and allows the Provisional Irish Republican Army to become a central actor in Northern Ireland.

Chapter 5 suggests that the appeal of republicans to significant numbers of Catholics reflects the failure of Britain to overcome the refusal of Protestants to share power with 'moderate' Catholics. In undermining moderates, Britain effectively vindicates the demand of republicans for an independent and united republic. It might seem that since republicans have fared little better, and often much worse than moderates, that they too would wither in the face of repeated defeats. But republicanism has developed a most tenacious ethos, one that allows it to count even its most ignominious 'failures' as 'successes' if they reaffirm the ideal of an independent and united Ireland. In spite of its romanticism, republicanism is determined, perhaps overdetermined, by Northern Ireland's most fundamental political and social relations. Republicanism begins by reacting to unionism and comes to reinforce it: their relationship is truly symbiotic.

Chapter 6 discusses why Protestants have rejected broadly based institutions designed to undercut republicans. These have often been proposed by Britain, and the fate of two of them – home rule in 1912– 14 and power-sharing in 1974 – is analyzed in terms of the relations of

Protestants to Britain and to Catholics. It is suggested that the reforms Britain advocates, by soliciting Catholic allegiance to the prevailing institutions, would jeopardize the discrepancy between Protestant loyalty and Catholic disloyalty at the heart of Protestant superiority. In this manner the conflict comes full circle; Protestants begin by excluding moderate Catholics from political power, which plays into the hands of militant republicans, which then 'justifies' the exclusion of Catholics in the first place. That this process is not some freak of Northern Ireland's politics is shown by a tentative comparison of Northern Ireland with South Africa. In both societies, the imperative to exclude and antagonize the native population is rooted in the structure of settler colonialism.

This analysis does not lead to predictions of happy endings. Rather than design a pleasing but impractical resolution of Northern Ireland's conflict, this work seeks to put the pieces of the puzzle into a coherent whole, to show the logic of a conflict that has, so far, managed to frustrate all the participants. In the concluding chapter, various contemporary proposals for Northern Ireland's future are evaluated, but few of these proposals get to the core of the conflict. The conflict has been going on in one form or another for four hundred years. There is no compelling reason to believe that it will end soon.

I now know why it is said that writing is the most social as well as private of activities. Many people have spent much time contributing directly or indirectly to this project – more time, perhaps, than is justified by the final product.

Ron, Dennis, Paul, and Eamon helped show me around Belfast, gracefully tolerating what must have been dumb questions and providing trusted friends in an unfamiliar environment. They personified the warmth and friendship that I will always associate with Belfast. In California, where I did most of the writing, Mary Dietz, Gregg Kvistad, and Bill Teterault read various chapters with sensitivity and care, and offered encouragement when the tedium of writing a dissertation became dispiriting. My thesis committee of Hanna Pitkin and Kenneth Jowitt was helpful and supportive, with Hanna setting standards of scholarship that I rarely reached but learned to respect, and Ken understanding what I meant to say and helping me to say it. And I must thank Dan Hallin who, I fear, sometimes read drafts more carefully than I wrote them, and who was an irreplaceable friend and critic. In Massachusetts, Wendy Brown has been a careful reader and an invaluable friend, offering far more than appears here. Two students at Williams College, Brad Shipp and Chris Sayler, served as research assistants, helping me to finalize the manuscript and putting up patiently with one request after another.

The political science departments at the University of California at Berkeley, the University of California at Santa Cruz, and Williams College furnished timely and essential financial assistance. Joel Krieger provided helpful editorial advice.

Finally, I would like to thank my parents for all their help and, most of all, Robin, for making this book possible.

Part I

1

The Luck of the Irish

I am haunted by the human chimpanzees I saw along that hundred miles of horrible country. I don't believe they are our fault. I believe there are not only many more of them than of old, but they are happier, better, more comfortably fed and lodged under our rule than they ever were. But to see white chimpanzees is dreadful; if they were black, one would not feel it so much, but their skins, except where tanned by exposure, are as white as ours.

Charles Kingsley, nineteenth-century Cambridge historian
describing a visit to Ireland

I

Political violence is a fact of daily life in Northern Ireland. It can strike anyone, anywhere, anytime. Drinking in a pub, travelling to work, sitting at home – no one is safe. Numbers alone cannot convey the danger, although the more than 2,300 who have died and the 24,000 injured in 43,000 separate bombings, shootings, and arsons represent a considerable toll for Northern Ireland's population of 1.5 million.[1] These casualties, compiled day after day for the better part of the past two decades, both express Northern Ireland's abiding political divisions and militate against their resolution. So pervasive and permanent has violence become that it serves less to change than to define Northern Ireland. The politics of Northern Ireland, as someone once remarked, is that of 'the last atrocity.'

The question is: why has this state of affairs emerged, why, in an integral part of the United Kingdom, has violence become the central fact of political life? On the surface, it seems most anomalous; endemic political violence is generally associated with societies caught between development and underdevelopment, unable to complete the shift from a traditional to a modern social order.[2] This hardly describes

Northern Ireland, for the simple reason that conflict, and more strikingly, violence, has preceeded, accompanied, and succeeded industrialization, parliamentary democracy, and the movement from 'traditional' to 'modern' forms of social organization. The parties to the conflict – Protestants and Catholics – are old, not new, rivals; they have both existed in Ireland for nearly four centuries, and for little of this period has the relationship been harmonious. Conflict between Protestants and Catholics cannot, in other words, be seen as an unfortunate concomitant of change but must instead be recognized as an unchanging part of Ulster's social order.[3] It is the rule, not the exception.

The question, then, persists: why, despite the trappings of 'modernity,' does fundamental conflict continue to dominate the politics of Northern Ireland? Religion obviously plays a paramount role in fostering and sustaining Northern Ireland's conflict, but if the importance of religion is beyond dispute, the same cannot be said of its meaning. That Protestants and Catholics are locked now as before in conflict is most certainly true, but it is not clear what this means. For it does not follow from their antagonism that Protestants and Catholics are therefore fighting about religion, or even that the groups identified as 'Protestant' and 'Catholic' are defined by religion alone. Indeed, two things illustrate the problem with such conclusions. First, conflict between Protestants and Catholics is scarcely normal in Western Europe, and so must be explained in something other than religious terms when it does occur. And secondly, in Northern Ireland people remain members of their 'religious' groups even if they drop their religion (thus ordinary speech recognizes that there are 'Protestant' and 'Catholic' atheists). This suggests that something more than religious affiliation forges the communities opposing each other in Northern Ireland. What is this 'more' and why does it result in endemic conflict?

The task, however, is not only to determine who are in conflict, and why, but also the reasons that the conflict has proved so intractable. Just because Protestants and Catholics, whoever they may be, are fighting, for whatever their reasons, does not mean that the dispute should be non-negotiable. After all, adversaries often reach agreements that, though not solving fundamental problems, at least contain them within manageable limits; that is what pluralist democracy is supposed to be all about. But such has not been the case in Northern Ireland. Even during periods of relative peace, there has been remarkably little consensus as to the legitimacy of the social order.

The Catholic minority of Northern Ireland, a full third of the population, may for prolonged periods have coexisted with the two-thirds Protestant majority without overt violence, but coexistence has never implied mutual acceptance of the status quo. Even during times of apparent stability, Northern Ireland was potentially – and perhaps fundamentally – unstable. So again the question of why poses itself: why has a compromise not been struck that allows the parties, whatever their other differences, to act together in matters of common concern?

It will be argued here that it is the lack of a consensual social order, and not, as some are wont to claim, a few terrorists in dire need of civics lessons that produces Northern Ireland's intense political violence. Its scope and duration indicate as much; were the violence not deeply rooted, it would have withered away by now. It thrives because Northern Ireland has two communities that are defined in contrast to each other: each community identifies itself as much by what it is not as by what it is, and what each is not is, above all else, the other. With the two communities set in opposition, intense conflict is built into the social order. Yet most scholarly work on Northern Ireland underplays the structural bases of the conflict, viewing the conflict instead as essentially unreasonable, as the result of tragic bigotry. If only, the thinking runs, reason could triumph over emotion, then moderates could gradually establish effective pluralist institutions. History suggests, however, that Northern Ireland's social order is unreceptive to pluralism and that attempts to reduce the violence by representing the aggrieved community in the decision-making processes precipitate disorders far worse than the normal violence.[4] This failure of institutional solutions, though quite disconcerting to the British government, stresses that the problem is more than individual 'terrorists'; the problem is a social order that renders 'terrorism' entirely commonplace.

The few mainstream scholarly analyses that seriously seek to connect the conflict with the social structure generally end up suggesting that religion – and religion alone – polarizes Northern Ireland. They begin with the perfectly accurate observation that Northern Ireland is divided into two hostile communities – one Protestant, the other Catholic. They then, with considerably less accuracy, go on to conclude that religion therefore causes the division. The conclusion, however, is not as apodictic as the explanations pretend; simply because polarization occurs along relgious lines does not mean that religion does the polarizing. That same polarization might be explained differently; religion might express as well as foster Northern Ireland's divisions. The meaning of religion is, again, the problem, but while it is unclear exactly how and why religion antagonizes the two communities, it is clear that religion has developed its meaning in a context that associated it with deeply secular interests and identities. The two 'religious' communities are separated by political, socio-economic, and cultural as well as religious differences. Thus to isolate religion from its context is to obscure the reasons, hardly self-evident, why religion has come to play the divisive role it obviously plays in Northern Ireland.

Religion in Ireland is enmeshed in, not insulated from, the social world. This is, of course, true in most societies, but has been especially true of Ireland from the time that Protestants established control over both state power and economic production in the seventeenth century. It was not until the late nineteenth and early twentieth centuries that Catholics finally overturned Protestant hegemony in most of Ireland, and even then Protestant domination remained intact in the area that became Northern Ireland. Thus historically Irish religions have conveyed deeply irreligious meanings: Protestantism meant privilege, while Catholicism implied deprivation. And because those equations have been – and indeed still are – upheld in Northern Ireland, the conflict that appears as religious becomes much more. It expresses the contradiction between powerful and powerless, as well as Protestant and Catholic.

Rather than competing interests more or less neutralizing each other in a universe of shifting coalitions, Northern Ireland reproduces one fundamental contradiction politically, socially, and religiously. Cleavages are mutually reinforcing, overlapping, and consistent, not cross-cutting, countervailing, and inconsistent. What must be explained, therefore, is what systematically sets Protestants and Catholics against each other. It is clearly not just religion; religion matters, but so do the interests with which it is connected. What matters most is what built privilege into the social order and conferred it on Protestants at the expense of Catholics, what brooked no mediation of the resulting conflicts, and thus what pitted Protestants and Catholics in irreconcilable contradiction. What counts is, in a word, colonialism: Protestants were colonizers, while Catholics were colonized. The conflict that appears as simply religious is at heart colonial, with the colonial actors donning religious attire to contest an order that systematically favors one and subordinates the other. This order must, as a condition of its existence, maintain the dichotomy between the two constituent communities, which means distinguishing between the privileged settlers and the deprived natives. It is the curse of religion in Ireland that it can draw the necessary distinction. Religion identifies the antagonistic communities that colonialism created.[5]

The point, however, is not that religion has no importance other than distinguishing settlers from natives – it does – but that because each community shares more than religion, each is more than a religious community. Yet each community defines itself in terms of religion, and it matters that this rather than some other characteristic – like race – identifies the communities to themselves and their adversaries. For Catholics the emphasis on religion invests immense authority in the Catholic Church, which expresses their collective identity: to be 'Irish' is, more or less, to be Catholic.[6] This association of religion with nationality permits the Church to speak on behalf of the 'nation,' giving it a powerful voice in the secular as well as the spiritual concerns of Catholics. In this respect Ireland resembles Poland; in one as in the other, an imperialist power to the east attacked the nation through its religion, which effectively made Catholicism synonymous with what it meant to be Irish or Polish. Thus the Church could pursue its interests without fear of anti-clerical challenges in the name of the 'nation.' But even this considerable clerical authority was prepared by political more than religious relations; the Church can claim to represent the Irish (or the Poles) largely because Britain (or the tsars) attempted to destroy the coherence of local culture by destroying the Church: the religious context is in both cases politicized by the invader.

The meaning of Protestantism is also deeply political in Ireland. Though Protestants obviously lack an institutional counterpart to the Catholic Church, Protestantism nonetheless integrates Protestants into one cohesive communal identity. Because Protestants understand, define, identify, themselves as Protestant (rather than, for example, as whites or English-speakers), Protestantism expresses what it is that molds Protestants of different classes, even sects, into one community.[7] This does not necessarily imply that Protestantism forms the collective identity but that it is believed to form it, a belief that, not incidentally, helps sanctify privileges that might otherwise appear less than righteous. Yet even though both Protestants and Catholics identify themselves through religion, and even though important implications follow from this as opposed to some other means of identification, the fact remains that the communities thus identified were – and are – forged by much else besides. They are colonial as well as religious.

The argument, then, is that the actors, stakes, and logics of the conflict in Northern Ireland are shaped by the legacy of colonialism. The actors are Protestant 'settlers' versus Catholic 'natives'; the stakes involve power and privilege and not merely religion; and the logic of the resulting conflict reinforces the poles at the expense of the middle. Religion serves, therefore, to reproduce the original and dominant conflict between the native and settler populations. The conflict became so tenacious because the Protestants were privileged by Britain since they, unlike Catholics, would act in British interests. Thus Britain inadvertently initiated a peculiar logic. Whereas the elites of most societies would prefer full to partial legitimacy, Northern Ireland's Protestants are threatened by the mere prospect of extended legitimacy. The point is not that other societies achieve full legitimacy, or even that it is actively pursued, but only that most elites would want full legitimacy were it available at an affordable price. In contrast, Protestants in Northern Ireland justified their political power and social privileges on the grounds of their 'loyalty' and Catholic 'disloyalty' to the established social order. The catch is that Protestant 'loyalty' is meaningful only in contradistinction to the 'disloyalty' of Catholics. Thus Protestants, especially the more marginal ones, have developed an enduring stake in sustaining the disloyalty of Catholics, even at the cost of chronic instability and violence. Violence poses less of a danger to some Protestants than does the threat of a social order accepted as legitimate by Catholics.

Hence the apparent 'irrationality' of Northern Irish politics: fundamental interests and identities not only lead to conflict but depend on it. To be Protestant is to be privileged; to be privileged is to require that Catholics be visibly deprived; and to deprive Catholics is to build the social order on overt as well as covert domination. Thus rather than a liberal society invoking universal 'rights' (whatever the objective inequalities), Northern Ireland is a colonial one based on invidious and abiding privileges. It is this, far more than religion, that constitutes the key to understanding Northern Ireland's politics.

II

Most interpretations of Northern Ireland either ignore or misunderstand colonialism. Those ignoring it usually claim that Northern Ireland's communities are fundamentally religious in nature, and are therefore fighting for religious reasons. But this overstates the importance of religion, for religion is not all that distinguishes – or antagonizes – the two communities, and to pretend otherwise is to rip religion from its historical, political, and socio-economic context. The point is understood by the second, socialist interpretation; what it does not grasp is the way religion fits into its context. Religion in this view is claimed to count not because it identifies real communities but because it creates them (more or less) artificially. In contending that religion represents false consciousness, however, the socialists end up isolating religion from its colonial context. Thus religion neither (as one interpretation would have it) constitutes nor (as the other suggests) conceals the context: instead, it expresses a larger whole.

The analyst who assigns the greatest weight to religion in Northern Ireland is probably Richard Rose. Rose has written two books and numerous papers on Northern Ireland, but his first book, *Governing Without Consensus*, contains the nucleus of his thinking. In 1968 (the year before the current wave of violence began in earnest), Rose conducted a series of interviews designed to determine the authority of the Northern Ireland government (Stormont) among its subjects. He discovered the obvious: Stormont's authority was divided. Protestants recognized it; Catholics repudiated it. Specifically, 68 percent of Protestants as opposed to 33 percent of Catholics approved the constitution of Northern Ireland.[8] This finding, that support for the government broke down along religious lines, should provoke little controversy. What is problematic, however, is *why* authority broke down in this manner. Rose assumes, but does not establish, that the two communities distinguished by religion are fighting *about* religion. 'What [Protestants and Catholics] disagree about is whether [Northern Ireland] should be a Protestant Christian or a Catholic Christian country.'[9] Religion, for Rose, causes the divisions that politics registers.

Rose's emphasis on the centrality of religion is curious in light of some of his other findings. If, for example, the Irish are fighting over religion, then it is to be expected that the correlation between religious fervor and political commitment would be high, or at least noteworthy. It is also to be expected that, if religion is really at stake, then members of both religions would be intolerant of the other's teachings. However, Rose's empirical findings disappoint the theoretical expectations that he raises; he finds that religious fervor has very little to do with political commitment, and that members of both religions are generally indifferent to the other's teachings.[10] These findings, though inconsistent with Rose's emphasis on the primacy of religion, do fit consistently with his evidence that religion is tied to national identity.

His survey indicates that while the overwhelming majority of Catholics regard themselves as Irish, only 20 percent of Protestants believe themselves to be Irish; the remaining 80 percent consists of 39 percent who think that they are British, 32 percent Ulster, and 9 percent who are not sure what they are.[11] But though Protestants disagree about who they are, they agree in professing loyalties consistent with their primacy in Northern Ireland. Whether they consider themselves British, Ulster, or even Irish, Protestants embrace politically what Catholics regard as foreign domination. Rose's statistics, in other words, suggest that there is as much, if not more, reason to call Northern Ireland's problems national as religious.

The problem, of course, is that Northern Ireland's divisions are neither only religious nor only national; they are both. Religion and nationality do not exist as two independent variables that sometimes correlate, but rather as two halves of one identity welded together by history. Catholics are generally the descendants of the indigenous Irish, while Protestants descend from Anglo-Scottish settlers. With neither religion nor nationality independent of the other, it is misleading for Rose to claim that 'Protestanism and Catholicism have created two communities.'[12] Rose understands Northern Ireland's problems to result from divided authority, but he grasps only the religious and not the colonial reasons for its divisions. He can correlate religion with political allegiance but cannot account for the correlation he uncovers: Rose does not explain *why* religion ties together with nationality to produce the divided authority which he believes to be the crux of Northern Ireland's problems.

While Rose tends to document the obvious sectarianism and ignore the more problematic reasons behind it, Conor Cruise O'Brien tries to understand what has made sectarianism into such an obvious part of everyday life in Northern Ireland. In *States of Ireland*, O'Brien presents a highly personalistic account of the violence exploding just as he was writing his book in 1971. Like Rose, O'Brien emphasizes the role played by religion in polarizing Northern Ireland, but unlike Rose, O'Brien hints at the connection of religion with other historical forces. Unfortunately, O'Brien does not develop his hints into a fully fledged argument; to the contrary, he backs off from them, aborting his insights and embracing a predominantly religious interpretation of Northern Ireland's conflict. Nonetheless, O'Brien's points can be sketched for future use, though it must be admitted that O'Brien himself repudiates the uses to which they will be put.

O'Brien assumes the polarization that Rose demonstrates. That Protestants and Catholics are now, and have long been, at odds is given; the problem is to understand what the terms 'Protestant' and 'Catholic' mean. O'Brien believes that their meanings are complex. While it is true to say that Protestants and Catholics are in conflict, he suggests that the use of religious terms may unduly stress the religious nature of a quarrel which is not altogether religious. Religion, he points out, is less important for what it is than for what it indicates.

> [T]he distinct communities indicated by the terms 'Catholic' and 'Protestant' are the prime realities of the situation. This is not the same as saying that religion is the main factor. Religious affiliation, in Ireland, is the rule of thumb by which one can distinguish between the people of native, Gaelic stock (Catholics) and those of settler stock from Scotland and England (Protestants).[13]

Religion is a sign, an expression, a 'rule of thumb' signifying the more basic difference between natives and settlers. It does not so much forge as identify Northern Ireland's two communities.

In arguing that religion is the means by which the more fundamental colonial contradictions are expressed, O'Brien equates its role in Irish history with the role played by race and color in colonial Africa and America.

> In regions like America and Africa, where the settlers were marked off from the natives by visible differences in pigmentation and other physical characteristics, the criterion presented no problem: a good light was all that was required. But in Ireland there were surely no distinguishable physical differences between the natives and the settlers. Genetically they were of the same mixed stock. The criteria [were] theological: settlers were Protestants, natives Catholics.[14]

With religion serving to manifest more basic colonial differences, its political salience would seem to be primarily derivative: religion is important because colonialism made it important. It identified the real, but otherwise unidentifiable, adversary. This rather unchristian function results from the seventeenth-century settlement that 'continues to dominate every aspect of the life of the region affected, and to permeate the politics of the whole island.'[15] As a result of that settlement the colonizers enjoyed – and enjoy still – economic, political, and social superiority over Catholic natives.

O'Brien's views as described thus far would suggest that he believes Northern Ireland's conflict to be fundamentally colonial. His use of terms like 'native' and 'settler,' his emphasis on religion as the means by which natives were distinguished from settlers, and his linkage of religion and political allegiance with economic positions deriving from the colonial settlement, would seem to lead O'Brien to interpret Northern Ireland in terms of colonialism. O'Brien, however, backs off; he rejects more than he accepts of the colonial interpretation.

> To say that it is a conflict of *settlers* and *natives* is to tell an important part of the truth, but only a part. It was a Reformation settlement in Counter-reformation territory. What kept alive the difference over the centuries, over a major change of language (among Catholics), and over the vast changes brought about by the industrial revolution – taking so many 'settlers' and 'natives' alike from the land they had fought over – was the factor of religion inseparably intertwined with political allegiance. . . . So we are brought back, inescapably, to what so many people seek to deny: the rather obvious fact of a conflict between groups defined by *religion*.[16]

Why O'Brien concludes by emphasizing religion over colonialism is unclear. It seems that he believes that despite the still 'dominant' character of the colonial settlement, colonialism itself is no longer divisive. When – and why – it stopped dividing is unspecified, but its importance now is only residual: colonialism matters because it defined religion in a way which, despite the passage of colonialism itself, still poisons religion.

The conclusion is not persuasive. That the communities are 'defined' by religion does not mean that they were created by, or are fighting because of, religion. O'Brien himself emphasizes that the communities identified by religion would exist separately and antagonistically even without the religious dimension. They are, because of privilege and deprivation, divided by more than religion. And to pretend, as does O'Brien, that the material contradictions are dissolved by religion is to overlook his most important point: religion identifies, rather than creates, the antagonists.

O'Brien emphasizes the prominence of religion in Northern Ireland's politics largely in response to the socialist republican emphasis on imperialism. Since James Connolly in the late nineteenth and early twentieth centuries, socialist republicans have contended that British imperialists and their mostly, but not exclusively, Protestant allies maintain political control over Northern Ireland (and historically over all of Ireland) in order to protect economic interests. The exact nature of those interests is murky,[17] but the socialist republicans believe that they involve the exploitation of Protestant along with Catholic workers. While the socialist republicans certainly do not mean to say that Protestants are exploited as harshly as Catholics, they do suggest that the exploitation of Protestants and Catholics alike portends the possibility of a working-class unity that would destroy the system of exploitation that truly benefits only the ruling class. To prevent the working-class unity that they themselves might cause, capitalist elites pursue a 'divide and conquer' strategy, deliberately fabricating the false but very useful belief that Protestant and Catholic workers have antithetical interests. Thus the religious divisions that Rose and O'Brien believe to be causal are for the socialist republicans only false constructs which split an otherwise united working class.

Socialist republicans believe that the conflict between Protestant and Catholic workers results more from elite machinations than from the structure of the situation. Were they not willfully divided by the exploiters, the two working classes would be one; as Liam de Paor argues, 'the working class in Ulster was divided, and the division was fostered and maintained by middle- and upper-class interests.'[18] Socialist republicans, therefore, confront an obvious problem: why, if religious divisions are essentially fabricated, have they proved so intractable? Socialist republicans answer that Protestant workers are favored over Catholics, especially in employment and housing, and that such discrimination divides the working class, 'giving Protestants a small but real advantage, and creating a Protestant "aristocracy of labour." '[19] Such advantages distract Protestant workers from the interests they share with Catholic workers, turning them against their real class and national interests. Thus for socialist republicans sectarianism conceals rather than reveals the central contradiction in Northern Ireland.

Socialist republicans admit, indeed emphasize, that the interests of Protestant and Catholic workers sometimes conflict. But such conflicts seem insignificant to them in view of the interests shared by Protestant and Catholic workers.[20] Were Protestant workers not duped by false consciousness, they would follow the interests disposing them to act with Catholic workers. The problem for socialist republicans, however, is that Protestant workers have a much greater stake in sectarianism than socialist republicans imagine. The gains that would accrue to Catholics from the demise of colonialism would most likely come at the expense of Protestant workers. Not only do Protestants hold jobs which Catholics do in fact covet, but those jobs tie Protestant workers to the British economy. The heavy engineering and shipbuilding sectors that produce the 'aristocracy of labor' have historically depended on British markets, and now depend on British subsidies. With Protestant workers dependent on Britain for their jobs, it is obvious that the Catholic demand for independence jeopardizes Protestant working-class interests as much as does the Catholic demand for equal access to jobs. The point, then, is that the sectarianism of the Protestant working class is grounded in its deepest interests. And that contradiction, more than religion or elite chicanery, sets Northern Ireland's two communities against each other.

In consequence, the real division in Northern Ireland is not, as socialist republicans argue, between British imperialists and Irish capitalists on the one hand and Protestant and Catholic workers on the other, but between Protestants and Catholics. Liam de Paor, for example, would have it that

> 'Planters and natives' can undoubtedly come to an agreement in Ireland. . . . What keeps the sterile quarrel of Orange and Green alive is the constant pressure of the third party, Great Britain.[21]

It is, however, taxing credibility to assert that Britain still manipulates Protestants for its own economic interests; it is much more likely, given the greater interest of Protestants in Northern Ireland, that they use Britain for their purposes. Protestants are not lackeys of Britain but independent actors pursuing their interests over and against those of Britain as well as of Catholics. Analysts such as de Paor do not, however, appreciate that Protestants hold interests and identities incompatible with those of Catholics, and habitually ignore the fact that Protestant elites need not invent ways to deceive the Protestant working class. The workers are themselves quite alert to, and alarmed by, Catholic advances, for those advances necessarily come at their expense.[22] Thus it is a fundamental misunderstanding of the dynamics of Northern Ireland to attribute Protestant working-class sectarianism to the machinations of their elites; certainly the elites do plot, manipulate, and try to divide Protestants from Catholics for their own purposes, but such strategies have succeeded not because of the gullibility of Protestant workers but because of their vulnerability to Catholics.

The criticism that socialist republicanism underestimates the material and overestimates the subjective bases of Protestant working-class politics is the starting-point for the work of a trio of state theorists. Paul Bew, Peter Gibbon, and Henry Patterson have individually and collectively challenged the 'red republican' interpretation of Irish history in general and of Ulster history in particular. Rather than accepting Connolly's view that Protestant workers are corrupted by the benefits offered them by imperialism, Bew et al. stress the role of the Northern Ireland state, known as Stormont, in reconciling the Protestant working class to the rule of the Protestant bourgeoisie. Their argument is that, far from being a solid and undifferentiated whole, Protestants are comprised of distinct, even antagonistic, social classes, and that the Northern Ireland state mediates the resulting contradictions on behalf of the bourgeoisie.

Bew, Gibbon, and Patterson argue persuasively that the unionism (that is, the commitment to union with Britain) of the Protestant working class reflects the consequences of Ireland's 'uneven development.' In contrast to the agricultural and relatively underdeveloped economy in the south and west of Ireland, the northern economy was industrial and developed, which tied the Belfast working class to the British rather than to the Irish economy. Thus instead of interpreting Protestant working-class unionism as irrational (as followers of Connolly sometimes do), Bew et al. see it as the expression of legitimate class interests. These interests do not themselves compel particular political configurations, but they do assist Stormont in what Bew et al. see as its essential task of containing and defusing class conflict among Protestants. Stormont's purpose is for them the same as that of any other capitalist state: to serve as the 'political organiser and unifier of the bourgeoisie, and disorganiser and disunifier of the proletariat.'[23]

In analyzing Stormont's role in maintaining the rule of the bourgeoisie, Bew et al. address specifically 'how in Northern Ireland the local Protestant bourgeoisie gained and held power, how it maintained a bloc or alliance of classes identifying with its rule, and how it divided and oppressed the classes and groups that opposed it.'[24] Their answer is that the Northern Irish bourgeoisie ceded control to a group of professional Unionist politicians who, by elaborating 'populist' policies, reproduced bourgeois domination. In this the Unionist Party was assisted by a very favorable deal from Britain, which enabled it to contain internal differences. In particular, the Unionist government established an independent military force (called the B Specials); received British subsidies for this and other 'populist' measures; and achieved effective autonomy over strategic jurisdictions, the most important of which was law and order.[25]

Much of this argument is persuasive, particularly its emphasis on the tensions among Protestant classes, its challenge to the view that Protestant workers are mere stooges for elites, and its understanding of Protestant workers as a class with interests not only independent of, but clashing with, those of the Protestant bourgeoisie on the one hand and the Catholic working class on the other. However Bew et al. do not explain why, if the Protestant working class was linked to Britain by the same economic interests as the bourgeoisie, the bourgeoisie needs to divide the working class. Nationality would seem to have served that purpose already. They claim that 'disunity between the Protestant and Catholic working class was Unionism's *sine qua non*'[26] but with the working class fundamentally split between those allegiant to Britain and Ireland, the prospects of working-class solidarity were minimal. Not only were Protestant and Catholic workers unlikely to make common cause, but the former had nowhere to turn to for allies except to the Protestant bourgeoisie. Thus while disunity was useful in consolidating the Protestant bloc, the state hardly needed to create it: disunity was built into the very fabric of Northern Ireland.

Bew, Gibbon, and Patterson rarely address this question, however, insisting instead that Northern Ireland under the Stormont government was an 'ordinary' bourgeois democracy.[27] Insofar as they are saying that the state in capitalist society tries to minimize class conflict, and that the Northern Ireland economy remained capitalist, the point is legitimate; but they mean to go beyond this to argue that the state in Northern Ireland is essentially similar to other capitalist states. This is precisely their problem, however, for capitalist states rarely depend on deep and abiding opposition from prominent minorities of the population for the stability of the ruling coalition. In contrast to the efforts of most capitalist states to extend their legitimacy, the Unionist government fed on illegitimacy. Unless Bew et al. can explain this anomaly, unless they can explain why full legitimation seriously endangered Northern Ireland's very social order, they cannot appreciate – still less explain – the genuine perversity of Northern Ireland.

This, like other problems for Bew et al., derives from their focus on intra-Protestant class relations to the near exclusion of Protestant–

Catholic conflict. Their reference to Northern Ireland as an 'ordinary' state is symptomatic of their misunderstanding. Ignoring the fact that Stormont's dealings with Protestants took place against a background of the exclusion of Catholics from political power, they do not explain how Protestants developed an abiding stake both in protecting what they saw as rightfully theirs from Catholic encroachments, and in maintaining the discrepancy between what they enjoyed and Catholics suffered. The gap between the statuses of Protestants and Catholics constituted the perceived interests and identities of Protestants. Hence the susceptibility of the Protestant working class to sectarian appeals; its interests are not only different from those of Catholics, but depend on subordination.

The deficiencies in their analyses notwithstanding, Rose, O'Brien, the socialist republicans, and Bew et al. do make important contributions to an interpretation of Northern Ireland. Rose's emphasis on divided authority in causing conflict is central to an understanding of politics in Northern Ireland. And O'Brien's linkage of religious identities with colonial statuses helps account for the divisions Rose discovers between Protestants and Catholics in Northern Ireland. For their part, socialist republicans identify the material and psychological privileges which give rise to the political processes discussed by Bew, Gibbon, and Patterson. Unfortunately, these insights have not been integrated into a more synthetic interpretation; the points stand separately rather than jointly. It would be useful, therefore, to elaborate an analysis explaining why the divisions occur along religious lines, why they are most intense between the two working classes, and why they have proved so enduring.

III

These questions, it will be argued, are best approached in terms of the two conditions that must obtain for Protestants to preserve their privileges. First, these privileges exist only in relation to their opposites; Protestant privileges, therefore, entail Catholic deprivations. Secondly, Protestant privileges evoke Catholic protests, which are contained only through British assistance. To secure the help that they need to retain their privileges, Protestants have proclaimed their loyalty to Britain and all things British. However, as the loyalty of Protestants is salient only in contrast to the disloyalty of Catholics, Protestants have historically held a vested interest in fostering

Catholic disloyalty. These incentives, moreover, are strongest for those who depend most directly on privileges over Catholics for their status, for, that is, marginal Protestants. The Protestant laboring classes were, and still are, particularly opposed to compromises that would concede Protestant privileges, since, they fear, the privileges that would be surrendered would most likely be theirs. For these reasons Protestants in general and Protestant workers in particular defend and maintain the colonial structures that shaped the history of Ireland, and especially that of Ulster.

Ireland was England's first colony; Northern Ireland may very well prove to be its last. This fact has fated Ireland to serve as something of a laboratory for British colonial policy, as lessons learned there were applied subsequently, and often more successfully, throughout the Empire. For if British sovereignty over Ireland has proved durable, it has not been easy. Britain has been harried by resistance from the moment it entered Ireland, and while hardly insurmountable – British rule, after all, spanned over three centuries for the whole of Ireland, nearly four centuries for the area that now comprises Northern Ireland – it was, and is, vexing. The extent of Britain's involvement in Ireland stems partly from the simple proximity of one to the other; being so close, Britain's impact on Ireland has been intense as well as prolonged. It did not merely disrupt, but obliterated, traditional Ireland, imposing over the ruins a colonial order that, though enduring, was – and in Northern Ireland still is – bitterly, even violently, resisted.

It is ironic that the proximity which deepened British involvement rarely resulted in effective control over Ireland. Much of Britain's problem has been that settlers rather than administrators have effectively ruled Ireland most of the time. The difference is important. Colonial administrators generally strive to serve the interests of the home country, which usually means expanding its prestige, excluding its rivals, or extracting the resources it desires as smoothly as possible, with the first two goals entailing little direct involvement in the colony, and the third more or less directing the home country to those regions possessing whatever resources are to be extracted. Settlers, on the other hand, want to turn the colony to their purposes, not those of the home country, which leads them to adopt a very different posture towards the colony. The home country views the colony as a means to other ends, while settlers regard the colony – and especially their control over it – as the inviolable foundation of their position. That is not to deny that settlers value the prestige of the home country, appreciate the need to contain rival colonial powers, or exploit resources, nor is it to minimize the ultimate stake of colonial officials in domination, but it is to suggest that the priorities of the two actors are decidedly different. The administrator subordinates the colony to the larger interests of the colonial power, while settlers, in case of conflict with the home country, emphasize the primacy of their interests over those of the home country.

As a type, administrators generally try to root their power in existing native institutions, in the hope of minimizing the dislocation they cause. The idea is that by protecting established native authorities these can, in turn, be used to protect colonialism. It is, of course, necessary to render the protected authorities dependent on the colonial power so that they do not threaten the home country, but this can often be accomplished through bribery, co-optation, and coercion.[28] Once subordinated, though, the vanquished authorities condone, even facilitate, the home country's continuing exploitation. Thus in West Africa, for example, Britain pioneered (and France subsequently emulated) a policy of indirect rule that 'assumed that African authority groups should have an established role in colonial government.'[29]

Britain had various reasons for this policy, among them the conviction that African colonies should be self-supporting (which meant that British administrators' means were limited) and the realization that indirect was easier than direct rule. Thus, with Britain disinclined to disturb matters more than necessary, 'most African societies maintained continuity through certain basic institutions. These continued to function despite the fate of larger political units.'[30] Their leaders were not replaced but converted into 'cogwheels between the colonial authority and the native peoples,'[31] and were forced to confer an otherwise elusive legitimacy on colonialism. As one British administrator put it,

> A great chief is a very valuable possession; his authority is an instrument of the greatest public utility, which it is most desirable to retain in full force.[32]

The argument is not that British colonialism in Africa was insignificant or altruistic, but that it posited an interest in preserving most indigenous authorities. Britain sought resources, prestige, or strategic advantage in Africa, not change. Certainly Britain suppressed recalcitrant chiefs, but the removal of specific authorities is funda-

mentally different from an indiscriminate attack on the established
structure of authority.

> [C]olonial regimes themselves tended to ally with the most . . .
> submissive chiefs, the custodians of law, order and hallowed
> custom . . . After all, the main preoccupation of those regimes
> was not to carry out social reform but primarily to control and to
> maintain law and order so as to facilitate economic exploitation.[33]

Even if European powers had developed the will to reform African
societies, they did not dispatch sufficient personnel. What has been
written of the Royal Niger Company in West Africa can be applied to
administrative colonialism in general:

> Though the regime undoubtedly bore heavily, indeed oppres-
> sively, upon the Africans under its jurisdiction, its effect was . . .
> almost totally negative. Little or nothing was done to change
> society, to alter beliefs or even to develop the economy.[34]

Settler colonialism operates according to a much deeper logic. If
administrators, lacking independent interests and regarding the colony
as an assignment rather than a home, remain what the home country
devised them to be – agents acting on its behalf – settlers rapidly
develop their own stakes in what they soon come to regard as their
permanent home. Specifically, settlers demand that their superiority
be maintained even at the cost of instability. While home countries
generally shook up traditional culture as little as possible (given that
the pre-eminence of colonial interests would inevitably shake it up
considerably), settlers attacked the traditional authorities that
appeared to them as a means less of controlling than of mobilizing
native resistance. Thus by challenging the authorities that home
countries were inclined to manipulate, settler colonies extended the
logic that administrative colonies preferred to mute.

It is here that settler colonialism becomes truly peculiar, for settlers
do not attack native cultural authorities with the purpose of turning
natives into settlers. That is, settlers do not want natives to adopt their
way of life, to become like themselves, to 'go settler.' Quite the
opposite, settlers deliberately keep natives different from themselves,
undermining the independence of native authorities not because they
impede the extension of settler culture to natives but because, actually
or potentially, they threaten settler hegemony. Natives are to be

weakened, not converted. For this reason, settlers insist that, if permitted to survive, native authorities be drained of their capacity for legitimate action, especially political action. Thus, consciously or not, settlers install a social order that not only fosters native disloyalty, but also roots their central interests and identities in the continuing antagonism of natives to their institutions.

This logic is particularly compelling for those settlers who realize that they would slip to the level of natives without colonial privilege. As Albert Memmi wrote, 'the daily humiliation of the colonized' is psychological as well as economic. 'Even the poorest colonizer [thinks] himself to be – and actually [is] – superior to the colonized.'[35] For this reason those settlers most susceptible to native competition, especially workers, insist on protection from natives. With their prestige as well as their jobs at stake, working-class settlers demand discrimination. And not only does the combination of institutionalized inferiority and political powerlessness antagonize much of the native population, but the antagonism of natives enhances the salience of marginal settlers to elites. The more threatening the natives, the more strategic – and thus the better rewarded – are those settlers who provide the elites with a mass base. Thus instead of trying to minimize disruption, the logic of settler colonialism accentuates it. This, much to the chagrin of the home country, puts native–settler relations beyond its control – not to say influence. Such, certainly, has been the pattern in Ireland, where after escalating from administrative to settler colonialism, Britain found that Protestants were likely to obstruct as well as serve British purposes.

IV

England's involvement in Ireland dates back to the twelfth century, but it changed qualitatively under the Tudors. As England emerged as a Western European power with global aspirations during the sixteenth century, it feared that one of its continental rivals might use Catholicism as an entrée into Ireland, and then launch an attack across the very narrow sea separating Britain from Ireland. The worry was not unfounded, for as the Tudors strengthened England, they excited the envy of European powers which seemed quite willing, and perhaps able, to use the Catholicism shared with the Irish as the foundation for a joint attack on the English upstarts. To prevent Ireland from serving as a staging area, the Tudors resolved to secure Ireland themselves.

It took the better part of the latter half of the sixteenth century for England to conquer Ireland. But conquest, achieved in 1603, presented the crown with another problem, for the expense of occupying the conquered territory would have overburdened the crown's limited budget. In consequence, England resolved on a dual strategy. First, it endeavored to use traditional Irish authorities for its purposes, restoring land that had been confiscated in exchange for submission in the belief that the conquest of Ireland would force them to honor the pledges that their fathers had previously ignored. Secondly, England eschewed costly military occupation for less expensive colonization, planting settlers on land confiscated from Irish opponents, real or suspected.

The results of both policies were at the outset ideal from England's point of view. The crown, by confiscating the land of those contesting its authority but confirming that of those recognizing it, was able to use traditional leaders to mediate English rule; meanwhile, by allocating to settlers land seized from the Irish, the crown created what was in effect a garrison of loyalists beholden to England for their land. And if settlers forgot their debt, the threat of the dispossessed Irish masses was enough to remind them that they needed as well as owed England. With both settlers and traditional Irish authorities dependent on England, the one was to be used to balance the other, thus allowing England to accrue the benefits without the costs of occupation.

There was, however, one flaw in this strategy. Since privileges distinguished Protestants from Catholics, Protestants tended to display them as conspicuously as possible. This seemingly irrational drive to antagonize Catholics in fact expressed the logic of their position as settlers in Ireland. Protestants were superior because England, after conquering Ireland, needed them to balance the Catholic majorities. In exchange for their services, Protestants were granted supremacy because they, unlike the natives, were ostensibly loyal to England. But because Protestant loyalty was salient only in contrast to Catholic disloyalty, Protestant settlers had an incentive to maintain the disloyalty of Catholic natives. If Catholics were reconciled to colonialism, Protestants would have become superfluous and lost their claim to special privileges. Protestants were, therefore, forced by the logic of their position to encourage native disloyalty – otherwise their loyalty was of little use to their British benefactors who rewarded them so handsomely for it. The resulting provocations, especially in conjunction with events in England, precipitated traditional rebellions in the 1640s and 1680s which were suppressed only by English armies. After the second rescue in 1690, Protestants resolved that it was not enough to put down rebellions; they had to be prevented in the first place.

The crux of the problem was that native authorities and settler interests were at cross purposes, and as settlers increased their power, prestige, and landholdings, they undercut the position of the traditional leaders whom the crown would rather have used. Irish, like other, traditions rested upon what Max Weber called 'piety for what actually, allegedly, or presumably has always existed.'[36] As Irish traditions passed from one generation to the next, they became 'inviolable norms of conduct.'[37] That is not to say that the traditional Irish order was benign – Weber, after all, is talking about 'domination,' not 'legitimacy'[38] – but that it was regarded as unchangeable. If affairs were not as they should be, they were at least as they 'had' to be.

Tradition is accepted unconsciously rather than consciously, and its strength lies in the fact that its venerability makes it seem immutable. The presumed immutability of tradition was, however, precisely what colonialism challenged. Even administrative colonies trying to tread gently by mediating their influence through traditional authorities sometimes traumatized a colony. The authorities that the administrators intended to use crumbled; once essential, they became contingent as the venerability that formerly comprised the core of tradition was desecrated by the new world of colonialism.[39] And with administrative colonialism inadvertently undermining the authorities it sought to protect, the open hatred of settler colonialism was that much more destructive. Such was the case in Ireland, as Protestants attacked not only specific Irish authorities but the traditions behind them as well.

In the eighteenth century Protestants subverted all traditional Irish authorities except for the Catholic Church. This, however, freed Protestants from their dependence on Britain, which Britain sought to restore with the Act of Union in 1801. Although the union did not shift real power from the Protestants to Britain immediately, it did render Protestants dependent on British, not Protestant, institutions. This, in turn, presented Protestants with a growing problem as Britain's interest in stability diverged from their commitment to superiority even at the cost of instability. As in the seventeenth century, when the crown tried to use traditional authorities for colonial purposes, in the nineteenth century Britain moved to include into the political process 'responsible' Catholic leaders. The Catholics, because indebted to

Britain for recognition, were expected to use their credibility with the Catholic masses to restore an order more amenable to British interests than the alternative disorder. The arrangement, if well executed, might have benefited both British and Catholic elites. It did create one not insignificant drawback, however: by cutting in the Catholic colonized, it cut out the Protestant colonizers.

The British strategy of selective inclusion hinged on a proposal for home rule that would, in essence, have given Catholics the political power necessary to overturn Protestant hegemony. That, combined with the decrease in Protestant legitimacy as a function of the increase in Catholic legitimacy, convinced Protestants that the very foundations of their hegemony were in jeopardy. Naturally this threat was opposed by Protestants throughout Ireland, but only in the six north-eastern counties of Ulster were there enough of them to oppose home rule, and later independence, effectively. Thus six counties of Ulster were partitioned off from the 26 (creating Northern Ireland), and given the Stormont parliament to legislate for and administer their internal affairs.

The new statelet of Northern Ireland reflected Ireland's, and especially Ulster's, development as a settler colony in decisive ways. First, Northern Ireland's dominant social, political, and economic institutions preserved privileges for Protestants and deprivations for Catholics, making Catholic inferiority the condition of Protestant superiority. This meant that Catholic gains would necessarily come at Protestant expense, confirming the traditional zero-sum quality of Ulster politics. The resulting disloyalty of Catholics to the Northern Ireland state was then used by Protestants to justify the subordination of Catholics in the first place. While the relationship of privilege to loyalty was, of course, not as one-way as Protestants pretended (for Catholics were not only deprived because disloyal but also disloyal because deprived), the important point is that the illegitimacy of Northern Ireland's dominant institutions among Catholics was functional, not dysfunctional. In Northern Ireland after 1921 as in Ireland after 1603, Protestants had a vested interest in sustaining the Catholic disloyalty that, first, legitimated Protestant privileges; secondly, accentuated the salience of Protestant loyalty to Britain; and thirdly, provided the threat that maintained Protestant solidarity. For these reasons Protestants maintained a fundamentally dichotomous social order in Northern Ireland. Two communities defined by centuries of colonial history still confronted each other as opposites – one prosperous, politically powerful, and privileged, the other poorer, weaker, and deprived – but after partition there was one essential change: Protestants were now a majority, not a minority.

V

The three centuries of colonial history that preceded independence-cum-partition in 1921–2 had defined Northern Ireland's two constituent communities in opposition to each other, dooming one – typically the Catholic – to frustration. As the satisfaction of one community necessitated the dissatisfaction of the other, the contradiction between them became insuperable within the context of colonialism. It could of course have been solved by Protestants liquidating Catholics, or by Catholics overthrowing Protestants, but as long as Protestants enjoyed colonial privileges over Catholics, conflict was built into the social order. The containment of such conflict was the reason for the creation in 1921 of the Stormont government that, though formally subordinate to Britain, was in practice allowed to govern however it pleased as long as it kept Irish problems out of British politics. With *carte blanche* in hand, Stormont did not bother with even the pretense of appealing to Catholics. In the circumspect language of Rose, Stormont 'did not seek to make [itself] fully legitimate by attracting the support of Catholics.'[40] In the more explicit language of its first prime minister, Stormont was a 'Protestant parliament for a Protestant people.'[41] As such, it systematically excluded Catholics from positions of political power, treating them not as interest groups to be aggregated but as subversives to be controlled.

Political differences were not, however, all that opposed Protestants to Catholics. Catholics were ostracized politically because, having been ostracized economically, socially, and culturally as well, they held interests that Protestants dared not let be expressed politically. In economic terms this meant that Protestants enjoyed higher incomes, more prestigious jobs, and less unemployment than Catholics; in social terms, that Protestants were privileged in services like housing, while Catholics were relatively deprived; and in cultural terms, that Protestants segregated neighborhood and workplace. Consequently, the social structure underpinning politics was dichotomized into two opposite and hostile communities, with each political, social, and economic difference reinforcing the others. What made this dichotomy especially gripping in Northern Ireland was that Protestants were not therefore isolated on top, but suffused throughout, the social structure.

In the country as in the city, in the working class as in the elites, the Protestant majority honored the colonial imperative to segregate themselves from their opposite.

Northern Ireland's segregation was the subject of a study by Rosemary Harris in the early 1950s. Harris found that the 'social networks of any individual are based overwhelmingly in most fields on ties with his co-religionists.'[42]

> [T]here exist, in broad terms, a Protestant social sphere and a Catholic social sphere, the separation between the two being manifested in the fields of kinship, education, [and] organizational membership.[43]

> Moreover, the tendency for the society to be divided in this way is made even more marked by the fact that the cleavage between Protestant and Catholic is so strong that as a consequence an awareness of religious roles exists whenever they meet. . . . The cleavage between religious groups is such that on almost every issue, local or national, there is a Catholic viewpoint and a different, Protestant viewpoint . . . . Thus all social relationships are pervaded by a consciousness of the religious dichotomy.[44]

The dichotomy of which Harris writes consists not only of spheres and viewpoints but also of more tangible cultural institutions, like schools, neighborhoods, and families. A family is Protestant *or* Catholic – rarely both. Protestants and Catholics rarely intermarry, and the exceptions are generally isolated from their original communities.[45] This means that ties of kinship, which in Northern Ireland often serve as the basis for social gatherings, reinforce sectarian divisions. Family ties Protestants to Protestants, Catholics to Catholics. So does neighborhood; cities are divided into Protestant and Catholic areas. Such physical separation militates against easy interaction between Protestants and Catholics, partly because of the inconvenience posed by the physical distance between the two areas, partly because of the psychological separation that accompanies physical separation. The other community seems – and in fact is – foreign, and to visit its territory is traumatic and potentially dangerous. Rather than enter unknown territory, people generally stay in their own areas, preferring to mingle, and especially live with those of their own kind. As Denis Barrit and Charles Carter observed,

there is a history of faction fights in the Ulster countryside and
. . . of rioting in Belfast, and common prudence suggests that one
should live with those who can be trusted to take the same side.[46]

The history of these conflicts is of course an important part of
children's education. Fortunately for the perpetuation of each community's myths, they are learned among one's own kind. Catholics
attend Catholic schools, while Protestants attend state schools which
are *de facto* Protestant, enabling socialization to be conducted amidst
political and religious homogeneity. To quote Barrit and Carter,

The education of the communities is almost wholly separate,
except at the university level. . . . This increases the opportunity
of impressing on the youth of each community the ideas of
religion and of history commonly accepted in that group, and of
preserving them from ever having to think about an alternative
view . . . . [In] each community it is possible for young people to
grow up, knowing many people as neighbours or as school
friends, and yet having no ties of friendship with any person of
different religious persuasion.[47]

Thus, like housing and kinship, education sustains solidarity with
one's own and hostility towards the other community.

Northern Ireland's segregation does not produce two separate but
equal communities. As Barrit and Carter found in a 1960 survey of
employment patterns in one city (Portadown), Protestants are
consistently better off than Catholics.

There is a marked difference in the economic status of the two
communities: the Protestants tending to provide the business and
professional classes, the larger farmers and skilled labour, and
the Catholics the small farmers and the unskilled labourers.
There are, of course, many exceptions to this, for instance
because a Catholic business and professional class has to exist to
serve the needs of the Catholic community . . . .[48]

But even the exceptions are revealing; while the Protestant middle
class is technical as well as service, the Catholic middle class mostly
serves the Catholic community, giving it a certain stake in the
dichotomization that shields it from Protestant competition.[49]

If sectarianism sometimes works to the advantage of the Catholic middle class, it consistently disadvantages the Catholic working class. Barrit and Carter found that Catholics comprised a disproportionate percentage of the unskilled and unemployed in Portadown. This finding of a working class stratified along religious lines in one city is confirmed by Edmund Aunger for Northern Ireland as a whole. Using data from the 1971 census, Aunger discredits the claim made by Rose (among others) that intra-working-class sectarianism is without economic basis.[50] Aunger discovers instead that Protestant workers earn higher wages, are more highly skilled, and are more likely to be employed than Catholic workers. Specifically,

> Protestants are disproportionately represented in the non-manual and the skilled manual occupations while non-Catholics are disproportionately represented only in the semi-skilled, unskilled and unemployed classes. . . . It is particularly note-worthy that, while the median Protestant is a *skilled* manual worker, the median Catholic is a *semi-skilled* manual worker.[51]

Class stratification thus reproduces the colonial disparity of Protestants and Catholics. Protestants dominate not only the upper classes but also the upper echelons of the working class, no small matter given that the settlers' two-to-one majority forces many to engage in manual labor. These privileges are not, of course, without benefit to the Protestant elites. By separating Protestant from Catholic workers, privileges tie them to the Protestant middle and upper classes in defense of the order that privileges Protestants at the expense of Catholics.

By systematically favoring Protestants over Catholics, Stormont sustained diametrically opposed political cultures.[52] On the one hand, Protestants, and especially those who have not made the disconcerting discovery that the British consider them Irish, loudly proclaimed their loyalty at every opportunity, toasting the Queen, displaying the Union Jack, and espousing the British way of life with a verve quite unknown in Britain. Nor were their words empty: Protestants made major sacrifices in the two world wars.[53] The meaning of their loyalty is more problematic than Protestants pretend, however, for Protestants expect in exchange for their devotion to be accorded certain perquisites from Britain, such as the freedom to handle the Catholic threat however they please. When Protestants are so favored, their loyalty to Britain knows no bounds (partly because it does not restrain their powers). But when Britain refuses them a free hand, Protestants complain, threaten, renounce; they even defy Britain on matters of the gravest concern – all, of course, in the name of loyalty to Britain's 'real' traditions.[54]

On the other hand, Catholics, though divided between 'nationalism' and 'republicanism,' were implicitly, if not explicitly, disloyal to Northern Ireland. Nationalists proclaimed unification of Ireland as their goal and parliamentarianism as their means. Unfortunately for nationalists, their means rarely promoted their ends. The parliaments they expected to grant independence rejected it instead. Unable thus to accomplish independence, nationalists contented themselves with futile attempts to reform Protestant superiority.[55] In contrast, republicans steadfastly rejected (and still reject) constitutionalism for physical force. However, this difference has not enabled republicans to succeed where nationalists have failed. They too have failed, often ignominiously, to establish an independent and united republic, but they have survived despite failure by making a virtue of necessity, that is, by using unavoidable defeats to glorify their ideals. The defeats derived from the simple fact that it was difficult, if not impossible, to devise a strategy by which the Catholic minority could overcome the Protestants or Britain, much less both together. But rather than surrendering in the face of superior force, republicans have martyred themselves in order to preserve the ideals they cannot realize.[56] This has made it as unlikely that republicans would submit as that they would triumph: their disloyalty, always present and often overt, mirrors Protestant loyalty. Thus the conflict between privileged and deprived is played out politically by that between loyalist and disloyalist.

The interaction of Protestant and Catholic political cultures meant that while Protestants ostentatiously – sometimes too ostentatiously – recognized British and Northern Ireland authorities, Catholics, whether nationalist or republican, openly defied them. And if Catholic defiance rarely amounted to much, that did not matter to Protestants, for Catholics had nonetheless flouted the traditions Protestants honored. It is the irony of Northern Ireland's politics, however, that Catholic disloyalty, precisely because it offended Protestants, benefited Unionism by sustaining its salience. Elections became little more than referenda on partition, enabling Unionist leaders to pursue social policies more conservative than those preferred by their working-class constituencies. For as long as Protestant workers perceived partition as beneficial, they were trapped into supporting a party that paid little heed to working-class interests. The implications of this strategy were fundamental, for, with Catholic disloyalty positioning Unionists to buy the support of Protestant workers cheaply, Unionists had strong incentive to sustain Catholic disloyalty, meaning that Stormont could not become fully legitimate. The conflict between Protestants and Catholics was the condition of its existence.

Protestants dominated Northern Ireland routinely as long as they remained unified. That presented Catholics with a dilemma, for their steadfast opposition to the border, whether electoral or violent, united Protestants against them. The resulting Catholic frustrations forced both nationalism and republicanism to give way, in the mid-1960s, to an emerging civil rights movement which declared that, like it or not, Catholics were British citizens. Playing down Catholic disloyalty, the civil rights movement undercut the rationale for Protestant domination. If Catholics were as loyal as Protestants, Protestants had no claim to special privileges.[57] This quandary fragmented rather than strengthened Protestant solidarity, with the Unionist Party splitting between a majority opposing reform and a minority, including the prime minister, succumbing to British pressure to introduce at least some reforms. Once implemented, the reforms turned out to be more symbolic than substantial, but they nonetheless symbolized the demise of heretofore unshakable Protestant hegemony. The point was not lost on Protestants, especially working-class Protestants; they protested.

The civil rights movement challenged the traditional justification for Protestant privileges, namely, the contrast of Protestant loyalty to Catholic disloyalty. That challenge, though disturbing to Protestants in general, threatened the Protestant working class in particular. While Protestant elites were elevated over Catholics by property as well as status, more marginal Protestants, such as workers, lacked property, and thus depended primarily on the status accorded them as settlers to establish their superiority over Catholics.[58] Status, however, depends on privilege for existence; without preferential treatment, status is lost. This psychological stake in colonial privilege combined with a more material interest in better jobs and housing to mobilize working-class Protestants in defense of colonial privilege. To upgrade Catholics was, Protestant workers realized, to downgrade themselves; the resulting riots forced Britain to send in the army in 1969.

Catholics initially welcomed British intervention. Not only did the army protect them, but the government recognized their key civil rights demands. It soon became clear, however, that civil rights, even when implemented, did not improve the lot of most Catholics noticeably. They might have achieved formal equality, but substantive equality remained as distant as ever. Thus civil rights reforms antagonized Protestants without satisfying Catholics. Facing this worsening political situation, Britain sought to calm the Protestant majority that was positioned to cause far more trouble than could the Catholics. Reassurance of Protestants, though, could come only by proving that Britain was not soft on Catholics, that is, only by doing the Unionists' dirty work. Thus, in attempting to satisfy Catholic grievances, Britain mobilized the Protestant reaction that forced Britain to increase the repression of Catholics. Events, in other words, had slipped beyond Britain's control.

Britain's essential problem is that it cannot straddle the colonial divide. As the question of civil rights indicated, even to attempt to appease Catholics was to trigger a Protestant backlash. Faced with the prospect of sustained Protestant protest, Britain chose what it regarded as the lesser of two disorders. Britain attacked Catholics to prevent Protestants from attacking Britain. However, repression of Catholics at the behest of Protestants had the natural effect of rallying more Catholics behind the most militant defenders of the besieged community, the Provisional Irish Republican Army. With widespread Catholic support, the Provisionals mounted a bombing campaign that may have failed to reunite Ireland but succeeded in forcing concessions (such as the abolition of Stormont in 1972) to Catholics. But if the concessions were important enough to draw Catholics away from the Provisionals, they were certain to provoke a Protestant backlash, thus beginning the logic anew. Unable to escape the vicious circle, Britain has become ever more frustrated in Northern Ireland. Its policy tends increasingly to flounder with no direction save that provided by the situation itself: as Britain moves in one direction, it mobilizes the forces that eventually drive it in the opposite one.

British policy is thus caught on the horns of the fundamental colonial dilemma: whatever pleases one community upsets the other. Hence the vacillation from reform to repression and back to reform. Britain is unable to settle on a viable policy because none is viable. The repression demanded by Protestants only strengthens Catholic militants, while reforms meant to undermine militants threaten Protestants without really satisfying Catholics. It is, indeed, difficult to imagine a policy acceptable to both communities; one community need only see that the other is satisfied to conclude that something is wrong. Britain, in other words, is trapped in the zero-sum game it established centuries ago; the social order is so dichotomized that the gains of one community come at the expense of the other. Protestants and Catholics are, therefore, locked in a contradiction that brooks no mediation. To attempt to mediate is, as Britain has demonstrated for the past decade, to flounder.

VI

Three questions were posed at the outset of this chapter: what conditions generate the conflict in Northern Ireland, how does religion help foster them, and why are they so intractable? The answer to each, it has been suggested, lies in the impact of colonialism on Ireland in general, and on Ulster in particular. By privileging colonizers over colonized, Britain dichotomized the social order into hostile communities, with Catholic inferiority the necessary corollary of Protestant superiority. This linkage of privilege, material and psychological, with religion divided Protestants from Catholics on secular grounds. Protestants were loyal and Catholics disloyal to the status quo. As a result of this overlap of privilege, political allegiance, and religion, one difference implied the others, creating a veritable Manichean divide between the two communities. Thus the communities identified by religion were – and still are – antagonized by much else as well: Protestants were colonizers, while Catholics were colonized.

In the face of this polarization, Britain has been unable to fashion a compromise between the two communities. To appeal to Catholics is to blur the contrast between the legitimacy of Protestant and the illegitimacy of Catholic aspirations, on which Protestants depend for superiority. With co-optation thus closed to Britain as a viable strategy for restoring order, Britain is unable to impose a solution to Northern Ireland's violence; it must instead rely on repression to contain the conflict it cannot mediate. Thus colonialism attains a life of its own beyond the control of the country that imposed it in the first place. The logic of colonialism becomes, from the British perspective, unreasonable.

2

The White Man's Burden

There were two Reigns of Terror if we would but remember it; the one wrought murder in hot passion, the other in heartless cold blood; the one lasted mere months, the other lasted a thousand years; the one inflicted death upon a thousand persons, the other upon a hundred millions; but our shudders are for the horrors of the minor terror, the momentary terror so to speak; whereas, what is the horror of swift death by the axe compared with the lifelong death from hunger, cold insult, cruelty, and heartbreak? What is swift death by lightning compared with slow death by fire at the stake? A city cemetery could contain the coffins filled by the brief Terror which we have all been so diligently taught to shiver and mourn over; but all France could hardly contain the coffins filled by the older and real Terror – that unspeakably bitter and awful Terror which none of us has been taught to see in its vastness or pity as it deserves.

Mark Twain

I

The last 400 years of Irish history have been shaped by the triangular conflict among Britain, Protestants, and Catholics. The particular motives and struggles of the various actors have naturally changed with the times, but they have consistently been rooted in the relationships generated by colonialism. British intervention forged two antithetical communities – one nationalist, Catholic, and poorer; the other loyalist, Protestant, and more affluent. The inevitable conflicts between them were then deepened by Britain's decision to empower Protestants because they, unlike the Irish Catholics, were loyal to Britain. This, in turn, enabled Protestants to maximize the benefits deriving from their loyalty by increasing Catholic disloyalty. Thus consciously or not, Protestants sought to preserve, not reconcile, the original conflict between Catholics on the one hand and both Britain and themselves on the other. It was the key to their interests and identities.

The conflicts between Catholics and the British–Protestant tandem were accentuated by a lesser but significant one pitting Protestants against Britain. Protestants were intended to serve as surrogates for Britain, but eventually resented the subjugation of their political and economic interests to those of Britain. They could not, however, attain parity with Britain without first defusing the threat posed to them by Catholics. Otherwise they were dependent on – and therefore were subordinate to – Britain for help in subduing Catholics. To retain the benefits but escape the costs of hegemony, Protestants ruled out policies of integration, assimilation, and inclusion as responses to the Catholic threat in favor of intensified oppression. Thus the conflict between Protestants and Britain exacerbated that between Protestants and Catholics, and vice versa. Protestants feared the internal threat issuing from Catholics and the external one from Britain and dreaded the day the two might unite against them.

II

Ireland had not been deeply affected by high feudalism, the centralizing state, and related developments in Europe before the Tudors. Various invaders, including Vikings and Normans, had landed, but they either perished, merged into, or coexisted with Gaelic culture. Of the invaders, the Normans exerted the greatest impact, and even they learned the Irish language, adopted Irish customs, and became, according to proverb, 'more Irish than the Irish.'[1] The proverb may have exaggerated the facts of the matter, but Norman worries that Irish culture was corrupting them eventually led them to enact the Statutes of Kilkenny for the purposes of maintaining and strengthening

> the barrier between the two races: alliance between them by marriage, concubinage or fostering of children was prohibited; Englishmen were not to dress or ride in the Irish fashion or take Irish names; neither the English nor the Irish living among the English were to use the Irish language; no Irish man was to be appointed to ecclesiastical office in the English areas. These measures . . . were . . . a desperate attempt to check the decay of the [Norman] colony and to preserve it from being completely

submerged . . . . [However] it proved, in the end, impossible to
maintain a rigid line of division between [Normans and Irish.][2]

Although the Normans could not seal themselves off from the native
Irish, they did retain their sense of a distinctive identity while
honoring the accepted Gaelic custom of aligning with one clan against
another and then fighting over the spoils. These practices had
continued for quite some time before the Tudors decided that to
protect their western flank, they had to change the rules of the game.
When the changes that they demanded – essentially recognition of
their sovereignty – proved unacceptable to Norman and Gael alike,
the Tudors initiated a process that culminated in conquest and
colonization.

Tudor interest in Ireland grew with Henry VIII. Henry certainly
had bigger fish to fry than Ireland, such as centralizing state power,
enhancing England's international status, disestablishing the Catholic
Church, and marrying and divorcing. But to accomplish his larger
purposes, he first had to make sure that Ireland could not interfere
with his plans. This did not mean that Ireland had to be re-made in
England's image or that traditional Irish authorities had to be
eliminated, but it did mean that they had to recognize the primacy of
English interests. To this end Henry sought to manipulate Irish
chieftains by the policy of 'surrender and regrant,' which gave the
clans' land to the chieftains in exchange for their fealty. Henry's plans
were, however, frustrated. Fearing the extension of English law to
Irish chieftains as an 'intolerable threat' to their privileged economic
and political position in Ireland, the Normans thwarted the crown's
policies.[3] This, in turn, encouraged the chieftains to forget their
promises of loyalty and to continue maintaining private armies,
defending their local autonomy, and interfering with English control.[4]
With the chieftains refusing to surrender their independence to
England's pleasure, first Henry, then Elizabeth concluded that
traditional Irish independence could not be eliminated by mere paper
titles. Ireland had to be conquered.

Elizabeth was reluctant to incur the expense of conquest.[5] She
clearly preferred diplomatic means and was particularly interested in
conciliating the Norman landlords who, despite their Catholicism,
proclaimed their loyalty to the crown. But their interests were
incompatible with those of English adventurers seeking Irish land,
and, unable to balance both, Elizabeth sided with the latter. Through
intrigue and negotiation as well as military force, she steadily

expanded the area under her effective control, prompting sporadic, but unsuccessful, rebellions that became pretexts for further expansions of English power.[6] This process continued from the 1560s through 1595, when Ulster, the most traditionally Gaelic part of Ireland, rebelled against spreading Anglicization. The uprising in Ulster soon extended to much of Ireland, leading England to answer with overwhelming military force. The ensuing war was directed at the Irish people as well as armies, with England burning fields, slaughtering cattle, and, according to their commander, 'trying to overcome [the Irish] by famine.'[7] Plague soon followed to depopulate large areas of Ireland; by the time the 'rebels' surrendered in 1603, Elizabeth 'had little left to reign over but ashes and carcasses.'[8]

The conquest of Ireland by England in 1603 marks a turning-point in Irish history, with the colonial state replacing the clan in power, if not in authority. In place of the social order based on kinship and tradition, English adventurers flocked to Ireland, imposed a coercive administration undiluted by loyalty, affection, or acknowledged law, and began taking land from the Irish. The crown consented, awarding large tracts of land to soldiers for their service in Ireland with the understanding that they would bring settlers from England or Scotland to work it. The idea was that these settlers would serve as an inexpensive garrison in Ireland, allowing England to pay settlers in Irish land for securing English interests.

The settlers who began arriving in the early seventeenth century differed from their Norman predecessors in three crucial respects. First, they were brought in substantial numbers and concentrated in particular areas, especially in Ulster, which helped them maintain their cultural identity. Secondly, they were Protestant, occasionally devout; where earlier settlers had, like the Irish, been Catholic, these were separated from natives by religion.[9] Thirdly, the religious cleavage reinforced that between expropriators and expropriated, dichotomizing the social order between two distinct and hostile communities. The resulting tension, while not the objective of British policy, was not dysfunctional. James I had embarked on colonization with the hope that the new Protestant settlers would integrate Irish customs and institutions into the new social order.[10] When their thirst for more land led them to reject accommodations with the native population, the power of the crown over Protestant settlers was actually strengthened. Protestants, by resisting the crown's plans for co-optation, fuelled the hostility of the Catholics who surrounded and outnumbered them. Consequently, Protestants rendered themselves dependent on, and thus loyal to, England for protection from rebellion.

The colonial order remained insecure throughout the seventeenth century. Catholics resented their new rulers, and the upheavals of seventeenth-century English politics twice afforded them unexpected opportunities to challenge England. In the 1640s the struggle between King Charles and the Puritan parliament spilled into Ireland when the king manipulated the Irish to recruit allies in his struggle with parliament. Fearing that Puritans would proscribe Catholicism and hoping to recover the lands confiscated in the first half of the century, Irish landowners rose in support of Charles. After several massacres in the initial rising, the rebellion spluttered on for several years under weak and divided leadership before it was finally and bloodily crushed by Cromwell, at the cost of the lives of perhaps a third of the Irish population.[11] In the aftermath of the rebellion, Cromwell instituted another wave of plantations and land confiscations, increasing the Protestant population from 100,000 in 1641 to 160,000 within a generation, and increasing the proportion of Irish land owned by Protestants from 41 percent to 78 percent.[12]

The pattern of troubled English kings manipulating Irish grievances recurred during the 'bloodless' Glorious Revolution. James II, uncertain of his base in England, ordered the formation of an army of Irish Catholics to pressure parliament, which backfired when the threat of using force to overthrow the Protestant constitution helped mobilize James's enemies.[13] They drove him from the throne to France, where Louis XIV equipped him with a new army that was dispatched to Ulster to join with the Catholics who were again rebelling with the crown against parliament, land confiscations, and Protestant hegemony. The Irish leaders who had survived the first two waves of land confiscation allied with James not because they were particularly enamored of him, but because they regarded him as a means by which they could protect their slipping position. To this end they backed James and fought his – and their – Protestant opponents in Ireland. The rebellion, like that of 1641, enjoyed early success; Protestants were massacred or forced to flee inside Derry city's walls, where they were subjected to a starvation siege that reduced the survivors to a diet of rats. These Protestants, huddled inside Derry's walls, symbolized the seventeenth-century settler experience. Encircled and beleaguered, their worst nightmares were realized. Protestants had always acted as though they were under siege; now they really were. The repressed returned, as Catholics shook colonialism to its foundation for the second time in 50 years. Soon, though, William of Orange broke the siege, drove James back to France, and restored Protestant rule in Ireland. While James suffered exile in Louis's court, his Irish supporters were left to the mercies of triumphant settlers who were determined that Catholics would never again become a threat needing to be beaten.

As part of the arrangement by which William secured the crown and parliament its rights, Irish Protestants received a parliament with effective control over matters internal to Ireland, which they used to destroy not only the fact but even the *possibility* of Catholic resistance. Traditional leaders would not survive with severely curtailed powers, as had happened during the Elizabethan and Cromwellian settlements; they would now be wiped out entirely. In contrast to previous settlements, the one following the Glorious Revolution denied traditional Irish leaders even subservient positions lest these be used for yet another rebellion. Protestants had learned that, despite conquest, colonialism was resisted by a web of traditional relations; that Ireland's political, social, and cultural relations were part of an interwoven way of life which rejected practices not fused to traditional norms. Protestants could not, therefore, capture political control without consolidating social and cultural control, for traditional social and cultural relations would, if permitted to survive, generate anti-colonial politics. To kill the body politic, the settlers cut out its heart.

Hence the settlers initiated, and the home country confirmed, a package of legislation known as the Penal Laws.

> The penal code, as it was actually carried out, was inspired much less by fanaticism than by rapacity, and was directed less against the Catholic religion than against the property and industry of its professors. It was intended to make them poor and to keep them poor, to crush in them every germ of enterprise, to degrade them into a servile caste who could never hope to rise to the level of their oppressors. The division of classes was made as deep as possible, and every precaution was taken to perpetuate and to embitter it.[14]

Protestants launched their attack because Catholicism, better than any other characteristic, distinguished native from settler. No other single criterion could perform the task; some Irish spoke English, so language would not do; the Irish were as Caucasian as the English, so neither would race; but all natives were Catholic – which provided a clear contrast to the settlers' Protestantism. That the conflict took religious form, however, does not mean that the conflict was fundamentally religious, but rather that religion identified the antagonists in a colonial conflict.[15]

The Penal Laws did, of course, attack the Church. Mass was proscribed. Clerics were banned, and those who violated the ban were subject to imprisonment, and, on second offense, were liable to be hanged, disemboweled (the settlers were serious about gutting Irish culture), and drawn and quartered. Rather than tolerating Catholicism as an opiate that would dull Catholics into accepting their oppression, it was assailed as a bastion of cultural resistance. But because religion guided rather than motivated the Penal Laws, they also extended to secular domains. Catholics were, for example, denied both primary and university educations. It was not enough, though, to keep the Irish ignorant. They had also to be cut from any institutions that might generate rebellion – including families. If, despite the confiscations, Catholics still owned land, it was immediately transferred to the eldest son should he defy his father and convert to Protestantism. Or if a man's wife converted, she legally passed beyond her husband's authority. Or if 'any child, however young, professed to be a Protestant, it was at once taken from its father's care.'[16] The idea was that, by undermining institutions that preserved the coherence of Gaelic tradition, the Irish could be pacified.

Land ownership, as the basis of traditional culture, was also subject to the Penal Laws. Catholics who had retained land through the Elizabethan and Cromwellian settlements were dispossessed by another wave of confiscations that left only 10 percent of the land in their hands, and that only because it was so impoverished that Protestants saw no reason to bother with it. The confiscations were extended partly out of greed and partly to prevent the eventual emergence of a landed class that might challenge settler hegemony. Accordingly, Protestants proscribed primogeniture for Catholics, denying them the power which would attend large landholdings. And to guarantee that Catholics would not buy property, its purchase was forbidden. Irish culture was to be uprooted from the land.

Lest provisions against Catholicism, education, the family, and land not annihilate the culture that Protestants found politically threatening, the Penal Laws expressly excluded Catholics from political life. They could not sit in either the British or Irish parliament. They could not vote. They could not practice law, judge law, enforce law, or sit on juries of law. They could not hold office (here the settlers were guilty of overkill, for without the franchise it was unlikely that Catholics would be elected to office in the first place). Catholics could not hold arms, or join the army or navy. They could not participate in politics because, in the opinion of the Lord Chancellor and the Chief Justice, 'the law does not suppose any such person to exist as an Irish Roman Catholic.'[17]

Collectively, then, the Penal Laws amounted to a full-scale onslaught against the social order that generated rebellion. They focused on religion because it was a convenient index separating native from settler, and it fitted well with the tenor of the age. Their purpose, though, was not to convert Catholics to Protestantism; that would have undercut the dichotomy underpinning settler hegemony. Had Catholics become like Protestants, the discrepancy between their loyalty and Catholic disloyalty at the heart of Protestant privileges would have evened out. The logic of their position thus disposed settlers to perpetuate Catholic disloyalty, while minimizing the resulting threat to themselves. The Penal Laws served the essential task of keeping the enemy alive but impotent.

III

Much ado is made of the lack of enforcement of the Penal Laws that began in the middle of the eighteenth century, but by then they had served their purpose; Catholics were debilitated. The very success of the Penal Laws, however, raised unexpected problems for their beneficiaries, for it eroded the threat that both united Protestants and rendered them dependent on Britain. No longer in dire need of Britain, Protestants pushed their interests against it to the verge of disloyalty. The crux of their complaint concerned the constitutional relationship tying Ireland to Britain. Ireland was subject to Poynings' Law, which stipulated that bills originating in the Irish parliament had to be submitted to the British Privy Council for approval, and that the Council could reject or amend Irish legislation at its pleasure. If rejected, the bill was dead. If amended, the bill was then returned to the Irish parliament for acceptance or rejection. The bill could not, however, be restored to its original form: Privy Council amendments were final. The dissatisfaction of Irish Protestants with their political subordination to Britain was accentuated by protectionist legislation taken by Britain against Irish industries that competed too success-fully with British industries. In the 1720s, these measures culminated in a bill that forbade all exports by the growing Irish woollen industry so that they could not compete with British exports. The act not only angered Protestants hurt by it directly, but also warned that the same fate might await any Irish enterprise successful enough to rival Britain.[18]

Settler dissatisfaction with Britain increased as trade limitations forced Ireland into excessive dependence on agriculture, worsening its already extreme poverty. The Catholic peasantry generally lived at bare subsistence level, and not always that well: the eighteenth century was punctuated by periodic famines. Although most Protestants were substantially better off than Catholics, their development was hampered by Ireland's general poverty; the drain of resources by absentee and wasteful landlords; and the consequent lack of capital.[19] Blaming trade restrictions for this condition, Irish Protestants pushed for an independent Irish parliament to bring free trade to Ireland. The demand met with little success until the 1770s, when the American colonies, voicing related complaints, rebelled against Britain and enabled Irish Protestants to threaten a similar course of action should Britain continue to ignore their demands. When Britain left Ireland unprotected by dispatching its garrison to America, Protestants took advantage of the situation to organize themselves into Volunteers that ostensibly guarded Ireland from foreign invasion, but in fact backed with armed pressure the demand for an independent Irish parliament.[20] The threat of Irish Protestants rising at the very time that Americans were already rebelling was too much for the British government; it capitulated, first granting free trade, then, in 1782, legislative independence for Ireland.

The Dublin parliament whose powers were expanded in 1782 was as unrepresentative as its predecessors. Although Protestants had solicited some Catholic support in pursuit of parliamentary independence, they were concerned less with Catholic rights than the prospect that Britain might try to rally Catholics against the proposed parliament.[21] When the independent parliament was established, Catholics were still deprived of the right to vote in elections, let alone to stand for office. Moreover, property qualifications, the system of rotten boroughs, and bribery effectively restricted influence to the crown and its wealthy landed allies, leaving the bulk of Protestants unrepresented. With the Protestant landed classes excluding from power the very Protestants on whom they depended for support, they put themselves in a precarious position. Discontent grew among the Protestant middle class and peasantry, especially where they were most heavily concentrated – in Ulster.

Ulster was different from the rest of Ireland. Because it had resisted conquest more fiercely, Ulster had been heavily colonized, and thus escaped the worst effects of the Penal Laws. Rather than treating its population as enemies to be weakened, Protestant tenants were regarded as allies.

> [L]andlords were willing to offer rather favourable terms in order to get Protestant tenants, who were presumed to be better risks from the standpoint of physical security and perhaps more attuned to 'English' farming practices. Protestants had been able to drive hard bargains with landowners, as most of the land in question was not particularly attractive – except to the descendants of its original occupiers. The Protestant tenantry thus imbibed the notion that they were especially important to their landlords and entitled to privileged treatment.[22]

The particular deals between Protestant landlords and tenants gradually evolved into a practice known as the Ulster custom which, while lacking the force of law, was a widely accepted usage that gave tenants a saleable interest in their holdings. Under the Ulster custom, a tenant

> could not be evicted without reasonable compensation; and he had some guarantee of a fair return for any improvements he might make, for either he would continue to occupy the farm himself, or, if he left, his improvements would add to the selling-price of the tenant right.[23]

This security was rare elsewhere in Ireland; if tenants improved the land, their rents could be increased commensurately, which removed any incentive to make improvements. Agriculture was, therefore, very rudimentary in most of Ireland. Ulster, however, produced surpluses that, once reinvested in agriculture or manufacture, prepared the base for an economy more varied and affluent than that of Ireland as a whole.

By sparing Protestant peasants from the poverty afflicting Catholics, the Ulster custom made them the sort of 'middle peasants' who were threatened by, but able to resist, the small clique of large landowning families that dominated the Irish parliament.[24] Protestant peasants resented their status as second-class settlers, ignored politically and discriminated against religiously if, as was often the case, they were

Presbyterian rather than Anglican. While the religious 'disabilities' were not nearly as onerous as those borne by Catholics, they combined with political powerlessness to generate significant disaffection among Protestant peasants. By the 1790s, the progressive wing of the Protestant middle class had convinced substantial numbers of them to enlist in the United Irishmen, an underground conspiracy advocating an independent and non-sectarian republic for Ireland. The agitation of the United Irishmen was facilitated considerably by the competition for land between Protestant and Catholic peasants that resulted from the repeal of the Penal Laws in 1793. With the standard of living enjoyed by Protestant peasants apparently under attack, the already low esteem in which they held landlords dropped lower. On these grounds the United Irishmen envisioned an alliance between the Protestant and Catholic peasantries under its leadership and supplemented by armies from revolutionary France. The combination might well have proved irresistable – had it held.

The inescapable problem confronting the United Irishmen was that the same forces disposing Protestant peasants against their landlords were also resuscitating sectarianism. To raise rents and make inroads into the Ulster custom, landlords were beginning to let to Catholics land traditionally held by Protestants. This offered the dual advantage of increasing rents while casting Catholics as the cause of the decline in living standards incurred by the Protestant peasantry.[25] Inevitably, competition between the Protestant and Catholic peasantries aggravated sectarianism, as exemplified by the foundation of the Orange Order in the 1790s. Comprised of peasants committed to protecting Protestant privileges by whatever means necessary, including intimidation and sometimes violence,[26] the Orange Order offset the republican and non-sectarian inclinations of many Protestant peasants. Thus the United Irishmen had overestimated the number of their adherents and underestimated the number of their adversaries among Protestant peasants. This, along with other miscalculations, was to cost republicans dearly.

The Protestants organized by the United Irishmen were supposed to enter into alliance with the Catholic peasantry. The Catholic peasantry, however, was essentially disorganized, belonging only nominally to the poorly organized Catholic Defenders. The Defenders were a collection of local, secret, agrarian societies that, despite similar principles and one name, had little or no central organizational structure. Although the Defenders agreed on the need to reduce rents and evictions by whatever means available, their various groups were too localized and politically untutored to act successfully on a national level. The United Irishmen, nonetheless, relied on the Defenders to organize the Catholic peasantry, which not only exaggerated their capacities but also overlooked the telling fact that the Defenders were the *Catholic* Defenders. Certainly the Defenders were concerned primarily with agrarian grievances, but having developed as a sectarian movement to protect Catholic peasants from the attacks mounted against them by Protestant peasants in Ulster, they tended to identify Protestants as their enemy. Thus the United Irishmen tried to organize the Protestant and Catholic peasantries along non-sectarian lines even though both saw themselves in sectarian terms, and then minimized the obstacles confronting them by underestimating the Orange Order and overestimating the Defenders. The United Irishmen had fewer friends and more foes than they reckoned.

If the Catholic and Protestant peasantries were to provide popular backing for an insurrection led by the Protestant middle class, the military muscle was to come from an outside element of some concern to both the Protestant landlords and the British government: French Revolutionary armies. Wolfe Tone, the most important leader of the United Irishmen, had convinced the French Directory that an invasion of Ireland would spark a mass revolution; drive Britain from Ireland; and cripple Britain's war effort against France. The British government, having thoroughly penetrated the organization of the United Irishmen, was aware of the conspiracy and appreciated the threat it posed. The British were, however, caught unaware by the departure of a substantial French fleet for the coast of Ireland in December 1796. But Britain received a stroke of good luck when much of the invasionary force, including the command vessel, was scattered by storms during the voyage to Ireland. When the still sizeable remainder reached the unprotected coast of Ireland, a combination of indecisive leadership and extraordinarily bad weather prevented the French from landing. With the French returning home, Britain unleashed a reign of terror that began in Protestant Ulster and eventually spread throughout Catholic Ireland. Martial law was declared, and the army employed widespread torture to uncover the membership of the United Irishmen.[27] This in conjuction with informers among the leadership of the United Irishmen broke the conspiracy. But rumors of extensive repression touched off the 1798 rebellion, in which disorganized and localized Catholic peasants rose in fear of the spreading repression.[28] The rebellion was too lacking in structure or purpose to challenge, let alone overturn, British rule, and rapidly degenerated into bands of Catholic peasants roaming the countryside in search of enemies, preferably Protestant.

Exaggerated reports that Catholic peasants were indiscriminately butchering Protestants combined with British repression to convince Protestants of the folly of alliance with Catholics. Rebellion, Protestants learned, was self-defeating as well as costly; the natives went wild, killing their benefactors.[29] Progressive Protestants believed that they had prepared an uprising against the colonial order that oppressed Irish regardless of religion, only to be massacred by ignorant mobs of Catholics still acting according to the colonial imperative that pitted members of one faith against those of the other. This object lesson in settler colonialism was not lost on Protestants. Those who had been lulled from vigilance by the passivity of Catholics remembered that their position depended on both British power and settler solidarity. Thus the 1798 rebellion, small though it was, marked the end of Protestant republicanism; thereafter no significant segment of the Protestant population threatened to join with Catholics against the colonial order. The fundamental colonial dichotomy was restored intact.

IV

The 1798 rebellion revealed both the importance and fragility of British control over Ireland. Though half-cocked, the rebellion reiterated, on the one hand, the strategic importance of Ireland to Britain and, on the other, the danger of radical Protestants channeling the desperation of the Catholic masses against Britain and its Protestant allies. Protestant radicalism had, clearly, been much tempered by the combination of British repression and Catholic sectarianism, but the misrule of Ireland by Protestant landlords nonetheless risked renewing it. Thus Britain moved to induce the Irish parliament to dissolve itself. This entailed threats, cajolery, promises of peerages, places and pensions of various sorts as well as overt bribery.[30] But these investments paid off when the Irish parliament voted itself out of existence with the Act of Union, which went into effect on 1 January 1801.

The Act of Union was designed to stabilize Ireland by integrating it into the United Kingdom. Having arranged the appropriate legislation, British interest in Ireland waned, allowing the executive organs of government to lapse into the hands of the same Protestants who had always controlled it. 'In every department of government, central and local, the Protestant landlords, their allies and dependants, remained in control.'[31] These Protestants tried to use the martial law that often prevailed in Ireland to maintain their previous position. In this they were only partly successful, for their formerly direct political power was rendered indirect by the Union. As the 1798 rebellion revealed the dependence of Protestant landlords on Britain for help in repressing Catholics, so the Union reinforced it by subordinating Protestants to Britain.[32] Protestants exercised political power not directly, but indirectly through Britain, reminding them of their loyalty to Britain and of the special privileges it conferred on them. This, in turn, revived the incentives for Protestants to deploy their power in ways that would sustain Catholic disloyalty, thus encouraging Britain to depend on them to maintain order in Ireland. Because the logic of the Protestants' position required the alienation of Catholics, 'any attempt to reconcile the majority to the union was almost bound to alarm the minority whose support was already secure.'[33]

British electoral laws helped Irish Protestants exclude Catholics from positions of political power. Although Catholics were finally entitled to vote, property qualifications and public balloting limited the significance of the franchise to countless Catholic tenants who, if eligible to vote, were pressured by their landlords to vote for particular candidates. Catholics could not, moreover, vote for their 'own kind,' since they were barred from parliament by the requirement that all members take an oath abjuring Catholicism. While the exclusion of Catholics from parliament was only a symbolic grievance to the masses of peasants too poor to vote, much less to sit in parliament, it did impair the articulation of the interests of the small but increasing number of Catholics who had managed to acquire estates or professions. Their deprivations were especially aggravating in view of British promises that Catholics would be accorded the right to sit in parliament in exchange for the hierarchy's endorsement of the Act of Union. But as often happened with British commitments to Irish Catholics, the government proved unwilling to honor them. The bishops, very concerned to prove their trustworthiness to the British, accepted the double-dealing meekly enough, but Catholic professionals were more militant.[34] They wanted the state opened to Catholic as well as Protestant elites, and eventually enlisted the participation of the Church in their campaign to this end. But even with clerical backing, Catholics with a direct stake in 'Catholic Emancipation' were far too weak to force through political reform. They needed the peasantry.

Catholic Emancipation was not of immediate concern to the

peasantry. Peasants suffered from the land system, not exclusion from parliament, and the election to parliament of Catholic landowners pledged to uphold the sanctity of property was unlikely to improve their conditions noticeably. However, the astute leadership of Daniel O'Connell and the organization of the clergy emphasized that Catholics were being discriminated against *as* Catholics, and therefore that all Catholics, even those unlikely to benefit from Emancipation, were obliged to support it. After a decade of unsuccessful effort, Emancipation caught on when, in 1823, O'Connell founded the Catholic Association, which recruited peasant members and assessed them nominal dues, giving them a sense of belonging. Having inspired the peasants to force Emancipation to a head, the movement was strong enough in 1828 for O'Connell to challenge the British government directly. He stood for election, and, when elected, refused to take the oath renouncing Catholicism. Threatened by the real prospect of rebellion over an issue whose significance was essentially symbolic, Britain relented and passed Emancipation. In exchange, O'Connell consented to an increase in the property qualification for the franchise, which disenfranchised many of those who had, at considerable risk to themselves, elected him.

Catholic Emancipation constituted the first major inroad into the structure of Protestant domination established centuries earlier and confirmed by the Act of Union. Britain retained sovereignty, the Anglican Church remained the established one, Protestants exercised effective control over political policy and owned most of the land, but finally Britain recognized the legitimacy of Catholic aspirations despite Protestant objections.[35] This, in turn, helped consolidate the moderation of the relatively few Catholics represented in parliament. Thus in one stroke Catholic Emancipation served the interests of Britain by promoting stability and of emerging Catholic elites by opening the state in principle, if not always in fact, to them. But it did little, if anything, for the Catholic peasants who constituted the overwhelming majority of the population.

Emancipation, though of great moment to Catholic elites, did not affect the more urgent matter of the land system. Since the seventeenth century most land had been owned by large, often absentee, landowners. The landowners, generally but not always Protestant, would in some instances divide and subdivide their land until tenants were brought to bare subsistence level, with any surplus scratched out by tenants serving as an invitation for another round of subdivisions. The small, overworked plots were cultivated by the most primitive agricultural techniques in Europe, as the practice of increasing rents commensurately with the value of any improvements made by peasants destroyed incentive to improve the land.[36] Inevitably, the productivity of the land entered a long-term decline that was only accelerated by a rapidly increasing population. Worsening land was supporting increasing numbers of people.

The linchpin of the land system was the potato, which peasants subsisted on while paying rent with commercial crops. This system was deeply unstable, however, as 70 percent of the rural population either lacked land or depended on inadequate holdings.[37] And in 1845 the linchpin was pulled out by a blight that ruined potato crops for the next four years. During this period Irish agriculture was not totally unproductive; several of the commercial crops enjoyed good years, but they were exported, leaving the peasantry little, if anything, to eat. Britain then availed itself of the opportunity provided by the famine to admit that Ireland was not an integral part of the United Kingdom after all: Irish, but not British, property was taxed for poor relief.[38] With the potato crop spoiled and Britain opposed to relief, the peasantry had scant choice but to emigrate or starve. Ireland lost a quarter of its population of eight million; one million emigrated (mostly to America) and another million died. Since those who died tended to be young (or very old) and those who emigrated tended to be young adults, Ireland lost not only a quarter of its population, but also a disproportionate number of people who were, or who would later have become, of childbearing age. This, combined with high emigration, continued to reduce Ireland's population; a century later it was half of what it had been before the famine.

The famine, however, did help to transform land relations. As peasants died, fled, or simply could not pay rent, landlords lost the labor of those who provided them with their income. Deprived of rents, the more wasteful ones were overwhelmed by their debts and started losing land to speculators, more efficient landlords, and the middle class, which was increasingly Catholic.[39] These new landlords soon began cutting into the protections won for peasants by the secret societies; shifting agricultural production from tillage to grazing; and consolidating holdings, with the latter two initiatives reducing the demand for peasant labor. By the mid-1870s the position of Irish peasants worsened further as technical developments (such as refrigeration) permitted the transportation of food across the Atlantic, forcing Irish agriculture to compete with more productive American farmers. The inevitable drop in prices produced a depression which, equally inevitably, produced evictions and starvation. This time, however, the peasantry eschewed agrarian terror for an effective national peasant organization, the Land League, that challenged – and eventually overturned – not only the symptoms but the system itself.[40]

The Land League was Ireland's first national peasant organization which

> resisted evictions, refused to pay their normal rents, and demanded that parliament make extensive alterations to the laws governing ownership and occupation of agricultural land in Ireland.[41]

In pursuing these objectives the Land League did not forego agrarian violence, but did subordinate it to political guidance that aimed to transform land relations, and not only remedy specific symptoms. By 1880 the 'land war' had neutralized landlord power, and the Land League had both assumed effective power over much of the country-side and had brought the land question to a head in parliament through an alliance with a parliamentary group led by Charles Stewart Parnell. The combination of popular and parliamentary agitation induced Britain to supplement the routine coercion acts with a serious attempt to solve the agrarian problem, once again validating the observation of an Irish politician: 'Violence is the only way of securing a hearing for moderation.'[42]

In 1881 Gladstone continued his reformist policy toward Ireland, which began a decade earlier with the disestablishment of the Anglican Church. He now introduced a Land Act that granted the '3 Fs' that comprised the program of tenant rights advocates: fixity of tenure; free sale by the tenant of his interest; and fair rent. While peasants still did not own the land they tilled, the act improved their long as well as short-term position, as Gladstone's original land reform act was followed by others in 1886, 1891, 1896, 1903, and 1909 that gradually transferred ownership from the landlords to the peasantry. These reforms were intended to bring peace and stability to the Irish countryside, and succeeded to an extent. Land agitation declined markedly, and the peasantry seemed willing to follow the constitutional nationalists politically. Meanwhile, Parnell shifted his careful balance of agrarian and political demands away from the land war.[43] Thus Britain was approaching a sort of neo-colonial solution to the Irish question. Economically, it would obtain what it wanted through

normal market mechanisms; politically, it would cultivate a social
base for a conservative Irish government to which it could safely
surrender partial control over Ireland. The solution was called home
rule.

V

Proposals for home rule took various forms, but all would have
provided Ireland with a separate executive and legislature with
jurisdiction over Ireland's internal affairs. However, 'all matters
affecting peace or war, foreign affairs or even customs and excise'[44]
were reserved for Westminster. Despite these reservations, Ireland's
delegation to parliament was overwhelmingly committed to home rule
from the 1880s through the First World War. Massive Irish support,
however, was insufficient to secure the passage of home rule in
Westminster; the Tories opposed, and the Liberals generally ignored,
home rule. In 1885, however, Parnell held the balance of power in
parliament and Gladstone was converted to the cause of home rule.
Gladstone, though, could not carry the Liberal Party with him, and
the Party split over this issue. In 1892 Gladstone pushed a second
home rule bill through the Commons, but the Lords vetoed it. Home
rule, despite the massive majority in Ireland pledged to it, then faded
into the background of British politics until the eve of the First World
War. But its popularity in Ireland was assured, regardless of its
failures in Wesminster, by the votes of the Catholic peasantry, the
leadership of the Catholic middle and lower middle classes, and the
organizational skills of the clergy. The peasantry worshipped the Irish
National Party for its role in forcing land reform through parliament;
the middle class craved the patronage that would be opened by home
rule; and the Church hierarchy realized that state patronage for
Catholics would inevitably sensitize the state to the interests of the
Church. Such, certainly, was the opinion not only of home rule's key
supporters, but also of its key opponents: Ulster Protestants and the
Tory Party.[45]

Ulster Protestants were as united in opposition to home rule as
Catholics were on behalf of it. Home rule, they claimed, meant 'Rome
rule.' And 'Rome rule' meant not only that specifically Catholic
doctrines would become matters of state policy, but also, Protestants
feared, that the secular interests of Catholics would be favored over
those of Protestants, and particularly that tariffs erected by Catholics
would hurt Ulster Protestants. In Ulster, unlike the rest of Ireland,

textiles and shipbuilding were important export industries, and both were tied to markets in Britain and the empire, and hence to the preservation of free trade.[46] Thus protection, while potentially attractive to the Catholic middle class, alarmed both middle and working-class Ulster Protestants. They feared that they would lose indispensable outlets for their ships and textiles, and these fears persisted even though the various home rule bills withheld from Ireland the authority to establish protective tariffs.

The other fears of Protestants were, however, more reasonable, for in admitting the legitimacy of Catholic aspirations, home rule struck directly at the very nexus of the colonial apparatus – political control.[47] Terrified that Britain was poised to deliver the state to Catholics, Protestants qualified their oft-professed loyalty to Britain and threatened rebellion, civil war, a unilateral declaration of independence. These threats were endorsed by Tories seeking an issue with which to oppose the Liberals. Ulster, as Randolph Churchill said in 1886, 'would fight and Ulster would be right.'[48] Or, as the leader of the Tory opposition observed in 1910, 'I can imagine no length of resistance to which Ulster will go, in which I shall not be ready to support them. . . .'[49]

The threats voiced by the Tory leaders were not idle. Each home rule bill was met by parliamentary and extra-parliamentary activity. The first was answered by riots, the revival of the Orange Order, the formation of the Ulster Unionist Party.[50] The second home rule bill encountered a similar response, and the third nearly provoked a major constitutional crisis. In 1910, Irish nationalists again captured the balance of power in parliament; this led to the introduction of a third bill, but the first that could not be rejected by the Lords (who were in the process of losing their veto). Ulster Protestant resistance, therefore, took especially desperate form. The Ulster Unionist Council (UUC), which directed both the parliamentary and popular movements against home rule, formed a paramilitary arm, the Ulster Volunteer Force (UVF). The UVF drilled, received shipments of illegal arms, and delivered ultimata about the rebellion that would follow any attempt to 'coerce' Ulster into home rule. As the threats became more brazen, the British army was instructed to intercept an illegal shipment of arms destined for the UUC. Many of the officer corps resigned instead, and the army's high command forced the government to promise that the army would not be used to put down a Protestant rebellion in Ulster.[51] With the assurance that 'loyalist' (as opposed, presumably, to seditious) rebellion would not be suppressed, the position of the UUC was strengthened immeasurably. In the ensuing negotiations the government offered to exempt Ulster from home rule for six years; denouncing this as a mere stay of execution, the UUC demanded that the exemption be permanent. As the stalemate was approaching a full-scale constitutional crisis, the First World War erupted. Home rule was passed into law, but suspended for the duration of the war. The question of Ulster's exclusion was to be decided later.

The passage of home rule capped a generation of struggle by constitutional nationalists, who had dominated Catholic politics since O'Connell despite persistent challenges from republicans. In contrast to constitutional nationalists, republicans embraced independence as an end and violence as a means. Home rule, they contended, would not only reduce the prospects for real independence, but partition would disfigure Ireland. Republicans, therefore, seized the opportunity presented by the war to stage an insurrection in 1916, the objective of which was less to attain independence than to revitalize the ideal of an independent Irish republic.[52] The rebellion initially failed on both scores. It was crushed within a week, and, more disturbing to the rebels, evoked derision in Ireland. What republicans could not manage, however, Britain accomplished. By executing the leaders of the insurrection, Britain converted them into martyrs and vindicated their cause.

In the aftermath of the rising, the government moved to mollify Ireland with home rule, but on terms favorable to Ulster Protestants. Six Ulster counties – including two with Catholic majorities – were to be separated permanently from the rest of Ireland. The home rule party acquiesced in this concession, which contributed to its collapse in the face of resurgent republicanism. Republicans swept the 1918 parliamentary elections, and then assembled in Dublin to proclaim a sovereign state. Their claims were backed, moreover, by a growing guerrilla campaign conducted by the survivors of the 1916 insurrection, now regrouped in the Irish Republican Army (IRA), which tried to paralyze British rule over Ireland by assassinating police officers and ambushing small groups of the irregular British forces called the Black and Tans.[53] The Black and Tans typically responded with indiscriminate terror directed against civilians. These tit for tat exchanges continued until IRA successes and Black and Tan excesses combined to galvanize the Catholic community, including the traditionally anti-republican hierarchy, behind the IRA. Isolated in all save the Protestant areas, beset by accelerating resignations from the police, and plagued by republican infiltration of its intelligence apparatus, Britain was driven to depend increasingly on terror, which only strengthened republicans. With its rule finally broken down in most of Ireland, Britain had to come to terms with republicans.

In 1921, after 125 years of struggle, republicans finally forced the British government to negotiate with them as the legitimate representatives of the Irish people. It soon became clear, however, that republicans were better fitted for struggle than negotiation. Britain was willing to confer the substance of power over 26 of Ireland's 32 counties to an independent Irish government, but insisted in exchange that the Irish government take an oath of allegiance to the crown and permit Britain to maintain two naval bases on Irish territory. Republican negotiators conceded both points, but a significant faction of the IRA rejected these concessions as desecrations of the republican tradition. Soon republicans split over the treaty, and a civil war broke out between the erstwhile comrades. The treatyists routed the anti-treatyists, though not before both sides lost most of their leaders. Meanwhile, the less symbolic but more important issue of partition was largely ignored.[54]

In 1920, Westminster had passed the Government of Ireland Act, partitioning Ireland between two home rule parliaments. The war of independence and the subsequent treaty voided the Act in most of Ireland, but in six of Ulster's nine counties it took effect, establishing the Stormont parliament. Originally the Unionist Party actively opposed the special parliament for Northern Ireland, preferring to remain directly under Westminster in the belief that the connection with Britain would be stronger if unmediated. But after sweeping the election to Stormont in 1921, Unionists discovered the usefulness of a separate government with control over security. They converted the UVF into a state force with the explicit purpose of suppressing Catholic 'rebellion' and proceeded to beat Catholics into submission to the new state. Northern Ireland was established.

VI

Irish history passed through three stages in the period that stretched from the Elizabethan conquests to independence with partition in 1921–2. The first stage was that of conquest, with England defeating Irish resistance militarily, challenging cultural authorities, and seizing the land. To accomplish these ends as cheaply as possible, England employed Protestant settlers to serve as its surrogates. The settlers were, however, dissatisfied with the endemic insecurity and periodic rebellions of the seventeenth century, and inaugurated the second stage of colonialism in Ireland, that of consolidation. In the Penal era Protestants attacked any and all Irish institutions that preserved the coherence of Irish tradition, and effectively destroyed the vitality of traditional Gaelic culture. Aiming to maintain their rule while simultaneously insulating themselves from Catholics, Protestants sought to secure their position by weakening Catholics without rendering themselves superfluous by reconciling Catholics to British rule. Unfortunately for Protestants, this led to incessant agrarian violence and republican uprisings, eventually necessitating the British reforms of the third stage and exposing fully the contradictions of their position.

British reforms were designed to stabilize Ireland by extending to Catholics the rights previously denied them. Settler colonialism is based, however, on privileges and deprivations, not rights. For Catholics to receive effective citizenship would at once have blurred the contrast between native and settler, and undercut the rationale for settler supremacy. Thus not Britain and not Catholics, but Protestants resisted a fully legitimate social and political order. The irony, of course, is that the sequence of British reforms – Catholic Emancipation, disestablishment of the Anglican Church, land reform, and finally proposals for home rule – had split the social and economic questions from the political. By granting land reform before resolving Ireland's constitutional relationship to Britain, Britain ensured that the largest class in a home rule or independent Ireland – the landowning Catholic peasantry – would be deeply conservative. Originally Protestants had rejected co-operation because Catholic demands were considered too disruptive, too radical; but even after land reform tempered these, Protestants refused co-operation with Catholics on principle. Thus when Britain proposed a social and political order that could have included loyal Catholics, Protestants blocked it. They yearned for domination, not inclusion.

The contradiction of settlers to natives survived and structured three centuries of Irish history: partition acknowledged as much. Rather than fading away, the original conflict was institutionalized in political, social, and religious relations. Politically, the natives were nationalists and the settlers unionists; socially, the nationalists were deprived and the unionists privileged; and religiously, the deprived were Catholic and the privileged Protestant. With the two communities locked in unnegotiable conflict, colonialism ultimately proved untenable in most of Ireland, leading Britain to propose a neo-colonial solution to the Irish problem. But because neo-colonialism jeopardized Protestant hegemony, it encountered the fervent opposition of unionists. In 26 of Ireland's 32 counties, Unionists lacked the base to prevent the co-optation of Catholic elites, but in Ulster, Unionists mobilized the Protestant majority to reject neo-colonialism for outright colonialism.

Colonialism derived its strength in Ulster from the pattern of the original plantation. In most of Ireland settlers were few and scattered; in Ulster they were numerous and concentrated. Since there were too many settlers in Ulster for most to belong to elites, many were forced into the laboring classes. The vitality of colonialism hinged on the allegiance of these laboring Protestants. To solicit their loyalty, Protestant elites conceded material privileges to them – initially the Ulster custom and later the better industrial jobs – that reinforced colonialism in two important ways. First, the higher standard of living provided by the Ulster custom generated surpluses that eventually gave rise to an industrial economy that was tied to the British economy for markets, and therefore disposed the Protestant laboring classes as well as the elites to support the colonial connection with Britain. Secondly, the benefits generated by Ulster's economy were directed disproportionately to Protestants. Class was stratified along colonial lines: on top were Protestant elites; in the middle were the Protestant working class and farmers and a smattering of Catholic elites; and on the bottom, menacing those above, were the Catholic laboring classes. Thus the Protestant working class and peasantry developed a material stake in supporting the colonial order that favored them over their historic adversaries, reinforcing the legacy of antagonism separating Protestants from Catholics.

Partition preserved Ulster colonialism from the anti-colonialism of the Catholic masses and the neo-colonialism of the British government. With effective, though not formal, independence from Britain in internal affairs, Protestants would consolidate their position in a manner similar in kind – though obviously not in degree – to that of their eighteenth-century ancestors. They staged a counter-offensive, driving Catholics from positions of authority, encouraging the Catholic disloyalty that justified the hegemony of Protestant loyalists, and invigorating the colonial contradiction. Northern Ireland became the last refuge of Protestant domination in Ireland.

3

The Gerrymandered State

'The reason the Irish are fighting each other is that they have no other worthy opponents.'

Tug McGraw

I

Partition resolved the colonial contradiction south but not north of the newly drawn border. In the 26 southern counties, it made possible the ascendancy of the Catholic middle class and *petit-bourgeoisie*, whose conservativism reassured Britain and the few remaining Protestants;[1] but in the north partition combined with devolution to shield unionists from friend and foe alike. Britain was able to ignore, and Catholics were unable to challenge, the internal politics in the six counties. Thus the creation of the Stormont government tightened the hold of Protestants on political power, but did not guarantee them security. For with Protestants refusing to pursue *rapprochement* with Catholics, they locked themselves into the colonial contradiction: but with a twist. Protestants, suddenly a two-to-one majority, could present their rule as that of the 'majority.' It is from this that one of Northern Ireland's most conspicuous anomalies arises: colonialism secured a 'democratic' facade.

Recently, considerable attention has been devoted to the events that took place between the inception of Stormont in 1921 and the outbreak of violence in 1969. The two most intriguing interpretations of this period do not, however, agree on the nature of the conflict between Ulster Protestants and Catholics. In fact, the differences between them are fundamental and pervasive, emerging particularly over the reasons why partition was instituted and why the Protestant working class endorsed it. On one side, Michael Farrell develops the standard socialist republican position, arguing that British machinations and the false consciousness of the Protestant working class account for the establishment and maintenance of the state in Northern Ireland. On the other side, Bew, Gibbon, and Patterson are joined by Belinda Probert in stressing the importance of Ireland's 'uneven development' and the deals made among Protestant classes to mediate their differences. Thus there are two central disputes between the competing positions: the first concerns whether partition constituted the dismemberment of Ireland or expressed Ulster's link to Britain; and the second, whether the Protestant working class acted according to false interests insinuated by its ruling class or according to its real interests.

Farrell's version of Northern Ireland's history emphasizes the importance of repression and false consciousness in installing and defending Stormont. According to Farrell, neither Catholics nor Protestant workers really wanted a separate state in Northern Ireland, but Catholics were forced and Protestant workers tricked into acceding to partition. In developing the latter point, Farrell argues that Protestant workers received privileges from the Stormont government, particularly in employment and housing, which tempered their militant class and national consciousness. This argument, however, raises problems. On the one hand, Farrell persuasively points to the significance of official and quasi-official violence in repressing wide-spread Catholic discontent and to the salience of privileges in shaping the politics of the Protestant working class. But on the other, Farrell becomes so convinced of the illegitimacy of the Northern Ireland state that he underestimates the interest of Protestant workers in partition and grossly overestimates their interest in republicanism. What appears in Farrell as the false consciousness of the Protestant working class is in fact a reasonable assessment of its most fundamental interests and identities.

Bew, Gibbon, and Patterson avoid these problems, but run into different ones. Rejecting Farrell's claim that the relation of Britain to Northern Ireland is imperialistic, they see partition as the result of Ireland's uneven development. Gibbon in particular argues that the economic basis of unionism was the 'contradiction between . . . town and country, industry and agriculture.'[2] Because Ulster, unlike the rest of Ireland, generated an industrial economy that depended on British markets, its working class developed distinctive 'political and ideological disposition[s].'[3] These, in turn, facilitated a genuine inter-class alliance among Protestants, which was dominated by the bourgeoisie, but also conferred real benefits on the Protestant working class. This argument is persuasive in accounting for both Protestant working-class opposition to home rule and support for the Stormont government. But it does not explain why Protestants excluded Catholics from political power. Protestant deals are obviously important, but they make sense only in the context of fundamental social, economic, and political divisions, and unless these are appreciated – which they are not by Bew et al. – the unionist alliance makes no sense.

II

From 1921 through 1968 Protestants rather effortlessly dominated Catholics. In those 47 years Stormont had only four different prime ministers – all Unionist. However, this continuity is indicative less of unity than of insurmountable divisions. After centuries as a minority dominating a majority, Protestants invoked the principle of majority rule to consecrate the exclusion of Catholics from political power. With the Unionist Party strictly Protestant, permanent Unionist control spelled Catholic powerlessness, which Catholics could do little but resent. The same majorities that rendered electoral strategies worthless also discouraged physical resistance, enabling Protestants to reproduce their hegemony as long as they could manage their internal differences.

Although Northern Irish history consists largely of Protestants routinizing their rule, the periods immediately preceding and succeeding its foundation are themselves quite eventful. On the eve of the First World War the British government was committed to home rule for Ireland and reluctantly conceded the temporary exclusion of six Ulster counties from the proposed parliament in Dublin. Unionist leaders, however, used their position in Britain's wartime coalition government to extract promises that the sacrifices displayed by Ulster loyalists (much of the Ulster Volunteer Force was wiped out in battle) would not pass unrewarded after the war, especially in view of the 'treachery' of the Easter rebellion. Hence when the Easter rebellion escalated the Irish Catholic demand from home rule to independence, Ulster Protestants were supported even by their erstwhile adversaries in Britain. Unionists were not, however, supporting each other at home.

In the aftermath of the First World War, Belfast was rife with labor agitation, especially among the most skilled sectors of the industrial working class – the Protestant shipyard workers.[4] Protestant workers demanded reforms similar to those the British working class as a whole was then demanding: higher wages, shorter hours, and the recognition of the rights of labor in capitalist society. By January 1919, these demands erupted into a series of major strikes. Workers in the transportation, power, shipbuilding, and engineering industries went on strike and offers of support from sympathetic unions nearly escalated the particular strikes into a general one. Confronted with this agitation, which was all the more disturbing in view of the accelerating drive of Catholics for independence, the employers offered minor concessions, summoned the army, and broke the strike.[5] Even then, however, Unionists could not rest comfortably. For after the strike collapsed, Protestant workers turned to the Labour Party in subsequent elections, rather than reverting to their previous unionism.

It was the good fortune of the Unionist Party, however, that the political independence of the Protestant working class was vulnerable to the growing threat republicans posed to Protestants irrespective of class. As previously independent labor movements were undercut by the specter of home rule, so was this one by the war of independence. Even though republicans were comparatively inactive in the north, their claim that the six north-eastern counties were rightfully part of an independent and united Ireland portended ill for laboring as well as other Protestants. Not only would they lose citizenship in what they regarded as their rightful nation, but they would suffer economically in two ways. First, Belfast's economy was integrated into that of Britain and the Empire. To separate from Britain politically was therefore to risk indispensable markets – and with them Protestant jobs. Secondly, Protestants held more and better jobs – 90 percent, for example, in the shipyards.[6] Since Catholics would naturally expect to gain from independence, and since their gains could come only at the expense of Protestants, Unionist elites could convert class conscious militancy into pro-colonial, anti-Catholic sectarianism. Unionist appeals were consistent, not inconsistent, with the established economic interests of Protestant workers.

These interests, moreover, were rendered especially insecure by the post-war depression then afflicting much of the industrialized world. Ulster was hit especially hard, with unemployment reaching 25 percent and sectarianism rising commensurately. Facing unemployment, Protestant workers decided that if work had to be lost, it was better that Catholics lose it. In July 1920 they forced 10,000 of Belfast's 90,000 Catholics from their jobs and allowed the Unionist Party, which championed the expulsions, to restore its leadership over them.[7] Thus the very economic hardships that originally contributed to working-class militancy eventually fuelled sectarianism; Catholics became scapegoats for the downturns of the business cycle.

By forcing Catholics to shoulder a disproportionate share of the economic burden, Ulster's colonial class structure diverted Protestant working-class militancy into sectarianism. If hurt badly by the depression, Protestant workers would have been still worse off had they not been able to take Catholic jobs. Thus when push came to shove, the conjunction of republicanism and a colonial class structure sent Protestant workers in Ulster scurrying back to their traditional leaders, suggesting that Protestant sectarianism resulted from more than the Unionist demagoguery that socialist republicans identify as its primary source. Farrell, for instance, contends repeatedly that Protestant workers would support republicanism were they not misled, and anticipates periodically that 'class conscious [Protestant] workers might throw in their lot with Sinn Fein.'[8] What Farrell does not realize, however, is that the class interests of Protestant workers are rooted in a colonial class structure; when that structure is threatened, the objective class interests of Protestant workers are also threatened. This, and not simply the brilliance of Unionist demagoguery, is why Protestant workers are so susceptible to Unionist sectarianism: class interests are determined by colonial interests.

These interests were protected by Britain with the passage of the Government of Ireland Act in 1920, which established one 'home rule' parliament for the 26 southern counties and another for the six northern counties. The partition of Ireland was obviously anathema to the Ulster Catholics, whom it turned into captives of the artificial Protestant majority, but they generally refrained from extending the war of independence to the north lest they get the worst of the bargain from Ulster's Protestant majority. Their discretion, however, proved fruitless; the election of a Catholic mayor in Derry touched off riots that soon spread throughout Northern Ireland. Through intimidation and violence, Protestants, who only a year or two earlier had been fighting among themselves, proceeded to make abundantly clear that in Northern Ireland they were to retain their traditional prerogatives and Catholics were to suffer their customary indignities. It was to be two years before order (Orange, naturally) was fully restored to the six counties.

In the summer of 1920 Protestants initiated indiscriminate attacks on Catholics, burning Catholic homes, driving Catholic workers from their jobs, and murdering Catholics randomly. When Catholics retaliated, Britain intervened to restore the peace. Britain, however, was simultaneously fighting republicans in the rest of Ireland, which disposed it to enter into *de facto* alliance with extra-legal Protestant organizations, including the Ulster Volunteer Force; the army and UVF even patrolled together.[9] It would, indeed, have been inconsistent of the British to act otherwise, for not only were Britain and the UVF fighting the same enemy, but the UVF was led by the very Unionists who were to control the separate government that Britain was trying to create in Ulster. The implicit alliance between Britain and Unionists became explicit when in late 1920 Westminster effectively converted the UVF from an extra-legal into an official organization (the Specials).[10] Consequently, Protestants were armed and Catholics disarmed; as the most important Unionist leader put it, '[i]n Ulster owing to the system of A, B, and C Constabulary, there is no reason why every Loyalist should not have arms to his hand, legally agreed to by the government.'[11]

The Specials were responsible not to the British but to the Stormont government, which was elected in 1921 and was controlled by the same Unionists who had threatened rebellion against home rule, formed the UVF, and condoned highly sectarian acts, including murder, against the Catholic community. Within a year, the alliance of Protestant vigilantes, the Protestant state, and the British army had beaten Catholics into submission. In Belfast alone 250 had been killed, 11,000 driven from their jobs, and 22,000 forced from their homes (out of a Catholic population of 93,000).[12] Unprotected and intimidated, the Catholic minority was not only stuck in Northern Ireland, but its exclusion from effective political power became the glue binding together the ascendant Unionist coalition.

III

The violence accompanying partition receded as it became clear to Catholics that the discrepancy between their weakness and Protestant strength was so vast that no matter what they tried, they could not overturn Protestant supremacy. Protests, whether parliamentary or extra-parliamentary, only backfired, intensifying the Protestant solid-arity that fostered their grievances in the first place. With Catholics doomed to impotence, Protestants ruled unimpeded as long as they maintained unity under the auspices of the Unionist Party. And from 1921 until 1968 Unionists remained united, turning Northern Ireland into an effective single-party system. It was the misfortune of the Catholic Nationalist Party to be the second party. Try as the Nationalist Party might to develop a coherent strategy to strengthen Catholics, it failed. Meanwhile Britain, relieved from the thankless task of 'governing' Ireland, turned a blind eye to the behavior of the Stormont government. The British Chancellor of the Exchequer, although routinely subsidizing the Northern Ireland state, reportedly did not even know the 'formula according to which the Northern Ireland Government gets its money.'[13] Given such lax supervision, Unionists could use British resources for their purposes.

The British government, according to the research of Bew et al., was initially divided over the question of partition, though by 1921 it decided that Ulster could not be 'coerced.'[14] Despite continuing differences over tactics and emphases, the only sustained British opposition to Stormont emanated from the Treasury, which was disturbed by Stormont's 'profligacy with public funds.'[15] This extravagance, according to Bew, Gibbon, and Patterson, resulted from Prime Minister Craig's deliberate strategy of establishing a state with a 'sectarian-populist flavour,'[16] the centerpiece of which was the B Specials. Bew et al. argue that Craig used the B Specials both as a relatively popular and expensive way of providing Stormont with an independent military capacity, and as a way of integrating the Protestant lower classes into the unionist coalition. By dismissing unpopular officers, for example, the Specials cultivated a populist, even democratic, image among Protestants that served as a model for the state as a whole.[17] Like the Specials, the new state was 'characterised by a combination of sectarian and "democratic" practices, and by a high consumption of public funds.'[18]

The strategy described by Bew et al. succeeded in assuring Unionist rule. From its foundation in 1921 until its suspension in 1972, Stormont was governed uninterruptedly by Unionists. Every government was Unionist; every member of every government was a unionist of one stripe or another; and every parliament had a unionist majority, with 32 of 52 seats the low-water mark for the Unionist Party. On average it held over 36 seats.[19] The resulting governments were remarkably stable; at the outbreak of the Second World War, four of the original seven cabinet ministers were still in office. Until both party and government factionalized in 1969 under pressure from the civil rights movement, there had been only four prime ministers in almost half a century. Northern Ireland was, *de facto*, a one-party state.

The party that controlled the state was shamelessly sectarian. A sample of observations offered by various premiers illustrates the point. Lord Craigavon, prime minister from 1921–40, boasted that 'we are a Protestant parliament and a Protestant state.'[20] Lord Brookeborough, prime minister from 1942–63, established his reputation with such injunctions as 'I recommend those people who are loyalists not to employ Roman Catholics, ninety-nine percent of whom are disloyal.'[21] And Terence O'Neill, who carefully cultivated an image for religious toleration while prime minister from 1963–9, revealed at the end of his career that 'If you treat Roman Catholics with due consideration and kindness, they will live like Protestants. . . .'[22] O'Neill's opinion, insulting though it was, did represent a departure from Unionist orthodoxy; previous Unionist governments had not even wanted Catholics to behave like Protestants. Better that Catholics sustain their traditional disloyalty, and thus justify Unionist sectarianism.

Rather than soliciting Catholic loyalty, Unionists sought to perpetuate disloyalty. In the subdued language of a sympathetic researcher, Craig 'made no attempt to associate the nationalist minority with the new state.'[23] Craig himself was more explicit. 'I have always said I am an Orangeman first and a politician and member of [Stormont] parliament afterwards.'[24] Such sectarianism was less the indiscretion of a tactless politician than the expression of party – and therefore state – policy. By confirming Catholic disloyalty, Unionists positioned themselves to make patriotic appeals to Protestant workers to defend the Union. As the sympathizer pointed out, '[i]n the last analysis, it was negative sectarianism and anti-nationalism rather than democratic organization and a positive social programme that held the unionist party together . . .'[25]

Sectarianism and anti-nationalism dominated Protestant politics well before the foundation of the Unionist Party in the 1880s. But in the 1880s Parnell and Gladstone, by advancing home rule to the forefront of British as well as Irish politics, forced Protestants to rally around Unionism. Unionism had, of course, been implicit in Protestant politics since the Act of Union abolished the Protestant parliament and rendered Protestants dependent on Britain in 1801. As long as both the Tories and Liberals maintained the constitutional status of Ireland, Protestants could choose between them along conventional class lines. Landlords tended to support the Tories, the middle class the Liberals. But when Gladstone committed the Liberal Party to home rule in the 1880s, the latent unionism of Protestants became overt and was, by necessity, forced into alliance with the Tory Party. Submerging their internal differences under their general interest in defending the Union, landlords, tenants, capitalists, and most, though not all, workers turned Unionist. This diversity inevitably strained the alliance. In the city, workers and capitalists disputed industrial issues, while in the countryside small landowners resented the supremacy of the large ones. These internal differences paled, however, in contrast to Protestant conflicts with Catholics. Catholics, in demanding political power, were trying to pull out the linchpin of settler hegemony and were therefore threatening mass as well as elite privileges. In the south Protestants were too few to do much against the Catholic masses, but in the north the Unionist coalition was decisive. After failing to block home rule for the whole of Ireland, Ulster Protestants abandoned their compatriots in the south in exchange for the superiority promised by partition.

In defending their superiority over Catholics, Protestants understood themselves to be defending a way of life under attack by papists intent on destroying political, civil, and religious liberty. Conceiving liberty as enlightened, industrious, and individualistic (that is, as essentially Protestant in nature), Protestants believed that the defense of Protestantism was tantamount to the defense of liberty. In practice, however, Protestants were defending secular traditions which, in Ireland, presupposed the subjugation of Catholics. What appears as religious bigotry was really interest, as evidenced by the fact that while the Unionist Party never nominated Catholics for office, and while only a handful of Irish Catholics were even admitted to the party, English Catholics were routinely accepted as members.[26] It was not Catholicism itself, but Catholicism tied to nationalism, that upset Unionists. The problem with Irish as opposed to English Catholics was that they opposed the 'Protestantism' – that is, the colonialism – of Northern Ireland. This connection was made quite neatly by the Orange Order.

The Orange Order was a fraternal society dedicated to opposing Catholicism; its sectarianism was so intense that its members were occasionally expelled for attending funerals in Catholic churches. Named in commemoration of the king who secured Protestant rule in Ireland, the Orange Order celebrated William's victory over King James II in 1690 with parades every 12 July. Meticulously decked out in the costumes of their fathers, Orangemen marched in honor of their heritage, part of which was the oppression of Catholics. Just to make sure that Catholics got the point straight, Orangemen would parade through Catholic neighborhoods, emphasizing Catholic inferiority and testing Catholic acquiescence. If the provocation of the Orange parades met with rock-throwing, stern measures were called for; if the parade met with nothing more than grudging resentment, the status quo was considered secure for another year.[27] While not calculated to win Catholic support, the parade did renew annually the commitment of Protestants to their distinctive heritage.

The Orange Order also figured quite prominently in Unionist circles, appointing a quarter of the members of the Ulster Unionist Council, the Party's governing body. The informal power of the Order was, if anything, even greater, as membership at the elite and popular levels of the two organizations was 'largely interchangable,'[28] and as all save a few members of the Unionist delegations to both Stormont and Westminster were Orangemen.[29] Moreover, Orange Halls were generally the 'meeting places' for local Unionist constituency associations and the location for 'what is generally called the "Unionist machine." '[30] In exchange for its influence, the Orange Order helped integrate Protestant workers into the Unionist Party, an important contribution given that Unionist conservativism was liable to spawn independent working-class politics. The Orange Order militated against this by attracting the working class to a 'populist' organization that was nonetheless controlled by conservative business and professional classes.[31]

Thus the Orange Order helped smooth over incipient conflicts among Protestants, and eased Protestant workers into a political system controlled by their traditional elites by bringing the ruling conservatives together with the less socially conservative working classes in a fraternal setting. But the elites had to pay a price for Orange support: the Orange Order was a relatively autonomous institution that, in addition to facilitating Unionist control over lower-class Protestants, also pressed the demands of the latter against the former. Lower-class Protestants were, therefore, in a position to have their cake and eat it too. The Orange Order and Unionist Party protected the populist character of the state and the traditional privileges due to Protestants over Catholics. This could have cost Protestant workers dearly, however, for it divided the working class and prevented it from claiming the benefits brought by class solidarity. But as citizens of the United Kingdom, Protestant workers received the full entitlements of the British welfare state. Thus they were cushioned from the consequences of their sectarianism; although divided from Catholic workers, Protestant workers still enjoyed the benefits won by the unity of the British working class – the post-Second World War welfare state.

If, however, Protestant workers could secure their essential privileges through the Unionist Party, they did not hold actual political power. The Protestant working class could apply pressure, but it could not make decisions. From its foundation, 'real control of the [Ulster Unionist Council] lay in the hands of a few land-owners and professional and business men';[32] Unionism extended substantive and symbolic privileges, but not procedural power to Protestant workers. Although they could often get what they needed from the Unionist Party, the party was subject to elite, not working-class, control; the 'democratic process [within the party] was at best a facade and at worst a fraud.'[33] Ten of the 35 to 40 Stormont seats under Unionist control were the preserves of individual families, with the rest subject to local elites that 'controlled every avenue through which patronage was dispensed.'[34] In a society with chronically high unemployment, this patronage was significant, and operated in conjunction with the republican 'threat' against the independent articulation of working-class demands. Election after election was converted into a referendum on partition as the Unionist Party dredged up the constitutional issue to win easy re-election for one Unionist government after another.[35]

The ease with which it won elections encouraged the Unionist Party to stick by the tried and proved electoral platform of preserving the constitutional link with Britain. With elections focusing on the constitutional status of Northern Ireland, a vote against Unionists was deemed tantamount to a vote for the inclusion of the six counties into the papist state to the south. This manipulation of the Protestant electorate was assisted immeasurably by the tactics of southern nationalist politicians. Periodically the dominant southern party (Fianna Fail) initiated campaigns to abolish the border separating north from south.[36] Although rarely amounting to anything more than propaganda for an inattentive international audience, they nonetheless lent credence to the republican specter that tied the Protestant working class to Unionism. The Protestant working class was thus trapped; if it did not vote Unionist, it felt its settler privileges in jeopardy; but if it did vote Unionist, it reinforced its subordination to Unionist elites.

IV

The reliance of Unionists on the constitutional issue, the Orange Order, and sectarianism reproduced Catholic disloyalty. It is the paradox of the Catholic predicament, however, that the stiffer their opposition to Stormont, the more they accentuated the salience of the union, enhanced the leverage of the Unionist Party over the Protestant working class, and justified their exclusion from power. Some Catholics did flirt briefly with recognition of the state shortly after its foundation; but apart from this aberration, Unionists confirmed the always implicit and sometimes explicit disloyalty of Catholics in ways that united Protestants around the Unionist Party. Thus by excluding Catholics, Unionists generated the Catholic disloyalty that secured Protestant loyalty: conflict facilitated rather than disturbed the colonial system.

The Nationalist Party was the opposite of the Unionist Party: Catholic rather than Protestant, anti-partitionist rather than partitionist, and powerless rather than powerful. It was, moreover, caught in a contradiction that precluded even the possibility of escaping powerlessness. On the one hand, it advocated the unification of Ireland through electoral means; on the other, two-thirds of Northern Ireland's electorate steadfastly opposed unification, and hence the Nationalists. Its electoral prospects were, therefore, limited. In the half-century of Stormont's existence, no Nationalist ever held a cabinet position and the only Nationalist bill passed into law concerned wild birds.

Lacking even the prospect of power at the provincial level, Nationalists could not hold themselves together. Organizationally, the party was weak, decentralized, and poorly led, never settling on a consistent policy towards Stormont; sometimes Nationalists attended, and sometimes they boycotted. From its establishment in 1921 through 1925 Stormont was boycotted by Nationalists; they began attending in 1925 only to walk out again in 1932. They were back in 1933 but by 1935 party discipline had broken down and members began attending or boycotting individually, until abstentionism triumphed again in 1938.[37] In 1945 Nationalists returned for lack of an alternative; and in 1965 they finally consented to become the official opposition. These shifts of policy resulted less from indecision – though that was certainly a factor – than from the futility of whatever policy was pursued. Inside parliament Nationalists were an impotent minority; outside they were senseless – parliamentarians without a parliament.

The Nationalist Party's inability to define a satisfactory relationship with Stormont derived primarily from the strength of the Unionist and the weakness of its own position. Stormont was not a pluralist institution that consulted and aggregated significant interests; it ostracized Nationalists. Catholic interests were routinely ignored (except in matters of education),[38] for it was the exclusion of Catholic interests that assured the unity of the Unionist Party. The Nationalists thus found themselves in the untenable position not only of recognizing the legitimacy of an institution that denied their own legitimacy, but also of violating the deeply held Catholic conviction of the fundamental injustice of partition and Stormont to no obvious benefit. Thus the tendency to boycott; but this tendency was, in turn, offset by pressure on Nationalists to represent Catholic interests as best they could.

The Nationalist Party reflected faithfully the views of local Catholic notables. In the country, the local associations were controlled by what passed for the elites of the rural Catholic community – farmers who owned a little extra land, shopkeepers, and teachers. In the city, the party represented the Catholic middle class. This class was not generally productive – it owned little capital – but its role in distribution and the professions, notably teaching, was assured by the polarization of Northern Ireland society and the specific instructions of the Catholic Church. Anxious to develop a Catholic middle class and fearful that Protestant professionals (such as doctors) might offer counsel inconsistent with Church teachings, the clergy put its full – and for Catholics unimpeachable – authority behind the middle class that it trained, nurtured, and advised. With the Nationalist Party thus representing middle-class Catholics who depended on sectarianism for clients, it developed a sectarianism that differed from that of the Unionist Party only in color – green rather than orange. In consequence, it played perfectly into the electoral strategy of the Unionist Party, 'proving' that the Church lurked behind nationalism.

The Nationalist Party's politics varied little from the time of partition until the late 1960s. It was adamantly, but peacefully, anti-partitionist. When the Unionist Party proclaimed each election to be a referendum on partition (and thus ignored social issues), the Nation-alist Party readily agreed and rallied Catholics to vote against partition. The party inevitably failed, but by accepting elections as referenda on partition, the Nationalist Party made no 'sustained effort to reach beyond the Catholic community and challenge for power on the basis of an economic and social programme.'[39] Indeed Nationalists subscribed to the conservative Catholic social teachings of the era, teachings that, while accepted because of the authority of the Church, conflicted with the interests of many Catholics as well as Protestants in such matters as trade unions and social welfare legislation. But its social conservatism notwithstanding, the Nationalist Party dominated the Catholic electorate in towns such as Derry. In this, Nationalists were aided immensely by the support of the Church. As one Derry Catholic wrote,

> The fear that it was possibly sinful to vote against the Nationalist Party was quite real. The party was closely associated with the church. Its basic unit of organization was not the electoral ward but the parish. The local parish priest would, in most cases, automatically, be chairman of the convention called to select a candidate.[40]

With the Church thus exerting itself on behalf of Nationalists, and with Nationalists subordinating social to national demands, the Nationalist Party obviously had negligible appeal to the Protestant working class. And without the support of Protestant workers, Nationalists were merely constitutionalists acting under a constitution that rendered them irrelevant: they posed no threat, real or prospective, to the Unionist Party.

V

The uninterrupted supremacy of one party is likely to breed stagnation under any conditions, but if, as was the case with Unionists, the party is from the outset deeply suspicious of any sort of innovation, then stagnation becomes the all but inescapable fate for the society ruled by the unaccountable party. It is not surprising, then, that decades of Unionist rule sowed social and cultural as well as political stagnancy. While such sluggishness proved quite congenial to the political interests of the Unionists, it proved more troublesome when extended to the economy. In the post-Second World War period, the shipbuilding and textiles industries that had sustained Ulster's economy began declining. These same industries were suffering a similar fate in Britain, but the Unionist Party was even less suited than were its British counterparts to reverse the downward spiral. It might not have posed much of a problem had Catholics absorbed the bulk of the layoffs, but the declining industries were Protestant industries with Protestant workforces – and that spelled Protestant unemployment.[41] Protestant unemployment, in turn, delivered the self-regulating political system a jolt from which it never fully recovered. In the hope of combating unemployment through foreign investment, a rejuvenated Stormont government projected Northern Ireland as 'modern,' 'forward-looking,' and 'progressive.'[42] While this image may have appealed to international capital, it suggested to some key Unionist constituencies that the Stormont government had become dangerously indifferent to the sectarianism on which they depended. Sectarianism, it turned out, had developed a logic quite beyond the control of the elites who had for so long manipulated it. Protestant workers balked at the ideological and political changes introduced to recruit foreign capitalists who were, predictably, not as committed to Northern Ireland's sectarianism as was the Protestant working class.

The economic problems that were to have far-reaching ramifications on Northern Ireland were only partially the fault of the Unionist Party. Like Britain, Northern Ireland was suffering the consequences of its previous pattern of industrialization. As the relative productivity of British plant and capital declined throughout the twentieth century, so did that of Northern Ireland. Relatively dependent on labor as opposed to capital, and unable to adopt new technologies because of obsolescent plants, British capitalism proved progressively less profitable, and those profits which were generated were invested disproportionately abroad. The outflow of capital in search of foreign profits exacerbated the original problem of ageing industry, depriving Britain of the investment necessary to modernize its economy. Thus British industry became steadily less competitive internationally, an especially severe problem for a country as dependent on international trade as Britain.[43] These structural problems were aggravated by a series of decisions in the 1950s and 1960s that hastened rather than reversed Britain's decline. Specifically, Britain maintained an overpriced currency that, first, diverted funds from investment, secondly, made British goods more expensive in the world market, and finally, further encouraged the export of capital.[44]

As an integral part of the British economy, if not polity, Northern Ireland suffered from the same problems of obsolescence and underinvestment. The problems, in fact, were worse in Northern Ireland than in Britain; not only were Northern Ireland's main industries the very labor-intensive ones that were deteriorating in Britain, but Northern Ireland had fewer industries than Britain to offset the descent of its core industries. This problem was aggravated by the flow of capital from Northern Ireland to Britain; as Britain's underinvestment was intensified by the export of profits abroad, this syndrome was reproduced as Northern Ireland's profits were exported to Britain.[45] With profits diverted from reinvestment, and with the pre-eminence of family over public firms obstructing the formation of capital,[46] Northern Ireland's industries became uneconomic, further reducing both profits and jobs. The employment statistics illustrate the point starkly. The three pillars of Ulster's economy were agriculture, shipbuilding, and linen. In agriculture employment fell from 138,000 to 67,000 in the period from 1949 through 1969; in shipbuilding employment dropped from 23,000 to 9,200 from 1945 through 1969; and in linen production employment dropped by 50 percent, as 31,000 jobs were lost from 1949 through 1967. By 1966 Northern Ireland's real income was 25 percent lower than that of Britain.[47] Yet Prime Minister Brookeborough, convinced that state planning smacked of socialism, refused to be shaken from his listlessness.[48]

By the late 1950s Unionist lethargy in the face of rising unemployment was beginning to cost them politically as well as economically. The 1958 elections were held against a backdrop of 10.7 percent unemployment and the Northern Ireland Labour Party won four seats in Stormont, including two previously 'safe' Unionist seats.[49] While the total was small, it alerted the more enlightened Unionists to the political costs of economic problems. In concert with both Whitehall and Stormont civil servants, these 'moderates' urged not only that Northern Ireland's economy be restructured to recruit foreign investment, but also that Stormont clean up its image. 'Backward' sectarianism was out; 'forward-looking' technocracy was in. These plans were, however, obstructed by the prime minister, who, with his long vacations and short hours, embodied the inactivity of Stormont, which often met only a few weeks a year.[50] As his Finance Minister later remarked, Brookeborough

> was good company and a good raconteur and those who met him imagined that he was relaxing away from his desk. What they didn't realize was that there was no desk.[51]

With some Unionists thus disenchanted with Brookeborough's indifference to Unionist political problems, and with the British Treasury disturbed that Brookeborough was doing nothing to reverse the economic problems that were forcing Britain to increase its subsidies to Northern Ireland, British civil servants combined with Unionist backbenchers to exert discreet but effective pressure to replace Brookeborough with his 'progressive' Minister of Finance, Terence O'Neill.

O'Neill was different from most Unionists. He was effectively English, having been raised in London and educated at Eton and

Oxford. After the Second World War he sought a Unionist seat in Westminster, but was rebuffed and ended up in Stormont instead, where he earned a reputation during the 1950s for understanding the economic realities of Northern Ireland. He became Finance Minister, worked well with civil servants in both the British and Northern Irish finance ministries, and seemed to have the background and temperament necessary to reorder Unionist priorities. He did not, however, have a very secure base in the Unionist Party, having not been elected but appointed, after the fashion of the Tory Party, by the Queen's representative.[52] It is questionable whether he could have won election; certainly neither he nor his policies were particularly popular in Unionist circles. But realizing that Northern Ireland had to recruit foreign capital to reduce Protestant unemployment and British subsidies, Britain was able to organize enough supporters to make him prime minister.

Foreign investment was not without its perils to the Unionist alliance. It not only meant trouble for the local family firms that had routinely delivered jobs to Protestant workers,[53] but it empowered actors with little interest in maintaining the patterns of discrimination that were essential to Ulster's class structure, and hence the Unionist Party. The task of recruiting (and therefore of minimizing the impact of) foreign investment fell to O'Neill's chief rival, Commerce Minister Brian Faulkner, which presented him with a problem. On the one hand, he had to protect Protestant jobs, since his political base lay in the Orange Order. On the other, he had to attract foreign investors who were indifferent to traditional hiring patterns. Faulkner proved equal to the task. By building plants in Protestant areas, justifying their location on the basis of superior infrastructure, and then renting them on very generous terms, Faulkner reconciled the conflict. The foreign capitalists, attracted by the subsidies and the developed infrastructure, located in heavily Protestant areas, where they hired the local population, thus perpetuating the traditional employment patterns. The problem was – or more accurately, should have been – solved. By steering foreign investment into the Protestant areas surrounding Belfast, O'Neill and Faulkner had shored up the class structure that had been weakened by the erosion of Northern Ireland's central industries.[54]

O'Neill realized that sectarianism and parochialism were not conducive to foreign investment. But as he could not include Catholics in the political system without triggering a dangerous backlash, O'Neill chose the next best option. He offered Catholics symbolic, not substantive, citizenship, making gestures that were intended to appease Catholics without upsetting the Protestant masses. As O'Neill wrote, he wanted Catholics

> [to see] me visiting Catholic schools, sitting beside their Cardinal at a ceremony in Armagh, visiting Catholic hospitals, greeting Prime Ministers of their Republic at Stormont, making concili- atory speeches.[55]

Thus without beginning to dismantle Protestant hegemony, O'Neill offered Catholics a sort of implicit citizenship. He talked of an 'opportunity state,' promised 'prosperity,' and 'progress,' and pleaded with 'Ulstermen' to 'shed the burdens of traditional grievances and ancient resentments.'[56] But he did not devise and still less begin implementing an effective strategy for reducing Northern Ireland's sectarianism. On the contrary: he reinforced the Protestant privileges he ostensibly deplored by pointing foreign investment to Protestant areas.

Even though O'Neill's gestures towards Catholics proved more symbolic than substantive, and even though they posed little threat to Protestants, they nonetheless unnerved workers in the traditional Protestant industries that were to be written off in favor of new industries. This provided the base for the first serious Protestant opposition to the Unionist Party since partition. Led by the Reverend Ian Paisley, this opposition was comprised of 'ultra-loyalists' centered in the Protestant working-class areas of east Belfast, where many of the shipyard workers lived. Combining denunciations of softness towards Catholics with populist demands, Paisley imputed worsening condi- tions to Unionist laxity on the Catholic question. Whether pelting the Republic's prime minister with snowballs after his meeting with O'Neill, or picketing Protestant churchmen involved in ecumenicalism, Paisley warned of the 'rebel' threat to increasingly receptive audiences. These sectarian and populist appeals enabled him to grow from an insignificant maverick in the 1950s into the dominant Protestant politician of the 1970s and 1980s. Meanwhile, Catholics, their expectations raised by O'Neill's gestures, began demanding more substance and less symbolism. It was, they argued, all well and good to recognize Catholics as citizens, but unless they were to be accorded the rights of citizenship, O'Neill's recognition amounted to little. Catholic unemployment, they pointed out, remained high and Catholic political power non-existent. Thus O'Neill had inadvertently stirred Catholics from their apathy only to disappoint them, while worrying Protestants unnecessarily. For this O'Neill – and Northern Ireland – were to pay dearly in the late 1960s.

VI

The proximate cause of O'Neill's troubles was his inability to balance Unionist sectarianism with symbolic gestures at reform. But this was just the expression of an underlying and more intractable problem: essential Unionist constituencies regarded Protestant superiority as indivisible. To play down the symbolic privileges, even while maintaining substantive ones, was to challenge the status of the less secure partners in the Unionist alliance, especially the Protestant working class. Protestant workers depended not only on state patronage for the privileges that defined their interests and identities, but also on the active exclusion of Catholics from the political rights of citizenship. The Unionist coalition worked, in other words, only if legitimacy was limited to Protestants. The point is not fully appreciated by Bew, Gibbon, and Patterson, who discuss incisively the deals struck by Stormont among Protestant classes but minimize the specific conditions of those deals. Stormont, as was soon to become clear, operated smoothly only as long as Catholics accepted and justified through their 'disloyalty' their exclusion from effective access to political power. For Catholics to recognize Stormont was not only to trip up the routinization of Protestant hegemony, it was also potentially to jeopardize the socio-economic and the political privileges which defined what it meant to be Protestant. The gravest danger to Stormont, it turned out, was not Catholic rejection but Catholic acceptance.

4

The Troubles

'The political center is like the Bermuda Triangle – whoever approaches it disappears.'

A French socialist

I

O'Neill's shift in the early and mid-1960s from overt to covert sectarianism earned him more enemies than friends. Protestants feared that their domination was ebbing, while Catholics were disappointed that it was not. This set the two communities on a collision course, with Catholics becoming increasingly impatient with the superiority that Protestants clung to ever more desperately. Caught between these cross-pressures, first O'Neill, and then Britain itself, found that whatever policy appeased one community incited the other. Failing to satisfy both communities, Britain has become enmeshed in an inescapable dilemma. To support Catholics is to antagonize Protestants (without necessarily winning over Catholics), but to support Protestants is to deliver Catholics into the hands of re-publicans. Either way Britain reinforces the logic it seeks to escape.

Northern Ireland's violence was precipitated by a movement that was itself non-violent. In the mid-1960s Catholics, realizing that partition was unassailable, rejected both nationalism and republicanism in favor of a civil rights movement which argued that it was better to accept partition (if only provisionally) and to make the best of a bad situation than to protest against a border that would not be changed no matter how indignant their complaints. If, the civil rights protesters contended, Northern Ireland was to belong to the United Kingdom, then they were entitled to their rights as British citizens.[1] This departure from the habitual Catholic rejection of partition may, as Unionists claim, have been only a ruse to disarm them of their traditional justification for the exclusion of Catholics from political power, but it succeeded anyway. Instead of reinforcing Protestant solidarity (as protests against partition had done), the civil rights movement exploited the divisions in the Unionist Party that had surfaced in the early 1960s. It trapped purported reformists such as O'Neill into backing earlier gestures with substantive reforms, while confirming the fear of the more traditional Unionist majority that one concession merely fuelled demands for more. Thus in discrediting the justification for Protestant domination, Catholics also shattered the formerly monolithic unity of the Unionist Party. For the first time since partition, Catholics deroutinized Unionist rule.

The civil rights movement held the initiative in Northern Ireland politics for only a year before it was superseded by a sequence of events it had itself brought about.[2] In that year, however, it awakened Catholics from their half-century of quiescence, destroyed Unionist unity, and forced Britain to commit its regular army. But these were the outcomes, not the objectives, of the civil rights movement. It pressed for:

1 universal franchise in local government elections in line with the franchise in the rest of the United Kingdom;
2 the redrawing of electoral boundaries by an independent commission to ensure fair representation;
3 legislation against discrimination in employment at the local government level and the provision of machinery to remedy local government grievances;
4 a compulsory points system for housing which would ensure fair allocation;
5 the repeal of the Special Powers Act;
6 the disbanding of the Ulster Special Constabulary (B Specials); and later
7 the withdrawal of the Public Order (Amendment) Bill.[3]

The civil rights movement was protesting against official discrimination at the local level (points 1–4), and against repressive legislation at the provincial level (points 5–7). The first point challenged municipal election laws that gave owners of businesses additional votes and denied votes to adults who were not heads of households. This obviously worked to the benefit of the more affluent – that is, Protestants – at the expense of the less affluent – that is, Catholics. The second point protested against blatant gerrymandering in several Northern Ireland cities, most conspicuously Derry. Unequal votes and gerrymandering enabled Protestants to control the municipal governments of several cities with Catholic majorities, and to use their control to allocate public housing and jobs to Protestants. Hence the third and fourth demands were designed to ensure the equitable allocation of municipal resources. The final three points challenged the repressive powers at Stormont's disposal. The crucial point, however, is that none of these planks challenged Protestant control of Stormont. While some of the more draconian powers of Unionists might have been curbed, their central institution was not challenged by the civil rights movement. Yet no matter how innocuous the civil rights demands were in themselves, they seemed subversive in the context of Northern Ireland. They posited equality; Northern Ireland reproduced inequality.

The call for Catholic equality, though unacceptable to the Unionist Party, was couched in such a way as to discredit Protestant supremacy. Previous Catholic protesters professed loyalty to an Irish republic in one form or another and, implicitly or explicitly, disloyalty to Northern Ireland, thereby justifying the denial of effective citizenship to Catholics. But once Catholics acknowledged their citizenship of the United Kingdom (albeit with less than complete sincerity) and demanded their rights, Unionists slowly divided between those willing and those refusing to entertain Catholic grievances. Unlike previous Catholic challenges that 'proved' the Catholic menace, and hence the need for Protestant vigilance, the civil rights movement had the opposite effect. It weakened Unionism's historic unity.

O'Neill's problem was less with the civil rights demands than with the Protestant reaction to them. Demonstrations were met with counter-demonstrations, and when O'Neill's rivals in the cabinet used the resulting threat of violence as a pretext for banning the original protests, the police dispersed the demonstrations that continued to occur. The result was riots,[4] and these riots, and especially the police overreactions, induced Britain to use the constitutional and financial powers at its disposal to press O'Neill for reforms. O'Neill consented in November 1968, offering a package of reforms that resolved several, but not all, of the grievances of the civil rights movement. In appeasing Britain, however, O'Neill had only antagonized Protestants without satisfying the more militant Catholics. Civil rights militants pointed out that the reforms were merely proposed, not implemented; that no commitment to the principle of 'one man, one vote' had been offered; that the Special Powers Act remained intact; and that the larger problem of unemployment was not even broached.[5] Meanwhile, recalcitrant Protestants both inside and outside the Unionist Party forced O'Neill to call an election that was, in effect, a referendum on his proposed reforms. He did not do very well.

Elections to Stormont were usually routine. Most constituencies were clearly Protestant or Catholic, so the candidate, once selected, was often returned unopposed. In the few constituencies that were evenly balanced, the elections were hard fought but insignificant (since whatever the outcome of the close races, the Unionist Party would easily control Stormont anyway). The February 1969 election was different. The Unionist Party split down the middle between pro-O'Neill and anti-O'Neill slates; Catholic constituencies likewise split between the Nationalist Party and the civil rights activists. The Nationalists were effectively destroyed by the civil rights candidates, but because Catholic influence in Stormont was negligible either way, the results of the Unionist split were much more significant. The results of the election were, in O'Neill's words, 'more indeterminate than I had hoped,'[6] as his slate won a bare majority over that of his opponents; his foremost critics in the party were re-elected; he himself was nearly beaten by Paisley; and his miniscule majority in Stormont melted into a minority as his followers realized there was a better future in reaction than in moderation.[7] In April, O'Neill resigned for the more dignified trappings of the House of Lords.

O'Neill's downfall was mostly the result of an impossible political situation. Continuing Catholic protests and police overreactions rendered Britain's hands-off policy untenable. But reforms that seemed unexceptionable to Britain proved unacceptable to Protestants, for the jobs, housing, and political power to which Catholics would become entitled had hitherto been reserved for them. Catholic gain would be Protestant loss.[8] With Protestant privileges threatened, those most dependent on them – the working class, Protestants in areas with Catholic majorities, and traditionalists – opposed reform, and so broke with O'Neill.[9] O'Neill was thus left in no-man's land. Britain encouraged him to advocate reforms that proved insufficient to Catholics and intolerable to the bulk of Protestants. O'Neill's fall thus illustrates the most enduring fact of Northern Ireland's colonial legacy: there is no base in the center – especially in times of confrontation.

Having forced O'Neill's resignation, the Protestant right wing, though as yet unable to make one of its own premier, was able to prevent an opponent from becoming prime minister. The compromise candidate was a cousin of O'Neill, James Chichester-Clark, whom the Unionist 'reformers' supported in preference to a representative of the

Unionist right. But as the demise of O'Neill had indicated the power of the intransigents, Chichester-Clark conceded the essence of their demands, and Britain went along with him lest he be replaced by his critics. Specifically, Chichester-Clark persuaded the British to consent to Orange parades in July and August 1969, despite the obvious dangers of inflammatory demonstrations in the midst of a tense political climate.[10] Thus Britain defended 'moderate' Unionists by, in effect, adopting the substance of right-wing Protestant demands. Predictably, the parades were more provocative than usual; the Catholic reaction was more defiant than usual; and the resulting riots more intense than usual. When Stormont could not restore order, the British government reluctantly dispatched the army to perform Stormont's job.

The fate of the civil rights movement suggests the futility of reformist solutions to Northern Ireland's problems. The demand for equality, while ostensibly moderate, in fact challenged the inequality at the heart of Ulster colonialism. Britain, not recognizing this, prevented the Unionist Party from ignoring the civil rights protest as it had ignored others, and drew O'Neill to a non-existent center. But though Catholics were tantalized by the promise of reform, the reality of official police repression induced them to withhold support until they saw results. Protestants, on the other hand, soon saw enough. They forced O'Neill's resignation, and his successor, while maintaining the illusion of reform, returned to the substance of repression. The police were unleashed on Catholics, and Orangemen allowed to march as they pleased.[11] Meanwhile, Britain feared that Chichester-Clark would be undermined unless allowed to adopt the policies of the intransigents. Britain reluctantly sanctioned sectarian provocations to avoid antagonizing the Protestants. This allowed the Protestants full opportunity to display their hostility towards the Catholics. The resulting violence forced Britain to intervene.

II

Britain was in an impossible political position. On the one hand, the Protestant riots in the summer of 1969 left it no choice but direct political and miltary intervention. On the other hand, Britain feared that any involvement in Northern Ireland would only deepen with time. As a compromise between the two extremes, Britain sought to minimize its unavoidable intervention lest it be 'sucked into the Irish bog.'[12] This meant that, irrespective of the merits of the two communities' grievances, the British government was disposed to upset the established order as little as possible. But to minimize disruption was, in practice, to maintain Unionist rule over Stormont. The only plausible alternatives – direct rule from Britain or Catholic power-sharing in Stormont – would, by forcing Britain to replace the Unionist Party as the predominant force in Northern Ireland's politics, have intensified the involvement that Britain preferred to escape. In consequence, Britain rejected both alternatives in favor of continued Unionist rule on condition that Stormont show more sensitivity to Catholic civil rights. In confirming the power of the Unionist Party, however, Britain minimized the impact of whatever civil rights were implemented, in effect putting the fox in charge of the hen house. When the resulting Catholic dissatisfaction took increasingly violent form, Britain shifted the army from protecting to repressing Catholics. Thus, the very reluctance to intervene in Northern Ireland that, on the one hand, induced Britain to let Protestants remain in control, resulted, on the other hand, in involving Britain in the repression of Catholics that Protestants demanded. Britain could not win for losing.

If Britain was eventually to side with the Protestants, it had no such intention when the British government first intervened. After putting an end to the rioting (at least for the time being), Britain sought to satisfy some Catholic demands. It agreed that Protestants had not only initiated the violence but had been actively assisted by the police and the B Specials. In consequence, Britain insisted on reform lest the army appear to Catholics to confirm Protestant superiority. As James Callaghan (then Home Secretary and, as such, the cabinet minister responsible for Northern Ireland) wrote later, he

> was certain that politically it would be a grave mistake to put British troops under the authority of the Ulster Unionist Government. Practically the whole of the Catholic population was by now thoroughly roused, and if the British Army were to appear to be an arm of the Ulster Unionist Government, the Catholics in their turn were likely to regard the troops with the same distaste as they regarded their Government.[13]

It was therefore

> unthinkable . . . that either the British Government or Parliament would have supported a proposal to hand over British troops to prop up a regime which had lost so much authority, unless reforms were made.[14]

To this end Callaghan proposed reforms of the police, of the allocation of public housing, of discrimination in public employment and of unemployment in general, and of the educational system; and finally he proposed the appointment of a Minister of Community Relations.[15] These reforms deeply troubled Protestants, for with the overt, even official, sectarianism that Stormont had habitually practiced unacceptable to Britain, their traditional privileges seemed in jeopardy.

While Protestants protested against the reforms, heckled British officials touring their areas, blustered in Stormont, and, in November 1969, rioted in the 'ultra-loyalist' Shankhill area of Belfast, Catholics were elated as much, it seems, by the humiliation of Protestants as by the reforms themselves. As Eamonn McCann wrote, Callaghan was popular among Catholics because he

> symbolized the political defeat of the Unionist Party. They were no longer calling the shots. The boss himself had arrived to put them in their place, and their discomfiture, of which his surly reception in the Fountain [a Protestant area of Derry] was seen as an example, was pleasant to behold. Things were going our way.[16]

This, indeed, was the crux of Callaghan's problem. To give Catholics even formal equality was to take from Protestants their hallowed superiority. Thus Protestants were threatened by the gestures directed at Catholics. Callaghan could disguise but not solve the dilemma. That was in effect his strategy: to oversell reforms which in themselves were modest.

The reforms initially appeared to both Protestants and Catholics to mark a fundamental change in the structure of Northern Ireland, but their significance was more symbolic than substantive. Symbolically, the reforms, by admitting the legitimacy of Catholic demands for equality, undercut the principle of Protestant superiority that had been the *raison d'être* of Stormont. But they did not threaten the substance of superiority. In material terms, Catholics had achieved only the opportunity to apply without prejudice for future openings in public housing and employment. In the meantime, Protestants were to retain not only a disproportionate share of the public jobs and housing already allocated, but also their privileged access to private employment. Their material, if not psychological, privileges remained more or less intact.

The British government realized that the reforms ultimately

protected Protestant privileges, but doubted that Protestants would realize this. What Protestants lost would be more salient than what they had kept. Britain therefore withheld more substantive reforms lest they enrage 'still further the mob element among the extreme Protestants.[17] As Callaghan was to note later, the reforms of the police – and by implication, the reforms in general – were

> scarcely revolutionary and did not warrant ... a furious reaction. But in a real sense they undermined the dominant world the Protestants had inhabited for so long, a world of entirely different assumptions and objectives. The Protestants had settled ideas about the nature of their society and their ascendancy over the minority, and felt this was all cut from under their feet by [reform]. Psychologically, it was very traumatic for them, and I tried to understand this.[18]

Retreating from the reforms necessary to actualize the promised equality, Britain disappointed the Catholic expectations that it had raised by promising reform. Callaghan himself admitted as much; Protestants had 'been in control for fifty years and were likely to *remain in control*.'[19] Thus both Protestants and Catholics had been deceived by the appearance of reform; Protestants had lost as little as Catholics had gained. It was to take several months before this became clear to the respective communities, but once realized it confirmed Callaghan's original warning: if the British army served Stormont, Catholics 'were likely to regard the troops with the same distaste as they regarded their Government.'

It was not long before Protestants and Catholics switched views on Britain and its reforms. At the outset Catholics celebrated the reforms as their first victory over Unionists in the half-century since partition, and the reforms were bemoaned by Protestants for much the same reason. As time wore on, however, and it became clear that the reforms did not undercut Protestant privilege, Protestants tentatively reaffirmed their loyalty to Britain, while Catholics reverted to their traditional disloyalty. Equal access to new openings in public housing and employment, even if fairly instituted, did not matter much given that there were comparatively few vacancies in public employment or housing, not to mention in the private sector. Improvements would, at best, have been very gradual; Catholics, however, especially the young, were impatient for results after they had first protested peacefully, next defended their neighborhoods physically, and had finally won what seemed an unprecedented victory. As McCann wrote, in

> a hundred other dusty streets in Derry and Belfast, things were [no] different. Reforms had filtered through on to the statute book. An Ombudsman had been appointed. Derry Corporation had been abolished and replaced by a Development Commission. A points system for the allocation of houses was in operation. Moderate Unionists could, and often did, point proudly to this record of progress. None of it, however, made any difference to the clumps of unemployed teenagers who stood, fists dug deep into their pockets, around William Street in the evenings. Briefly elevated into folk-hero status in the heady days of August, praised and patronized by local leaders for their expertise with the stone and petrol bomb, they had now been dragged back down into the anonymous depression which had hitherto been their constant condition. For them at least, nothing had changed and they were bitterly cynical about the talk of a reformed future. 'We'll get nothing out of it. The Orangemen are still in power.' Occasionally they would stone the soldiers. It was small-scale stuff.[20]

McCann attributes this increasing Catholic dissatisfaction to the failure of civil rights, despite the ballyhoo, to improve social conditions by very much. Unemployment remained extremely high for Catholics, especially teenagers, and prospects for future employment were as dim as ever. Meanwhile housing, already inadequate throughout Northern Ireland, had been worsened by the dislocation following the August riots. The housing segregation that had been the norm in Northern Ireland had eased somewhat during the 1960s, but the riots drove Catholics back to those areas where insufficient housing had been an important impetus for the civil rights movement in the first place. With their expectations having been raised by the initial successes of the movement, Catholic demands now shifted from formal rights to effective power.

Catholics blamed their continuing frustrations on Unionist rule; as McCann records, Catholics complained that 'Orangemen [were] still in power.' The complaint was not without justification. Britain had, it is true, put an end to the gerrymandering that enabled Unionists to control Catholic majorities in a few areas, most notably Derry. But Derry was the exception, not the rule. In most areas, and certainly for the province as a whole, Unionists had no need to gerrymander: the majority supported them already. Thus while disbanding unfair election rules had a definite symbolic effect, it did not fundamentally affect the distribution of power. Unionists could win fairly as well as unfairly. At both the local and provincial levels of government,

> the structure of power was left intact. Catholics might get fairer representation than before; but they would still be a permanent minority, with no prospect of taking part in government at the centre, and no entitlement to seats on public bodies except by Protestant grace. Indeed, with the patronage these reforms placed in the gift of the central government, the power of the unreformed Stormont actually increased.[21]

The problem, however, was not so much that the reforms were not implemented in good faith as that the Catholics were upset by their insufficiency and the Protestants by their excess. Under these circumstances, the best Britain could do was to cultivate one community at the expense of the other, and it did not even accomplish this, as the riots provoked by preliminary Orange parades in late June 1970 proved. Most of the fighting occurred between Protestants and Catholics, with the British army caught in between, endeavoring, without much success, to keep the two sides apart.[22] In other words, Britain acted in the riots in the same way as it had acted during the preceding year: its policy swerved first one way, then the other, as it was trapped between the mutually exclusive demands of the two communities. Since Britain was committed less to one side or the other than to the restoration of order, it favored whichever side was currently threatening stability. The consequences of British vacillation were apparent in the riots. Britain had not only failed to satisfy both communities; it had failed to satisfy either. Confronted by the simultaneous increase in both Protestant reaction and Catholic resistance, Britain dropped the carrot for the stick – repression replaced reform.

The shift from symbolic reforms to repression coincided with a change in Britain from a Labour to a Conservative government. Within two weeks, the Tories permitted the army to escalate a routine search for arms into a major riot, declared a curfew for several days, and, finally, as if to make sure that Catholics got the message straight, allowed the army to chauffeur two 'beaming Unionist ministers . . . on a tour round the subjugated Falls [area of Belfast].'[23] The 'Falls curfew,' as the incident was called, signified a decisive reversal in policy; previously Protestants and Catholics alike had believed that the army protected Catholics from Protestant attacks (although by this time Catholic confidence was fast fading). Now, however, both communities perceived that the army had reversed sides, that the Catholics it had once protected were to be subordinated to the exigencies of Unionist politics. The switch was soon confirmed by increased army harrasment of, and inequitable prison sentences for, Catholics.[24] The effect of such discriminatory treatment was, however, very different from that anticipated by the Unionists who urged it on the British. Instead of daunting Catholics, it deepened their opposition to the army that was backing an unrepentant Stormont. By clearly defending Protestant superiority, by occupying Catholic but not Protestant areas, and by refusing to insist on further reforms, Britain persuaded Catholics that it could no longer be trusted to protect their interests. Such, of course, had always been the point of the republicans: the British delivered Catholics to the emerging Provisional Irish Republican Army.

Prior to the outbreak of violence in the summer of 1969, northern republicanism had been in eclipse for decades. Its most important task – the protection of Catholic areas in case of Protestant rioting – had lost its urgency for most Catholics, as had its goal of unifying Ireland.[25] Catholics made this point unmistakeably clear to the IRA when they ignored its bombing campaign that began in the mid-1950s and lasted until the early 1960s. The indifference of Catholics, in turn, induced the IRA in the mid-1960s to re-evaluate the efficacy of physical force against the border and to conclude that partition could be ended only by the united efforts of the Protestant and Catholic working classes. Consequently, the IRA not only made extremely unsuccessful overtures to Protestant workers but also demilitarized[26] and drove traditionalists opposed to such innovations out of the organization. The traditionalists, still convinced that the connection with Britain caused all Northern Ireland's problems and that it could be severed only by physical force, were vindicated in 1969 when the very Protestant workers whom the socialist republicans were invoking as allies invaded Catholic areas, and the IRA, which was supposed to protect Catholics under such circumstances, proved unable to perform its duty: it had sold its guns. With the socialists thus discredited (in Belfast the graffiti ran: 'IRA = I Ran Away'[27]), the traditionalists reorganized as the Provisional (as opposed to the Official) IRA. By

1970 the Provisionals were mobilizing the resistance that increased along with British repression.

The Provisionals insisted that the struggle was the same as always: the Irish against the British army. This belief had few adherents among the Catholics when the British rescued them from Protestant rioters, but became increasingly plausible as the army responded to Protestant pressure by escalating the harassment of Catholics. By harassing Catholics on behalf of Protestants, the army confirmed the Provisional's diagnosis and remedy: the problem was Britain and the solution was physical force. Such an interpretation was, moreover, much more consistent with Catholic political traditions than with the civil rights movement. Civil rights, after all, implied Catholic recognition of British authority, and while recognition had successfully divided Unionists, it did conflict with the deeply held conviction of Catholics that they were rightfully Irish, not British, citizens. The resulting confusion deepened when the army acted against Protestants on behalf of Catholics. For while Catholics certainly enjoyed the spectacle of Britain disciplining Protestants, some had misgivings about rooting for Britain. When the army turned to repressing Catholics, however, traditional Catholic identities were confirmed and 'people were almost relieved gradually to discover that the guiltily discarded [republican] tradition on which the community was founded was, after all, meaningful and immediately relevant.'[28]

As support for them grew, the Provisionals turned from an essentially defensive to an offensive force. By early 1971, they were planting bombs, attacking patrols, and forcing Catholics to choose between parliamentary and violent protest.[29] Meanwhile Protestants, enraged by the Provisionals' attacks on their lives, property, and institutions, demanded that the army 'do something.' And the army, itself frustrated and at a loss for what else to do, increased arms raids, beatings, and occasional killings,[30] thereby playing into the Provisionals' hands. For while the attacks were too wild to hurt the Provisionals, they confirmed the need for protection that the Provisionals answered.

The escalating repression strengthened the Provisionals indirectly as well as directly. Directly, they benefited from behavior that intensified the colonial dichotomy. In confirming the Catholic belief that it was 'us' versus 'them', the British induced Catholics to support the Provisionals not only as part of 'us,' but also as the part providing protection from 'them.'[31] Indirectly, repression hampered the exercise of normal civil authority, reducing the government's capacity to discharge such mundane tasks as the maintenance of social services, the allocation of public housing, and the defense of law and order in Catholic areas. These tasks devolved increasingly onto the IRA, not so much because the IRA wanted, for example, to allocate housing, as because the task had to be done and with the breakdown of public authority no other organization in the Catholic community was both willing and able to do it.[32] Thus the IRA, though hardly a government in the orthodox sense, was by virtue of its military role expected to perform many of the responsibilities normally associated with government. It was as if Catholics had adopted the Weberian definition of a state; recognizing the IRA's violence as legitimate, they expected it to discharge the other functions attendant on the organization monopolizing legitimate violence. This role, which in the first instance reflected the authority of the Provisionals among the Catholics, in the second reinforced that authority. By filling the void created by the shift of the British from the Catholic to the Protestant side, the Provisionals assumed *de facto* control of Catholic working-class areas.

Catholic working-class areas of Belfast, Derry, and other cities were 'no-go' areas. That is, the British army respected the barricades that Catholics had erected to keep the police out, allowing the Provisionals to operate with near impunity in their areas. From these sanctuaries the Provisionals conducted what they fancied to be an 'economic' war which, by escalating the financial costs of British involvement, would force Britain from Ireland. To this end, the Provisionals occasionally destroyed a plant of economic significance, but mostly bombed small businesses owned and frequented by Protestants such as pubs. While effective economically,[33] the bombing campaign was even more effective politically. Unionist associations, backbenchers, and opinion demanded that Chichester-Clark extend 'law and order' to the republican sanctuaries.[34] This of course required British approval. But Britain balked at the implications of such a move, leaving Chichester-Clark in an untenable position; his hold on the party, never strong, weakened irretrievably as Unionists insisted on action that he could not deliver. When Britain vetoed the escalation demanded by Chichester-Clark, he resigned and was succeeded by Brian Faulkner.[35]

Faulkner initially made a gesture towards the Social Democratic and Labour Party (SDLP), the Catholic political party formed in 1970 to replace the discredited Nationalist Party. The offer, which would have given the SDLP control over several committees in Stormont, was accepted by the SDLP. But before the deal was implemented, the

British Army killed two Catholics under questionable circumstances, leading the SDLP to withdraw from Stormont.[36] Having failed to co-opt moderate Catholics, Faulkner then returned to a policy of pure repression, insisting on more troops, tougher methods, and, most of all, internment of suspected republicans. Britain, and especially the army, was reluctant to authorize internment, for the army realized that intelligence about the Provisionals was unreliable and internment would likely cause more trouble than it would prevent.[37] But rather than undermine a third Stormont premier, the British government overruled the military and authorized internment.

Internment permitted the arrest and imprisonment of persons suspected of terrorist offenses without the formalities of a trial. The lists of those to be interned were drawn up by the Stormont Minister of Home Affairs, who was responsible for co-ordinating the security forces. With Faulkner heading this ministry as well as the government, internment expressed his dual objectives of pre-empting the Unionist right wing by crushing the Provisionals. It was Faulkner's misfortune, however, that these objectives were incompatible, that in attacking Catholics, apparently at the behest of sectarian Protestants, Faulkner intensified the colonial dichotomy and united the Catholic 'us' (which included the Provisionals) against his government. Moreover, the lack of accurate information on the Provisional leadership led the British army to arrest many Catholics with little, if any, connection with the Provisionals,[38] with the inevitable result of an increase in the number of Catholics financing, protecting, and joining the Provisionals.[39] Rather than crushing the Provisionals, internment exacerbated the grievances that led Britain to repress Catholics in the first place, as was made perfectly clear by a series of demonstrations that culminated in Derry on 30 January 1972. That day's demonstration was banned by Faulkner, and amidst the fairly routine rioting that followed the attempt to disperse it, the army killed 13 Catholics and wounded a dozen more. The details of the shooting were disputed, although even the British commission investigating the killings found that at least nine, and probably even 11 of the dead were definitely unarmed.[40] But whatever the truth may have been, the killing of 13 demonstrators protesting against a policy that violated British constitutional principles, convinced the British government that it had performed Stormont's dirty work long enough. Repression had sullied Britain's international reputation, fuelled a bombing campaign that weakened an already depressed economy, and revitalized the forces it intended to repress. With the costs of repression disproportionate to its gains,

Britain reversed course yet once again. It tried to mollify the Catholics by redressing their paramount grievance: Britain abolished Stormont.

III

The 'Protestant parliament for a Protestant people' was technically 'prorogued,' in fact abolished, on 28 March 1972, and replaced by 'direct rule' from London.[41] Once again, however, Britain was caught in a predicament in which concessions to one side brought prompt retaliation from the other. And this time Britain put itself squarely between the two sides. The Provisionals (not to say Catholics) interpreted the abolition of Stormont as a sign of British weakness, from which they concluded that more bombs would achieve unification. Protestants likewise saw the end of Stormont as a step by Britain towards the unification of Ireland, and fearful that Britain was about to abandon them altogether,[42] Protestants flocked to the emerging Ulster Defence Association (UDA) and Ulster Volunteer Force (UVF). These paramilitary organizations, which were especially attractive to Protestant workers, engaged in direct action of various kinds, including the murder of Catholics, who were regarded in intent, if not always in fact, as republicans.[43]

In response to the murders of increasing numbers of Catholics, the Provisionals retaliated against Protestants, inaugurating the tit-for-tat murders that set the backdrop of Northern Ireland's politics for the next decade, and creating a major problem for British policy.[44] Britain had disbanded Stormont to drive a wedge between the Provisionals and their supporters. The idea was that Catholics, though not enamored of the Provisionals, supported them because of the sectarianism of Stormont. Britain concluded from this that the elimination of Stormont would entice Catholics from confrontation to compromise. The immediate results were, from Britain's perspective, encouraging, as signs emerged that Catholics were exerting pressure on the Provisionals to drop 'armed struggle.' Tired of the costs of urban political violence, and convinced that the Provisionals, in destroying Stormont, had won most of what could be won through violence, Catholics pressured the Provisionals to enter into a truce with the British army. The truce proved short lived and the Provisionals returned to the bombing campaign in earnest a month later. But their reversion to violence after such a brief respite fundamentally weakened their position. On the one hand, Catholics were beginning to worry that the Provisionals preferred war to peace, and on the other, the army was able to exploit Catholic dissatisfaction with the Provisionals to enter the 'no-go' areas and to deprive the Provisionals of secure bases for their operations.

The decision of the Provisionals to pursue a strategy that was increasingly less popular among Catholics cost them dearly, but they were spared from paying the full political price by the random murder of Catholics committed by the Protestant paramilitaries. The army was unable (and the police perhaps unwilling) to stop these, which reaffirmed the dependence of Catholics on the Provisionals for protection. In this period it was not possible to prevent a gang of men from travelling several blocks from one area to the next, grabbing a victim or tossing a bomb, and then returning to the home base before the casualties had even been counted. It was possible, however, to hope that retaliation against the attackers' community would discourage more killings of Catholics. The consequence of this was that Protestant paramilitaries, by responding to the abrogation of Stormont with direct attacks on Catholics, strengthened the Provisionals at the very time when British concessions had weakened the Provisionals among Catholics. Even British successes turned to failure.

Britain's inability to contain, still less to eliminate, the violence that followed the abolition of Stormont convinced it of the need for new governing institutions that would assure Catholics a role in governing Northern Ireland. To this end Britain issued a two-pronged proposal to establish a new provincial government in late 1972. First, Britain dropped its earlier contention that the Irish government had no legitimate interest in Northern Ireland. The British government offered, and the Irish government agreed, to establish a commission comprised of British, Irish, and Northern Irish representatives to consider matters of joint concern to the Irish and Northern Irish governments. The powers and jurisdictions of the new Council of Ireland were ambiguous, but its formation acknowledged the interest of the Irish Republic in Ulster's affairs.[45] In exchange, Britain expected more co-operation from Dublin in combating the IRA. Secondly, Britain proposed to sanction an Assembly for Northern Ireland on condition that representatives of the SDLP be included in the executive of the government. Britain intended, by guaranteeing Catholics a share of institutional power, to fashion effective institutions to cause Catholics to press their demands through the SDLP, not the Provisionals. By weakening republicans, Britain hoped to undercut those Protestants depending on republican excesses for their position.

Power-sharing and the Council of Ireland constituted Britain's first attempt to end the violence through the inclusion of Catholics in a government of Northern Ireland. Originally Britain had granted civil rights to Catholics, but in practice this had amounted to formal, not substantive, equality, with the institutions that were to protect Catholic gains (such as they were) remaining under Unionist control. Britain had next abolished Stormont, but the disbandment of the institution which denied Catholics political power was not the same as extending power to them. It was this deficiency that power-sharing was to redress. Britain recognized Catholics as legitimate citizens with legitimate claims on the government. Legitimacy, however, is precisely what Protestants, and especially those most dependent upon colonial privileges for their interests and identities, were determined to deny Catholics. To appeal to Catholics, as Britain discovered, was to mobilize Protestants in general and workers in particular in opposition to its plans.

Catholics endorsed the power-sharing government for the very reason that Protestants were to reject it: the new executive would have constituted their first effective representation since partition. Despite the opposition of the Provisionals, the SDLP easily carried the Catholic vote in the elections to the Assembly and subsequently suffered none of the conflicts that were beginning to beset the Unionists. The Unionist Party, however, balked at sharing power with the SDLP, which forced Faulkner to split from his party if he was to fulfill his ambition of heading the new government. Although Faulkner was able to carry enough supporters with him to become prime minister, he and his Protestant backers were now facing a hostile and united community. Protestants had voted decisively against power-sharing and the Council of Ireland in elections to the Assembly, and when power-sharing was installed anyway, the Protestant working-class spearheaded a general strike. The strike soon brought Northern Ireland's economy to a stop, partly because of widespread compliance among Protestant workers and partly because these workers controlled the most important jobs by virtue of sectarian hiring patterns. Meanwhile, the Protestant paramilitaries assumed overt control of Protestant working-class areas, establishing roadblocks, dispensing work permits, and allocating food. In response, both British and Northern Irish governments blustered, issued counter-threats, bemoaned the economic calamity, and vowed never to surrender to such blackmail. Two weeks later the power-sharing government resigned.

The success of the strike dashed British hopes of co-opting 'responsible' Catholics. Power-sharing depended, obviously, on co-operation among Protestant and Catholic politicians; if Protestant politicians were unwilling or unable to co-operate, British plans were caught in an unsolvable dilemma. Britain recognized, on the one hand, that the formation of institutions based broadly among both Protestants and Catholics was the only alternative to conceding the Provisionals enough support among Catholics to continue their campaign indefinitely. But, on the other, Protestants destroyed these same institutions in the name of opposing creeping republicanism. Thus by the mid-1970s Britain, having failed with both repression and moderation, and having admitted to itself that no other policy was available, sought to·cushion itself from the costs of failure. Thereafter, its overriding concern was to minimize its commitments in Northern Ireland: it sought to disrupt matters as little as possible, to appease whichever side could cause more trouble. However, this choice also carried costs, for in effectively upholding the established structure of Protestant privilege, it assured the Provisionals of their base among Catholics.

IV

From the outbreak of riots over civil rights through the demise of the power-sharing executive, violence was a means used in pursuit of goals that were tacitly, if not actively, supported by much of one community or the other. With the collapse of power-sharing, however, the violence entered a stage that extended through the rest of the decade, one in which violence became less a means to other ends than an end in itself. The three main actors – Protestants, Catholics, and Britain – disagreed deeply on what constituted an acceptable solution, with Protestants having blocked reform, and Catholics having shown the futility of repression unaccompanied by reform. British policy subsequently oscillated between the poles of reform and repression, raising fears among both Protestants and Catholics that Britain would join with the other. To reduce the likelihood of this possibility, elements of both communities used violence to remind Britain of the perils awaiting unpopular initiatives. The centrality of violence to Northern Ireland's politics, moreover, brought to the fore groups that were more adept at killing people than at organizing them. These groups, having seized the initiative in one community, then reinforced their counterparts in the other. The violence of loyalists justified and necessitated that of republicans and vice versa, as Northern Ireland's politics steadily degenerated into that of 'the last atrocity.'

Faced with the failure of reformist policies in the wake of the general strike, Britain first denied, then resigned itself to the worsening situation. Britain initially decided to try again; it called for a constitutional convention to establish a new government that would include power sharing, an Irish dimension, and recognition of its right to veto legislation. But when the ensuing elections to the convention were swept by a coalition of unionist parties implacably opposed to power-sharing, Britain tacitly acknowledged defeat and moved to cut its losses. Having already decided that the only viable solution to the violence was to include both communities in a devolved government, and having failed to establish such a government, Britain made the best of a bad situation. It opted for a series of measures designed to shift from itself the worst consequences of the conflict. Britain would allow Northern Ireland to stew in its own mess.

This meant that for the remainder of the 1970s, Britain half-heartedly explored alternatives to direct rule, generally by testing various proposals among the established parties in the hope of discovering consensus for devolving some governmental functions back to Northern Ireland. Failing repeatedly in this task, Britain avoided threatening Protestants with unification unless they consented to power-sharing in favor of a policy of 'Ulsterization' that decreed Northern Ireland's violence to be criminal, not political, in nature,[46] and as such, to be the responsibility primarily of the police, not the army. The attraction of 'Ulsterization' to Britain was that, by reducing Britain's role in Northern Ireland, it diminished the possibility of a major calamity.[47]

Britain's most costly decisions had been those, such as internment and power-sharing, that mobilized one community or the other against it. In contrast, Ulsterization allowed Britain to minimize these dangers, although at the price of deepening the morass that increased long-term costs. For in guaranteeing Protestants that unification could come only with their consent, Britain encouraged them to block power-sharing while keeping partition. And in thus weakening Catholic moderates, Britain strengthened the Provisionals.

Britain's strategy of distancing itself from Northern Ireland allowed unionists to retain the link with Britain, block power-sharing, and veto British initiatives, but prevented the formation of institutions that they could control. Clearly, Britain wanted to begin devolving powers onto Northern Ireland, yet it dared not do so until moderate Catholics were brought into the picture. Thus in vetoing power-sharing and frustrating moderate Catholics, unionists deprived themselves of institutions in which they would have exercised predominate, if not exclusive, influence. Protestant unity extended no further, however, than the demand for 'majority rule' and the rejection of anything less. Beyond this, different actors pursued different ambitions, as the Ulster Unionist Party and the Democratic Unionist Party (DUP) of Paisley competed for electoral ascendancy, and as the paramilitaries struggled to maintain their position. In the latter half of the 1970s and the early 1980s, loyalist paramilitaries were hurt by internal corruption and arrests. But their essential problem was that support for them derived from the failure of unionist politicians to stave off British initiatives, as is shown by their popularity in the period between the elimination of Stormont and the collapse of the power-sharing executive. But the success of the paramilitaries was, paradoxically, their undoing, for having established to Britain's satisfaction the price of reform, Britain dropped reformist policies and reduced the need for the services provided by the paramilitaries. The paramilitaries survived anyway, ready to surface in case of British 'betrayal,' but in the meantime their foremost function was to help the Provisionals by killing Catholics randomly.

The combination of Protestant intransigence and British inattention limited the options available to Catholics. Catholic support for the Provisionals dwindled largely because they continued to bomb away regardless of the circumstances. Having squandered much of their earlier popularity among Catholics by emphasizing violent to the exclusion of political strategies, the Provisionals left themselves vulnerable to the increasingly sophisticated counter-insurgency tech-niques of Britain. The conjunction of their excesses and British restraint hurt the Provisionals severely; donations, solidarity, and the quality of recruits declined. The Church reiterated that membership in the Provisionals was 'a mortal sin which will one day have to be accounted before God,'[48] and the SDLP consolidated its hold on Catholics. Here, however, Protestant intransigence intervened to save the Provisionals. No matter how far their popularity among Catholics fell, the Provisionals could survive as long as Catholics had no other way of redressing their grievances. And unionists, by refusing to share power with the SDLP, frustrated effective alternatives to the Provi-sionals. This, in turn, invited the fate the Protestants most dreaded: sustained republican violence.

Even though their political base was ultimately protected by unionists, the Provisionals floundered through the 1970s until, like the martyrs of 1916, they salvaged their fortunes through desperate self-sacrifice. In 1981, after a dozen years of violence, the last nine of which had produced no victories of note, the Provisionals resorted to one of their favored means of protest: the hunger strike. Republican prisoners demanded that those among their number who had been incarcerated since 1976 receive the same political status as those imprisoned before then. When this demand was rejected, some engaged in hunger strikes, with 11 ultimately dying without achieving political status. Britain, displaying its inimitable capacity to misread the political situation in Northern Ireland, declared a major victory over 'terrorism,' only to discover that the symbolism of republicans sacrificing themselves for their cause reversed the losses of a decade. In the decade between the abolition of Stormont and the hunger strikes, the Provisionals had floundered; since the strikes, the Provisionals have, for reasons to be discussed below, recovered the political initiative among Catholics and presented Britain with an intractable enemy. For if the Provisionals often salvaged defeat from victory (as in the wake of Stormont's abolition), they also drew inspiration from their defeats (as in the hunger strikes), which makes them as unlikely to surrender as to prevail. Throughout the 1970s, the Provisionals maintained the struggle they could not win.

V

The argument in this chapter has been that the violence in Northern Ireland results from the enduring conflict of Protestants and Catholics over the vestiges of colonial privileges. Protestants demand a structure of domination, which Catholics resist. Caught between these conflicting pressures, Britain has alternated between reformist and repressive policies. Although neither policy has succeeded in restoring stability to Northern Ireland, both did address the essential problem of the dissatisfaction of Catholics with their subjugation. By the middle of the 1970s, however, both policies had exhausted themselves. The futility of repression unattended by reform was exposed by the failure of internment, and the infeasibility of consensual reform was asserted by the general strike. In response to these failures, successive British governments refrained from pursuing significant initiatives for the remainder of the decade. But this course also failed, since it encouraged violence as the only effective means of political expression. What cries out for explanation, therefore, are the reasons, on the one hand, that unionists thwart accommodations with moderate Catholics, and on the other, that republicans regenerate themselves through apparent failure. Why do both persist in the behavior that reproduces violence?

Part II

5

Rebellion as a Cause

'It is not those who can inflict the most, but those who can suffer the most who will conquer.'

A republican hunger striker

I

The argument so far has stressed that the social order of Northern Ireland privileges Protestants at the expense of Catholics, links class interests to national and religious identities, and renders cleavages mutually reinforcing. With social relations systematically reproducing the contradiction of Protestants to Catholics, the social base for co-operative politics is lacking. Instead of being integrated into one mutually acceptable society or insulated in autonomous sectors, Northern Ireland's two communities are linked by the domination of one over the other. It is this domination which precludes one of the most discussed forms of power-sharing, that of 'consociational democracy.' Consociational democracy, as one of its most influential analysts points out, consists of deliberate efforts by elites to 'turn a democracy with a fragmented political culture into a stable democracy,' usually by forming coalition cabinets. This, according to Arend Lijphart, occurs only when no single 'subculture' is strong enough to establish 'clear hegemony.'[1] In Northern Ireland, however, unionists are able to posit, defend, and maintain their hegemony over Catholics, meaning that instead of an understanding to encourage agreement on some matters and the agreement to disagree on others, Protestants press for clear and decisive supremacy. Thus they proclaim the sanctity of the union with Britain that underpins their position, and Catholics, whether through nationalism or republicanism, challenge the union for the same reason.

Republicanism and unionism express the opposite experiences of colonialism, the one challenging and the other defending it. For this reason they are interlocking, not separate, politics. By excluding even moderate nationalists from real and symbolic power, unionism strengthens republicans, and the stronger republicans become, the more desperate Protestants are to exclude Catholics. As intransigents in one community reinforce those in the other, unionism and republicanism play out the original Protestant–Catholic contradiction politically. This is attributable less to the peculiarities of Northern Ireland than to the dynamics of settler colonialism, as is suggested by the similarities of Northern Ireland to South Africa. In both, settlers separate and privilege themselves, enabling the otherwise vulnerable settler working classes to use the resulting native threat to increase their leverage over elites. This means that native disloyalty is functional for Protestant and Afrikaner workers, giving them political as well as psychological incentives to exclude their rivals. It is for this reason that Protestants in the 1912–14 Ulster crisis and the 1974 general strike frustrated British initiatives to extend effective political power to Catholics. Defining their identities as well as their interests in contrast to those of Catholics, they depend on the distinction between the legitimacy of their, and the illegitimacy of Catholic, aspirations. This, in a nutshell, is why from the seventeenth to the twentieth centuries Protestants have steadfastly demanded the exclusion of Catholics from established political power; they realized that to legitimate Catholic interests was to delegitimate Protestant hegemony.[2]

Unionists normally emphasize their loyalty to Britain, praising the Queen, flying the Union Jack, and staging loyalist parades. These professions are by no means disingenuous, as Protestants sincerely wish Britain to honor them as they honor it. But should they be forced to choose between loyalty to His or Her Majesty's government and to their special privileges, unionists not only defend their privileges but actively challenge British authority. While at the outset constitutional, their challenges rapidly turn unconstitutional unless Britain relents on its reforms. For the relationship of Protestants to Britain is ambivalent; on the one hand, Protestant hegemony depends on Britain's tacit, and sometimes active, consent, while on the other it can clash with British interests. Subject to the dual threat of British betrayal and Catholic rebellion, Protestants are caught in a position that is never fully secure. And when their latent insecurity becomes overt, Protestants act with a desperation belying their professed deference to Britain and all things British. 'Loyalism' incites loyalist rebellion.

The insistence of Protestants on reserving political power for themselves means that certain political tendencies, even if supported by a majority of Catholics, remain insignificant politically. In particular, Catholic parliamentarians are frustrated by the enduring fact that, both before and after partition, they were a permanent minority in Westminster and Stormont. As a minority accepting that majorities rule, Catholic parliamentarians, even if supported by most Catholics, were doomed to irrelevance; they were parliamentarians without a parliament. And on those rare occasions on which Catholics were backed by Britain, as happened with home rule and power-sharing, it mattered not a whit, for unionists were not about to allow parliamentary headcounts to undercut their superiority.[3] The consequence of the defeats incurred by 'responsible' Catholics is that the strength of republicans is disproportionate to their numbers. Although typically a minority of the Catholic population, republicans are well positioned to exploit the grievances preserved by Protestant intransigence. Even if republicans fail as ignominiously as parliamentarians, they can survive; they have developed an ethos that does not depend on political power, but, because it thrives on adversity, can sustain the struggle it has yet to win.

II

British governments have a difficult time making sense of Irish republicanism, which is not surprising given the differences between republican and British history. While the history of the republicans is about rebellion, British history has not only produced few rebellions, but has sought since the Whig interpretation of the Glorious Revolution, to understand even these as final, desperate recourses justified by the need to put institutions back on track, as the exceptions that restore the rules. No wonder, then, that Irish republicanism confounds Britain; for instead of resorting to rebellion to restore normality, republicans rebel as a matter of course, continuing to resist Britain no matter how overpowering the forces arrayed against them. In this manner republicans have created the central paradox of their movement. On the one hand, they incur defeat after defeat and leave a trail of destruction, but on the other, they keep coming back for more and assure that no defeat is final. Thus if republicans cannot win for losing, neither can they lose for winning.

The difference between republican victories and defeats would seem to be clear enough. Having posited an independent and united republic as their goal, republicans presumably would win if they achieved an Irish republic and would lose if they suffered high and continuing casualties without establishing one. But republicanism defies such easy classification; its history is comprised of many more defeats than victories, and its main victory – independence-cum-partition – is rejected as a failure. That republicans have actually survived raises two fundamental questions. First, why do people join a movement that has suffered centuries of real and perceived failures? And secondly, what has republicanism had to become to survive the string of failures that results from British repression, Protestant determination, and Catholic indifference?

The answer to the second question is that republicanism has adapted successfully to its unhappy tradition, that it has constituted failure as success and used its most abject defeats to revitalize the cause. Republicans act against such great odds that they not only fail to seize power, but often end up dead. Republicans, however, take this as evidence less of failure than of success, their point being that their sacrifices succeed if they are remembered, and they have learned how to memoralize failure and use it to recruit new support. But however skillfully republicans blur the distinction between victory and defeat, they are successful only because objective conditions are ripe for such interpretations, because Britain tacitly and actively backs Protestant domination. In consequence, Britain, by denying Catholics self-determination and equality, sustains the needs that republicans claim to answer.

The Act of Union in 1801 ostensibly made Ireland an integral part of the United Kingdom, though it has since then been treated as an alien trouble-spot best kept at a distance (whether through repression, manipulation, or reform). To this end, British governments have explored every option in Ireland save for complete withdrawal, and some have entertained even this at pivotal moments of Irish history (such as the 1920s and perhaps the early 1970s), only to defer to Protestant objections. These objections create Britain's foremost problem and republicanism's greatest opportunity. For once Britain allows Protestants to block unification, it ends up preserving Protestant hegemony, frustrating the Catholic desires for national self-determination and social equality, and thus vindicating the republican dictum that Britain is Ireland's 'radical vice.'

Republicans have been demanding separation from Britain since they formed the United Irishmen in the 1790s. The United Irishmen was, ironically, founded by Protestant burghers and yeoman farmers in protest against the subordination of their interests to those of British commerce and Ascendancy landlords. Their grievances were hardly new,[4] but eighteenth-century developments made them unusually combustible, for the Penal Laws had by the end of the eighteenth century subdued the Catholic threat that had previously enforced both Protestant unity and Protestant dependence on Britain. Free to protest the domination of Irish landed and British commercial interests, the Protestant middle class turned republican under the influence of the French Revolution. With the ambitions of the Irish, like the French, middle class thwarted by the ascendancy of birth and land, it too demanded an independent republic; equality would replace inequality, independence would replace dependence. In the words of Wolfe Tone, leader of the United Irishmen, 'England [is] the radical vice of our Government, and consequently . . . Ireland [will] never be either free, prosperous, or happy, until she [is] independent, and . . . independence [is] unattainable whilst the connection with England exist[s].'[5] Republicans realized, of course, that an independent republic could not be established peacefully, but they believed that an insurrection joining their United Irishmen organization, the Catholic peasantry's agrarian societies (known collectively as the 'Defenders'), and French revolutionary armies could, in the words of Wolfe Tone, 'substitute the common name of Irishmen in place of the denominations of Protestant, Catholic, and Dissenter.'[6] Hence occurred Ireland's first republican, as opposed to traditional Gaelic, rebellion.

It was a fiasco. The United Irishmen were thoroughly infiltrated by British informers, leading to the arrest of their leaders and the repression of their followers well before the rebellion was launched. The Defenders were never more than local, ill-organized bands of peasants lacking both the consciousness and the organizational wherewithal to form a disciplined fighting force. And the French never provided as much military assistance as Irish republicans had expected. The result was that leaderless Catholics in several counties were panicked into rebellion by the repression that the British were applying to prevent rebellion. Armed mostly with their traditional pikes, they haphazardly flailed at their traditional enemies, Irish Protestants.[7] Needless to say, this, along with the abiding contradiction of Protestant and Catholic interests, hardened Protestants against republicanism; when resurrected as a broadly based movement in the 1860s, republicanism drew most of its support from Catholics.

The United Irishmen nonetheless left an indelible imprint on the character of republicanism. In the first instance the United Irishmen stressed separatism at the expense of other issues, emphasizing Ireland's relation to Britain and de-emphasizing a definite social program. Thus the land question, which was of literal life-and-death importance to much of the peasantry, was given short shrift by the United Irishmen – this in spite of both the obvious connection between the land and national issues and the centrality of land to peasants whose support was indispensable to republican success. Republicans did not defend the land system; they did not think about it much. Their approach was expressed quite neatly by Wolfe Tone in his casual remark that 'Our independence must be had at all hazards! If the men of property will not support us they must fall; we can support ourselves by the aid of that numerous and respectable class of the community – the men of no property.'[8] While Tone seems to be suggesting the wisdom of appealing to the peasantry, his wording reveals this as something of an afterthought. He would bring down landlords because of their stance on the national, not the land, issue. Similarly, he would rally peasants not because he associated republicanism with their class interests, but because their enemy was his. The point, however, is not only that the class interests of early republicans were those of a bourgeoisie whose development was frustrated by British and Ascendancy interests, but also that the resulting indifference to the land question insinuated into republicanism an enduring aversion to social questions. Beginning with the United Irishmen, republicanism has tended to subordinate class interests to the national demand.

In the second instance, the United Irishmen defined the objectives that survive unchanged to this day, seeking in the words of their founder to 'subvert the tyranny of our execrable government; to break the connection with England, the never-failing source of all our political evils; and to assert the independence of my country.'[9] British rule was deeply unpopular and constitutional incrementalism could do little about it, and this opened considerable space for a movement seeking a fundamental transformation of Ireland. By staging Ireland's first modern rebellion, republicans claimed this space for themselves, securing the status of republicanism as the radical alternative to the status quo and setting the essential agenda for two centuries of Irish revolutionaries. In losing the battle, the United Irishmen transformed the war.

Republicanism was converted from a brief episode into an enduring tradition by the Irish Republican Brotherhood (IRB) or Fenians in the 1860s. In between the United Irishmen and the IRB, republicans had staged 'rebellions' in 1803 and 1848, but both were so lacking in organization and appeal that they served less to challenge British rule than to symbolize Irish helplessness in the face of British power. Robert Emmet and Smith O'Brien – leaders of the respective 'rebellions' – could offer only desperation, which the Fenians recognized was not enough. Much more determined and tenaciously organized than their Protestant predecessors had been, the Fenians expanded as well as revived the popular presence of republicans. Certainly they never approached the popularity of the Home Rule Party or the Land League, but the IRB extended enduring roots among the peasantry and lower middle class by supplying both organizations with essential political skills and frightening British governments into dealing with them.

But whatever help they offered others, the Fenians failed to install the republic in either fact or the popular imagination. They were eclipsed by home rule, defanged by land reform, and embarrassed by their inability to mount a serious challenge to Britain. To reverse this half-century of decline, what remained of the IRB focused its energies on preserving and purifying its ideals. It feared that a generation and more of Irish support for home rule was corroding the ideal of a separate and independent republic and recognized that past rebellions served, if not to create a republic, as least to keep the hope alive. The conclusions republicans drew from this – that their ideal was created and sustained by periodic sacrifices – was dramatized brilliantly by the young republican playwright William Butler Yeats, in the play 'Cathleen ni Hoolihan.'

Yeats's play concerns a 'good, steady' young man named Michael who is soon to marry Delia, a fine woman bringing a handsome dowry with her. As Michael's family sits discussing the uses to which the dowry might be put, an old woman enters and tells that strangers have taken her house and land, leaving her to wander day after day with no place to rest. She then tells of the many men who have died for their love of her; more, she says to the disbelief of her audience, will die for her tomorrow. Taking pity, Michael's parents offer her a little silver, which she declines: 'If anyone would give me help he must give me himself, he must give me all.'[10] But, she warns,

It is a hard service they take that help me. Many that are red-cheeked now will be pale-cheeked; many that have been free to walk the hills and the bogs and the rushes will be sent to walk hard streets in far countries; many a good plan will be broken; . . . many that have gathered money will not spend it; many a child will be born and there will be no father at its christening to give it a name. They that have red cheeks will have pale cheeks for my sake; and for all that they will think they are well paid.[9]

She then leaves with a song:

They shall be remembered for ever;
They shall be alive for ever;
They shall be speaking for ever;
The people shall hear them for ever.[12]

'Good, steady' Michael is spellbound by the promise of everlasting fame to those who help the old woman recover her fields and expel the strangers from her house. Forgetting that he is to be married the next day, he follows the applause he hears outside, and though his family implores him to stay, he does not hear a word they say. Delia grabs him, he is about to yield, and then hears the old woman's voice: 'they shall be remembered for ever; the people shall hear them for ever.' Michael leaves, and his father asks his brother, who has just returned inside, whether he saw an old woman going down the path. The brother replies: 'I did not, but I saw a young girl, and she had the walk of a queen.'[13]

Yeats's old woman, Cathleen ni Hoolihan, is an ancient peasant symbol for Ireland. For Yeats the woman, though old, destitute, and homeless, is like Ireland, too proud to accept silver and too pure to need it. She can promise her lovers little, not wealth, not life, not even her bed, yet they follow her anyway. She is temptation, seducing young men from their worldly responsibilities and pleasures – land, home, and family – to sacrifice themselves for her sake, not theirs. Her charms are so powerful that even in shriveled skin she need not deceive: she admits honestly that not only will her followers probably die in her service, but will lose their youth first. 'They that had red cheeks will have pale cheeks for my sake.' She guarantees only that through suffering young men will attain a purpose and fame otherwise unattainable.

The posthumous fame held out by the old woman contrasts with the more mundane inducements offered by Michael's fiancée, young Delia. Reversing most stereotypes, the older woman is the temptress and the younger her victim. Delia is as substantial as Cathleen is ephemeral, representing the money, comfort, and family which stand in the way of the heroic life. While Cathleen's charms are otherworldly, Delia's are worldly; she can be held, possessed, known. The old woman, however, is as intangible as a fantasy, offering her men only unfulfilled pursuit which, precisely because unfulfilled, preserves the attraction. As opposites, Michael must choose between the two women; he could no more have both than he could have two wives. Nor may Michael go back on his choice; in choosing one over the other, he is defining who he is and what kind of life he will lead. Thus in choosing Cathleen, Michael opts for pursuit over outcome, and moreover, for a pursuit whose inexorable outcome is romantic death. And, Yeats teaches, such a death is more meaningful than life with Delia, for Michael not only achieves fame but restores 'the walk of a queen.'

By finding success in what appears as failure, 'Cathleen ni Hoolihan' advocates Michael's choice. Despite – or perhaps because of – the military defeat to which Michael is marching, he will successfully revive Ireland's national spirit. Yeats's interpretation of Irish history, while ignored by most of the nation, was embraced by enough to make it politically significant. The play, in fact, was re-enacted a dozen years later – for real. A group of republicans, many of whom were directly and almost all of whom were indirectly influenced by the play, staged an insurrection which the leaders knew to be doomed to failure. Yeats's audience was prepared – more prepared than he – to renew Ireland by shedding its own blood.[14]

III

In 1916 a few members of the IRB decided that unless their generation rose in a dramatic rebellion, republicanism would fade into oblivion. To garner support for the rebellion that the rebels thought was necessitated by the very indifference of most Irish to rebellion, the IRB infiltrated the National Volunteers, an open paramilitary organization designed to counterbalance the opposition of the Ulster Volunteer Force to home rule. The IRB's infiltration was so effective that, unbeknownst to the Volunteers, it nearly succeeded in involving them in the rebellion. At the last moment, however, the leadership of the Volunteers got wind of the plot and countermanded the orders designed to set the rebellion in motion.[15] Undeterred by the loss of the 10,000 men upon whom they had been counting, the IRB used the 1,000 men still under its direct control to occupy various buildings in Dublin, whereupon they declared a republic. The rebels were bombarded into surrender a week later.

Judging from the response of the Irish to the Easter insurrection, the rebels were right to fear for the future of their movement. The rebellion was met by an indifference that soon turned to derision, with the defeated rebels jeered by Dublin crowds when they were marched to prison. This was, indeed, the very reason for the rebellion, for the leaders of the IRB believed that only insurrection could shake republicanism from the lethargy enveloping it. The hope that Irish republicanism could rise like a phoenix from the ashes of failed rebellion was developed most fully by Padraic Pearse, the 'president' of the provisional republic who, better than any of his comrades, embodied the cause for which the insurrectionists marched to their inevitable defeat. Pearse aimed not to overthrow the British – unrealistic though he was, Pearse knew this to be impossible – but rather to pick up where Yeats left off. Where Yeats preached that the pursuit was all and the realization nothing, Pearse practiced it. Where Yeats promised glory to those who would fight for Ireland, Pearse sought it. But where Yeats backed off from his prescriptions and bemoaned the insurrection his play helped to inspire, Pearse carried Yeats to the logical conclusion of desperate and hopeless rebellion.

Pearse had a personal morbidity that fitted well with his republicanism. As a boy he and his brother vowed to free Ireland or die fighting; as an adult he always wore black, founded a school to rear boys on the tales of ancient Irish heroes in preparation for heroic feats of their own, and converted republicanism into something akin to a sacred doctrine. Pearse maintained that the national demand of Ireland is 'fixed and determined; that that demand has been made by every generation; that we of this generation receive it as a trust from our fathers; that we are bound by it; that we have not the right to alter it or to abate it by one jot or tittle . . . '[16] To change, to modify, even to adapt republicanism to changing conditions is to desecrate a commitment that is less political than religious. Patriotism, wrote Pearse, is 'of the same nature as religious faith.'[17] The tone of this religious faith is, of course, distinctly Catholic, emphasizing hallowed traditions, redemptive suffering, and martyrdom. Hence the scheduling of the insurrection for Easter Sunday: like Michael, Pearse meant to affirm through his death what he could not reach in his life.

Pearse argued that martyrdom carries both intrinsic and extrinsic rewards. By turning 'their backs to the pleasant paths and their faces to the hard paths,' and following 'only the far, faint call that leads them into the battle or to the harder death at the foot of a gibbet,'[18] republicans confer a form of sainthood on themselves; those who die for country 'stand mid-way between God and men.'[19] In illustration, Pearse points to Robert Emmet: 'No failure, judged as the world judges these things, was ever more complete, more pathetic than Emmet's. And yet he has left the memory of a sacrifice Christ-like in its perfection.'[20] 'Be assured that such a death always means redemption' for one's people as well as oneself.[21] As Christ's blood cleansed man of his sin, so does the republican's cleanse the Irish of theirs; sacrifice absolves the nation of the guilt resulting from its subjugation.

> Life springs from death; and from the graves of patriot men and women spring living nations. The Defenders of this Realm have worked well in secret and in the open. They think that they have pacified Ireland. They think that they have purchased half of us and intimidated the other half. They think that they have foreseen everything, think that they have provided against everything; but the fools, the fools, the fools! – they have left us our Fenian dead, and while Ireland holds these graves, Ireland unfree shall never be at peace.[22]

By thus glorifying defeats not only in the face of, but because of, failure, Pearse helped sustain a tradition long on failure and short on success – at a high cost.

In maintaining the demands of 'our fathers' without alteration, Pearse also maintained the subordination of social to national demands. To put the interests of one particular group (like the peasantry or working class) over those of the 'nation' as a whole would for Pearse detract from the purity of national objectives. For this reason Pearse praised the parliamentary leader Charles Stewart Parnell for manipulating the peasantry's demand for land into support for the nation.[23] Not only is it right and just for class demands to be used on behalf of national demands and wrong and unjust to use national demands on behalf of class demands, but Pearse says nothing about the possibility that the origins of the two kinds of grievances are linked. Rather than elaborating an analysis of, say, imperialism, that would allow republicans to appeal to class interests, Pearse developed the romantic, even mystical, elements of his tradition to win support.

Mysticism becomes especially conspicuous in Pearse's discussion of violence. The point is not that Pearse advocated violence to achieve the republic – this, after all, is part and parcel of republicanism – but that as Pearse converted martyrs from means to ends in themselves, so did he convert violence into an end in itself. Thus, he applauded indiscriminately the possession and use of arms, congratulating the Orangemen then arming themselves against home rule for establishing the precedent of Irishmen holding arms,[24] and regretting that 'Ireland has not known the exhilaration of war for over a hundred years.'[25] The use of weapons, according to Pearse, converts an otherwise effeminate people into men:

> I should like to see any and every body of Irish citizens armed. We must accustom ourselves to the thought of arms, to the sight of arms, to the use of arms. We may make mistakes in the beginning and shoot the wrong people; but bloodshed is a cleansing and a sanctifying thing, and the nation which regards it as the final horror has lost its manhood.[26]

Violence thus becomes tantamount to a moral obligation, exempting its perpetrators from mundane morality; giving – or taking – life, even innocent life ('shooting the wrong people'), visiting a Christian holiness on those who do the giving and taking.

Having pressed their cause by violence, and died in consequence, Pearse and his comrades joined the pantheon of republican martyrs who define the republican code of honor. But one critical difference distinguishes the rebels of 1916 from their predecessors. Where earlier republicans had risen in the hope of winning Irish independence and had died as the price of their defeat, the martyrdom of the Easter insurrectionists was deliberate; martyrdom was not the price of victory: it was victory. The 1916 rebellion was meant not to seize power but to inspire future generations to rebel. And oddly enough, it succeeded in this enterprise. Although jeered by Dubliners as they were marched to prison, the rebels were soon accorded respect, then honor as the British executed suspected leaders over a span of two weeks. The British, in other words, gave Pearse his martyrdom and vindicated his most optimistic predictions, delivering the Irish people to the surviving (and on the whole shrewder) republicans. The failure of 1916 thus led directly to the success, albeit partial, of 1922, which saw *de facto* independence for 26 of the 32 Irish counties and partition for the other six. The conditions attached to their victory were, however, as unacceptable to some republicans as they would have been to Pearse. Like him, they preferred purity even at the cost of failure, to corrupting 'successes.'

IV

The executions of the Easter rebels had an even greater effect than Pearse imagined, transforming as well as preserving the republican movement. Hitherto it had been ridiculed when not ignored, but thereafter it was actively backed by most Catholics in the 1921–2 guerrilla campaign against British rule. By 1921, republicans, now organized in the Irish Republican Army, had effectively paralyzed civil authority throughout Ireland (save, of course, for Ulster), forcing Britain to negotiate with the IRA lest it be drawn into a prolonged, and perhaps interminable, military occupation of Ireland. The negotiations were slow and confusing,[27] but eventually produced a treaty giving Ireland *de facto*, but not *de jure*, independence; permitting Britain to retain two naval bases in Ireland; and partitioning six Ulster counties (two with Catholic majorities) from the rest of Ireland until such time as a border commission was appointed to adjust the border according to the sentiments of the affected populations.[28] The treaty, in other words, fell short of a united and independent republic, but still offered Ireland more than it had enjoyed since the Elizabethan conquest. It also split the IRA down the middle.

Although their negotiators had worked out the terms with the British, republicans divided over acceptance or rejection of the treaty. Those accepting the treaty argued that while not ideal, it offered the best deal available under the circumstances (the 'freedom to become free,' according to its most important advocate), and that the British would unleash the 'terrible' war that Lloyd George threatened were it rejected. Those rejecting the treaty ignored the pragmatism of the treatyists to argue that the provisions requiring the Irish to recognize the king (as part of Britain's *de jure* sovereignty) and to permit two naval bases constituted an unconscionable betrayal of the republican dead. After intense debate, the republican parliament narrowly ratified the treaty, prompting the withdrawal of the anti-treatyists amid threats of civil war. For the next several months an uneasy truce prevailed until the pro-treaty government, succumbing to British pressure, routed its erstwhile comrades in a short but decisive civil war.[29]

The civil war proved the capacity of republicans to seize defeat from the jaws of victory. Not only did they split over the treaty, fight among themselves, and kill several key leaders, but the row resulted from differences over symbolic, not substantive, compromises. The important compromise provided for by the treaty was partition, but this was generally ignored, with republicans fighting instead over the symbolic and short-lived concessions that allowed Britain to retain two naval bases and conferred Commonwealth status.[30] Thus the obvious questions are why republicans split, and why they split over symbolic issues rather than the substantive (as well as symbolic) one of partition. The answer to the latter is that southern republicans, their rhetoric notwithstanding, seemed to view Ulster as Protestant and not really Irish. Certainly they knew Catholics lived there, but preferring to avoid the problems raised by Ulster's majority, they accepted uncritically Britain's hollow promises that the border would be adjusted to accommodate northern Catholics. It was much cleaner to denounce the treatyists for accepting less than a full republic than to raise troubling questions about the role of Protestants in Ireland.

If republicans split over symbolic rather than substantive issues, it remains to be explained why they split in the first place. The argument here is that republicans divided at the prospect of victory for the same reason that they survived the experience of defeat. Having built their movement around martyrs, the catharsis of failure, and the primacy of struggle, their hands were bound, with some republicans inevitably seeing pragmatic concessions as betraying their heritage. What had been functional became dysfunctional when it became clear that by conceding a little republicans could gain a lot. But these concessions, whatever the arguments for or against, struck purists as desecrations of the dead. Thus the purists were repudiating not only the specific compromises mandated by the treaty, but the very notion of compromise as well, leading them to hold out for complete victory, to lose the civil war, and to regroup in the IRA. Republicanism had learned from Pearse to choose the fate of Sisyphus rather than the costs of political pragmatism.

The custodians of the republican tradition blamed 'politics' for their defeat, accusing the treatyists of betraying their dead for mere political gain. Hence Michael Collins, the leader of the pro-treaty forces, was not only assassinated but purged from the honor roll of republican martyrs – this even though he led republicans in the war of independence more effectively than they had been led before or since. But in spite of opting for a course more likely to bring defeat than victory, republicans were ill-prepared for the ramifications of partition. In the south they were rendered largely irrelevant by the achievement of *de facto*, if not *de jure*, independence; and in the north they were frustrated by the permanent unionist majority set against them: partition tied the hands of republicans for two generations.

The IRA did not renounce politics altogether in the aftermath of the civil war. In the 1930s the depression revived the socialist republicanism of James Connolly, which enjoyed considerable success inside and outside the IRA until purged by orthodox republicans a few years later.[31] The traditionalists then embarked on an ill-conceived, poorly organized, and utterly stupid bombing campaign in Britain on the eve of the Second World War. After this campaign collapsed, the traditionalists regrouped for the 'border campaign' of 1956–62, which was another débâcle. Although fancying itself at war with Northern Ireland, the IRA accomplished little but the death of 19 people and the destruction of several border huts. So futile was the border war that Protestants ignored it, with the traditional beneficiary of republican violence, the Unionist Party, actually losing several seats in Stormont to the Northern Ireland Labour Party.[32] With republicanism not only dismissed as irrelevant by most Catholics but ignored by Protestants skilled in detecting republican conspiracies, the more politic republicans argued the desirability of de-emphasizing traditional physical force republicanism in favor of socialist republicanism.

The socialists presented two essential arguments: that Ireland's problems, north and south, resulted from capitalism as well as partition, and that these could be redressed only by the united efforts of the Protestant and Catholic working classes. Since the latter requirement suggested to republicans that they begin seeking ways of co-operating with Protestant workers, the IRA in the mid-1960s quietly de-emphasized its opposition to partition and discreetly backed the civil rights movement. Both developments greatly distressed IRA traditionalists, the former for obvious reasons and the latter for implicitly recognizing the legitimacy of partition.[33] The result of these rival understandings of republicanism was to split the IRA in 1969 into two distinct organizations, the reformist Officials and the traditionalist Provisionals, with the Provisionals steadily eclipsing the Officials in popularity.[34]

While the Officials have been exploring alternative definitions of republicanism, none of which has won significant support, the Provisionals have depended heavily on violence, often to the exclusion of other means. The Provisionals, of course, understand their violence as a strategic choice; by routinely bombing small businesses, assassinating police, and occasionally blowing up spectacular targets or ambushing British soldiers, the Provisionals believe that they are inexorably wearing down Britain's will to maintain the union of Britain and Northern Ireland.[35] But Provisional violence accomplishes more than this; it also proves them determined, resolute, and ruthless heirs to the republican tradition. And this tradition sometimes outweighs considerations of mere prudence.

V

The Provisionals' greatest triumph was undoubtedly the abolition of the 'Protestant parliament for a Protestant people' in March 1972. Having mobilized Catholic outrage against British repression – most notably internment and 'Bloody Sunday' – and having forced Britain to recognize Stormont's manifest incapacity to govern, that is, to control them, the Provisionals enjoyed unrivaled prestige among Catholics as a whole and working-class Catholics in particular.[36] And not only had the Provisionals undermined Stormont, but the decision to abandon Stormont was taken by the Conservative Party. The Provisionals had thus won a double victory over the Unionists; they destroyed Unionism's most important political institution, while at the same time estranging the Unionist Party from its closest British ally. Not bad for an organization representing at most one-third of the population against the British army as well as the Protestant majority.

But success creates problems for republicans. Although the Provisionals had achieved as much as could be reasonably expected in triumphing over Stormont, they had not won their stated objective – Northern Ireland remained part of the United Kingdom – and hoped that 'one more push' might achieve independence. Britain had, after all, already betrayed the Protestants once by 'proroguing' Stormont and seemed capable of betraying them again, as was indicated by remarks that Harold Wilson, then between governments, was making in parliament about transferring the six counties to the Republic.[37]

This prospect dimmed, however, in light of Catholic as well as Protestant reactions to the disbandment of Stormont. With the constitutional status of Northern Ireland apparently in doubt for the first time since 1921–2, Protestants counter-attacked, holding rallies, forming paramilitaries, murdering Catholics, and in general making it abundantly clear to Britain that they were to be pushed no further. Moreover, the abolition of Stormont weakened the resolve of Catholics while fortifying that of Protestants; Catholics had withstood arms searches, arrests, killings, the disruption of their lives to win this victory over Protestants. As they could scarcely expect to win any more against the combined opposition of the Protestant majority and the British army, Catholics thought it time to enjoy the fruits of their labors: they demanded a truce from republicans.[38] The Provisionals, worried, however, that while a truce would imply the recognition that they sought from Britain, it might also make them soft, cost them the initiative, and, worst of all, render them irrelevant.[39] Nonetheless, Catholics were so anxious to escape the travails of war that they prevailed on the Provisionals for a truce in June 1972, which brought a two-week respite to Catholics before a minor incident erupted into violence.[40] As neither the Provisionals nor the British semed to know whether the renewed hostilities resulted from confusion or malice, however, hope of repairing the truce remained alive for several weeks. That hope, along with the republican sympathies of many Catholics, was exploded on 'Bloody Friday.'

On 21 July 1972, 22 bombs were planted in downtown Belfast by the Provisionals. There is some dispute whether the Provisionals telephoned warnings for all of the bombs; the British agreed that warnings were given for some but denied that warnings were given for all the bombs, and the Provisionals claimed that warnings were given for all the bombs, but that the British, in an effort to discredit the Provisionals, refused to relay the warnings for some. Either way, the Provisionals clearly planted an exceptional number of bombs in civilian targets with the knowledge that civilian casualties were quite possible. In the event, nine people died, over a hundred were hospitalized, and Protestant and Catholic felt a terror unusual even in Belfast. Thus the Provisionals played into the hands of those British officers who allegedly withheld warnings of the bombs by showing themselves to lack compunction against blowing up innocent civilians, and confirming the misgivings which even their supporters were beginning to harbor about the unceasing bombing campaign.

'Bloody Friday' marks a turning-point in the fortunes of the Provisionals. Whereas they had previously constituted the dominant force in the Catholic community, they subsequently suffered one setback after another. The local support on which the Provisionals depended declined; fewer doors by which snipers might make good their escape from the British were left open at night, less money was dropped in the collection tills, and so forth. Meanwhile, the British army was able to enter the 'no-go' areas previously off limits to it, thus depriving the Provisionals of prestige and territorial bases at the very time when their renewed campaign was eroding support among Catholics. By counter-attacking just as the Provisionals overstepped their bounds, the British dealt the Provisionals a blow from which they did not really recover until the hunger strikes a decade later..

With the Provisionals foremost among 'Bloody Friday's' casualties, the question is why: why, despite the emergence of a powerful Protestant reaction, despite the growing opposition of Catholics, despite criticism even from individual Provisionals, why, despite this, did the Provisionals renounce negotiations in pursuit of a complete victory they could not realistically hope to achieve? The obstacles presented by British counter-insurgency, Protestant reaction, and Catholic misgivings would suggest that this decision was not motivated primarily by a concern for tactical advantage. After all, the bombing campaign had already given them the political initiative; it could do no more. But rather than using their initiative to maximize their negotiating position, the Provisionals returned to 'armed struggle' in part because they could not get what they wanted through negotiations. Negotiations by definition involve conceding part of an objective in order to secure other parts, and the objective sought by the Provisionals – an independent and united republic – was indivisible. Irish sovereignty was by nature an all-or-nothing affair, leaving little for republicans to discuss with their enemies.

But the Provisionals were motivated by more than this. They not only doubted the feasibility of negotiating an acceptable compromise with Britain; they further rejected compromise in principle. To compromise was to betray a trust consecrated by the blood of generations, to lessen the cause for which republican martyrs had died. Thus the Provisionals dismissed political (as opposed to military) strategies as at best mere talk, at worst treachery.[41] This absolutism, moreover, provided its own justification, for it both militated against success by renouncing the give and take of politics, and gave purpose to sustained and relentless violence. The Provisionals, by converting violence from a necessary and legitimate means of establishing the republic into an end in itself, believed that they were performing their duty as republicans: they were transmitting their ideal to the next generation, untarnished by either compromise or implementation.

Given the greater resources available to their enemies, it might seem that the attachment of the Provisionals to violence would be self-defeating, that their refusal to compromise in the face of the superior forces arrayed against them would lead to their demise. The whole experience of republicanism suggests otherwise, however; success, not defeat, has most tested republicans. As the victories won in the war of independence prepared for the 'sell-out' by republican leaders, so Provisional successes in 1970–2 opened new possibilities for betrayal.

Lest this occur at the expense of the ideals that had sustained republicans during decades short on victory and long on defeat, the Provisionals, like their predecessors, decided to preserve rather than compromise their ideal. If, as was then manifestly the case, an independent and united republic was beyond the reach of the Provisionals, they would not grab what they could but would instead reaffirm the cause which so many had affirmed before them. It was this respect for traditional republican absolutism that the Provisionals reaffirmed in blood on 'Bloody Friday.' The heroic myth got the better of political prudence.

VI

Catholic support for the Provisionals began slipping in the summer of 1972 first and foremost because they had exhausted the potential of violence without politics. Having destroyed Stormont, the Provisionals needed political ideas, strategies, and organizations to achieve the more difficult objective of unifying Ireland, especially in view of Britain's improved strategies for countering them. Militarily, the British army had learned that the indiscriminate repression of Catholics played into the hands of the Provisionals, which encouraged it to target the Provisionals in particular and not Catholics in general. Politically, the British government recognized the SDLP as the responsible alternative to the Provisionals, though this would have accomplished more had unionists agreed to share power with the SDLP. Nonetheless, the conjunction of British backing for the SDLP and the Provisionals' political bumbling helped foster the illusion that the SDLP could accomplish more than the IRA and at a considerably lower cost to Catholics. Thus the Provisionals found their very success turned against them by Britain. After constituting Catholics as a force to be dealt with, the Provisionals let the SDLP do the dealing.

Britain's strategy was to isolate the Provisionals as criminals. Previously Britain had recognized the Provisionals as a political organization, most conspicuously by awarding special status to republican (and also loyalist) prisoners and by negotiating directly with IRA leaders. In the mid-1970s, however, Britain reversed course; it revoked political status, decreed the Provisionals a criminal conspiracy, and accordingly shifted primary responsibility for security from the army to the RUC. The latter change not only scaled down Britain's presence in Northern Ireland, but also reflected its desire for more accurate intelligence on the Provisionals, a function which

Britain regarded as belonging to the police rather than the army. Thus encouraging the RUC to acquire as much information as possible, Britain allowed it to use whatever interrogation techniques proved most productive, turning a blind eye to widespread allegations of police brutality. By 1976–7 these developments had exacted a significant toll on the Provisionals. While able to sustain a high level of violence, the Provisionals were doing so with less support, with recruits more susceptible to the temptations of gangsterism and informing, and a divided leadership.

The Provisionals, however, not only survived their trials but, by making three important changes, turned them to their advantage. The first and most decisive was a change in leadership. Until the mid-1970s, the Provisionals were led by older men, typically southerners who had joined the IRA in the 1950s or even 1940s, and understood their project in narrowly conventional terms. They were sworn to a 32 county Gaelic republic; they were deeply averse to politics and indifferent to social issues; and they were comfortable with 'armed' struggle and uncomfortable with any other kind. The reverses of the mid-1970s, however, exposed this generation to challenge from younger northerners who were concerned with political and social issues as well as republican shibboleths. Many of these emerging leaders had participated in the civil rights movement before joining the Provisionals, had then assumed substantial responsibilities for day-to-day operations in the early 1970s, and had reshaped their understanding of republicanism after being imprisoned. Once released, they captured and transformed the Provisionals by restructuring the 'active service' units, reviving Sinn Fein (the so-called 'political wing' of the IRA), and politicizing both.

Secondly the new leadership dismantled the IRA's 'battalions' in favor of cells, which reduced contact among 'volunteers' and minimized the damage caused by loose lips. Finally, these security measures were then supplemented by more sophisticated political organizations, programs, and strategies, as the Provisionals began seeking the support of working-class Catholics by espousing socialism in addition to republicanism. Certainly the content of their version of socialism was vague, but it involved substantial work on social issues, which broadened both the popularity and outlook of the Provisionals. Meanwhile, the Provisionals were organizing on behalf of republican prisoners denied political status, partly to improve the condition of their prisoners and partly to cultivate support among Catholics who were opposed to IRA violence but recognized it as political.

Republican prisoners, female as well as male, had from the first refused to wear the prison clothes that symbolized their criminality. When their protests were ignored by British and nationalist opinion alike, the prisoners embarked on the 'dirty' protests, in which they smeared their waste on the walls of their cells. When these protests too were ignored, the prisoners – evidently over the objections of the regular leadership – reverted to the reflexive response of republicans to apparently hopeless situations: self-sacrifice in the form of hunger strikes. In the same way as the insurrectionists of 1916, the hunger strikers would purify and affirm their cause through their deaths.

There were two distinct waves of hunger strikes. The first occurred in late 1980 but faltered amidst widespread confusion, instigating the second and more famous wave in 1981 and reinforcing Thatcher's refusal to 'give in to terrorists.' The inflexibility of Britain was meant to force the hunger strikers to relent, which was to serve the dual purpose of vindicating law and order and discrediting the Provisionals. But Britain misjudged its adversaries; instead of yielding in the face of Thatcher's intransigence, the Provisionals, by carrying the strikes to their conclusion, turned back the tables on Britain. Britain expected the Provisionals to suffer isolation as a result of the 'defeat' of the strike; in fact, however, the Provisionals polarized opinion, presented themselves as victims of British insensitivity, and recovered much of the esteem they had lost in the years since 'Bloody Friday,' as was shown when Bobby Sands, the leader of the hunger strikers, was elected to parliament six weeks into his fast. All of which raises one obvious question: why did the hunger strikes accomplish so much?

The hunger strikes succeeded for an array of reasons having to do with the issues at stake, the courage and symbolism of prisoners starving themselves to death, and the political situation. The issue dividing the two sides was clear-cut: were republican prisoners guilty of criminal or political acts? On the one hand, the British government insisted that 'terrorism was terrorism was terrorism,' while, on the other, republicans argued that the motives and content of their 'crimes' were political, as Britain itself had recognized through the special judicial procedures used to convict republicans (and loyalists). Whatever the merits of the respective cases, most Catholics not only viewed that of the Provisionals more sympathetically, but their passions were inflamed by Thatcher's refusal to discuss the issue. Thus the symbolism was ideal for republicans. They received massive publicity in their most self-sacrificing moment, which helped them to escape their image as terrorists while 'establishing' the wanton disregard of Britain for the lives of its prisoners. To Irish Catholic audiences schooled from childhood in the sacrifices of 1798, 1916, and the like, the meaning was unmistakable. These like the other republicans appeared to be dying for Ireland, and their deaths confirmed the republican claim that Britain caused Irish suffering. Thus the strikes 'proved' that, far from mere 'gunmen,' republicans were more devoted to their cause than to their lives.

The hunger strikes, although the ideal way of resuscitating the Provisionals, succeeded only because Catholic support for the SDLP was soft. Having declared for objectives that Protestants blocked, the SDLP did not convert British and clerical recognition into headway on either of its two main objectives, power-sharing and an 'Irish dimension': it failed to deliver the goods. Nor was this its only problem. As the SDLP understood,[42] Britain entertained the SDLP as an alternative to the Provisionals, which meant that the SDLP depended on the vitality of its most bitter competitor to secure an audience with its benefactors. Without the Provisionals, the SDLP's attraction to Britain would have vanished. Thus the SDLP was caught in an impossible dilemma: to succeed among Catholics it had to rout the Provisionals, but this, even if possible, would deprive it of leverage over Britain. Unable to win for losing, the SDLP remained vulnerable to the Provisionals if they struck on the right issue at the right time – as they did with the hunger strikes.

The hunger strikes (with the indispensable assistance of Thatcher) restored the initiative the Provisionals lost on 'Bloody Friday.' In the interval between these two events, the Provisionals highlighted the peculiar mix of success and failure at the heart of republicanism. Their decline commenced when, after destroying Stormont and forcing Britain to negotiate with them, they did not convert military success into political gains. Failing to consolidate their victories, partly because in practice they were too weak to achieve their goal of a republic and partly because in principle they rejected politics for 'armed struggle,' the Provisionals stumbled from one mishap to another, spared collapse only by Britain's inability to achieve the political solution that would freeze them out. But continuing Protestant hegemony sustained the possibility of a Provisional revival, which was seized through the self-sacrifice with which republicans respond to adversity.

VII

The basic problem confronting the Provisionals is that, like northern
Catholics, they have been dealt a losing hand. No matter how they
play their cards, their opponents hold the trumps. The Provisionals
see Britain as the important player; it is argued here that the
Protestants manipulate Britain, but either way Catholics face two
opponents whose combined resources are unbeatable. Catholics are
therefore caught in the difficult position of failing whichever direction
they turn; neither nationalism nor republicanism can redress their
abiding grievances. Failure, however, hampers nationalists more than
republicans, for unlike the Provisionals, the SDLP accepts the
legitimacy of the institutions that doom them to impotence. In
contrast, the Provisionals actively defy the prevailing authorities,
which is why they opt for violence: it not only attacks British rule
instrumentally, but repudiates it existentially.

Republicans can reasonably argue, moreover, that violence has
accomplished more than peaceful protest, having contributed to land
reform, independence for the 26 counties, and the abolition of
Stormont. But violence has failed to achieve either the full republican
demands or concessions acceptable to the Provisionals. For the
Provisionals reject concessions that would maximize their influence in
Northern Ireland in favor of the all-or-nothing, indivisible objective of
a sovereign Irish republic. Anything less is merely a temptation to
break faith with their republicanism. In the face of this disparity
between what they want and what they can get, republicans survive
now as before by glorifying their sacrifices, by sanctifying their
failures, and by making a virtue of necessity. This can cost republicans
dearly, however, since the belief that martyrs purge republicanism of
corruption (much as hunger strikers purge their bodies) disposes them
to substitute self-sacrifice for politics and to denounce new departures
as insults to the dead.

The link between the experience and the glorification of failure is
something of a chicken and egg question: do republicans fail because
they romaticize failure or do they romanticize failure because they fail?
Obviously both factors are at work, but the essential problem
confronting republicans is that Northern Ireland's social order
prepares their defeat. Like the Catholic minority, the Provisionals are
hampered by the dynamics of settler colonialism, which maintains the
superiority of Protestants at the expense of Catholics. Consequently,
Catholics are unable to reform Protestant hegemony, are driven to

support republicans, and are left no alternative but to reinforce the contradictions that frustrate them. But if Catholics are damned if they do and damned if they do not embrace republicanism, republicans at least create meaning out of Catholic powerlessness. As McCann writes,

> [I]f the traditional Republican account of Irish history has been most fervently believed in the Catholic ghettos of the North, . . . it is because the people who live there, ground down by oppression and with no apparent possibility of escape, have needed an ennobled history, have needed to postulate a line of continuity between the glorious struggles of the past and a liberation yet to come.[43]

And that is both the strength and weakness of republicanism in Northern Ireland. Although offering Ulster Catholics their only historically effective way of acting, republicanism sometimes becomes less a strategy of liberation from colonial oppression than one of coping with it. It finds solace inside Protestant hegemony and offers the illusion of escape, even if unknowingly fortifying the colonial garrison.

It is for this reason that the Provisionals resort to violence. The point is not just that violence might materially advance the republic, but that even failure is success, that transferring the struggle to ensuing generations revives the conditions of future struggle. As irrational as republicanism might thus seem, it survives because of the disparity in power between Catholics and Protestants. The glorification of sacrifice and the cult of martyrs are republicanism's way of dealing with its weakness, turning cause for despair into inspiration. And this is why the Provisionals press their struggle when strong as well as weak; having evolved to survive hard times, republicanism has trouble capitalizing on good times. Its demand for total victory, while inspiring when facing imminent defeat, is not conducive to cashing in at the optimal moment. Hence instead of betraying itself by making the best available deals, republicanism reproduces the contradictions of settler colonialism. To criticize it is, therefore, to criticize the social order that denies Catholics other options.

6

Unrequited Loyalty

'We are all children of wrath.'

Ian Paisley

I

It is often claimed that republicans and unionists are much alike, that the intransigence of one mirrors that of the other. The point is valid to the extent that republicans use unionists to secure their political base, and vice versa. However, one critical difference between republicans and unionists deserves note. While Catholics have demonstrated repeatedly that they would abandon republicans if satisfactory compromises were available, most Protestants clutch to the privileges elevating them over Catholics as to their very identities. Thus the appeal of republicans to Catholics results from unionist intransigence, but that of unionists to Protestants reflects the commitment of Protestants to their uncompromised superiority.

Two episodes illustrate starkly the refusal of Ulster Protestants to compromise with Catholics: the crisis over home rule in 1912–14, and the general strike in 1974. In 1912–14, unionists carried their opposition to home rule to the verge of physical rebellion. As this expressed the sentiments not of a handful of aspiring martyrs but of a community united in defiance, Protestant claims of unadulterated loyalty are obviously thrown into question. This does not mean that Protestant loyalism is merely a charade. Rather, Protestants are caught in a genuine dilemma, loyal both to themselves and to Britain. Their dilemma is exacerbated not only because these dual allegiances sometimes conflict, but because the privileges defining what it means to be Protestant rest on British support. This is why home rule so disturbed Protestants: by extending political power to Catholics, home rule would have undercut the privileges that shaped the meaning of

Protestantism. As a consequence of this 'betrayal,' Protestants felt absolved from their duty to obey their sovereign, and compelled to resort to rebellion in defense of their traditional hegemony. The home rule crisis, in other words, exposes the limits – and contradictions – of Protestant loyalism.

The imperative to exclude Catholics from any meaningful participation in political institutions was reiterated by the general strike in 1974, but this time Protestants rejected a proposal intended to confirm rather than to overturn their primacy. Thus, as the home rule crisis displayed the paradoxical relation of Protestants to Britain, the general strike revealed that of Protestants to Catholics. The institutions that Protestants overturned had been shaped both to reconcile Catholics to a subordinate role in Northern Ireland and to protect the essential interests of Protestants. The north would remain separate from the south and would receive a new government in which unionists would exercise preponderant influence – if only they agreed to participate with Catholics. But this concession, despite its moderation, was unacceptable to Protestant workers: they staged a ruthlessly effective general strike against the power-sharing government. The very success of the strike, however, exposed Protestants to familiar problems, for in excluding Catholics from political institutions, they preserved both the grievances of Catholics and the appeal of the Provisionals. Having staved off one challenge, Protestants not only made another inevitable, but denied themselves the security that they craved. Protestants, in a nutshell, curse themselves to perpetual insecurity.

II

The 'loyalty' of Protestants is ambivalent because they depend on a benefactor whom they cannot fully trust. In the face of Ireland's hostile Catholic majority, Protestants worry that, someday, they may require British help to suppress Catholic rebellions. But Protestants appreciate that Britain is less committed to their hegemony than are they, and suspect that at a decisive moment it might try to buy peace with Catholics by betraying them. The fear is not unfounded, for though originally British surrogates, Protestants have become superfluous to, even incompatible with, Britain's interests. With their dependence unreciprocated, Protestants have developed a fervent but unsteady commitment to Britain. Prolonged periods of loyalty are punctuated by moments of veritable rebellion as Protestants, sensing the knife at their back, challenge the country which they ordinarily claim as their own. Take, for example, the crisis over home rule.

To enlightened British opinion home rule appeared the very essence of judicious reform, thorough yet moderate. The Catholic majority of Ireland would acquire limited authority over most domestic affairs, while Britain would retain authority over such 'imperial' matters as trade, defense, and foreign policy. Because reformist rather than revolutionary, it is perhaps difficult to appreciate the passions excited for and against home rule, when, in 1886, the Irish delegation in parliament assumed the balance of power between Conservatives and Liberals at the very time Gladstone was concluding that only home rule could establish lasting peace in Ireland. Gladstone, though, could not carry his party with him, and home rule failed in the Commons. In 1893 a subsequent Gladstone government passed home rule through the Commons, only to have the Lords reject it resoundingly. It was there that matters rested until the Liberals routed the Conservatives in the 1906 elections. The scale of the Liberal victory at first portended ill for Irish home rule, for, freed from dependence on Irish support, the government lacked incentive to open the pandora's box of Irish politics. But when Lloyd George challenged the Lords on the budget, the Irish scored a double victory; first, the elections called to resolve the budgetary stalemate left the Liberals dependent on the Irish for a parliamentary majority; and, secondly, the Liberals and their Irish backers were able to force the Lords to surrender its veto over Commons legislation.[1] Thus in the process of indebting the government to them, the Irish had abolished the most significant constitutional obstacle to home rule.

These developments were much more disturbing to Protestants than were previous home rule proposals. While Unionists had opposed home rule in 1886 and 1893 through extra-parliamentary as well as parliamentary means, they recognized that the Lords would block it ultimately. Once deprived of the Lords' protection, however, Unionists escalated beyond the customary riots to threaten rebellion in 1912–14, with the threats drawing more support from Protestants than any previous rebellion had from Catholics; loyalists, it seemed, made better rebels than did the rebels. Certainly they prepared better; beginning in January 1912, Unionists openly formed, drilled, and armed the Ulster Volunteer Force (UVF) with the express purpose of keeping Ulster in a United Kingdom free of home rule. As Edward Carson, leader of the Unionists, put it.

We will defeat the most nefarious conspiracy that has ever been hatched against a free people. . . . We must be prepared . . . the morning Home Rule is passed, ourselves to become responsible for the government of the Protestant Province of Ulster.[2]

This threat of secession was supported in the most respectable British quarters, as the Conservative Party sought to manipulate the mounting Ulster crisis to the disadvantage of Liberals.[3] The thrust of the anti-home rule movement, however, was Unionist and extra-parliamentary, not Tory and parliamentary. In July 1912, Protestants rioted in Belfast, and in September, nearly 500,000 Unionists signed 'Ulster's Solemn League and Covenant,' vowing, in the name of the King, to use 'all means which may be found necessary to defeat the present conspiracy to set up a Home Rule Parliament in Ireland.'[4] Then, in 1914, the army's officer corps indicated that it would resign (that is, mutiny), rather than 'coerce' Ulster (that is, enforce an Act of Parliament). In the face of these escalating costs, the government offered to exempt six Ulster counties from home rule for six years; the Unionists, realizing that defiance was paying off, rejected the concession, which precipitated a fully-fledged constitutional confront-ation over the implementation of home rule in late August 1914. On one side were arrayed the Unionist and Conservative parties, with the tacit support of the army; and on the other were the Liberal government, the Irish home rule party, and the writ of parliament. In the event, of course, the First World War interceded, and Unionists rallied behind the flag, using their position in the wartime coalition government (they were, obviously, forgiven their earlier excesses) to win the partition of six of Ulster's nine counties from post-war Ireland. Thus Unionists not only retained the link with Britain but even ended up with a parliament of their very own, *gratis*: the fruits of defiance more than justified loyalty.

Two points are noteworthy about the 'Ulster crisis': the intensity of Protestant resistance to home rule and the resulting defiance of Britain. The problem for Protestants was that the threat of home rule issued from Britain as well as Ireland. Catholics had been routinely returning massive home rule majorities to parliament for more than a generation, but these did not matter as long as the two main British parties ignored them. Once the Liberal Party endorsed home rule, however, strategic segments of the British elite switched their support from Protestants to Catholics, which together with the removal of the Lords' power to veto legislation, converted the erstwhile source of

Protestant salvation into the source of danger. This, in turn, fundamentally distinguished twentieth-century Protestants from their ancestors. While both anticipated renewed siege, the parents expected rescue where the children feared betrayal.

It is not without irony that uncertain backing from Britain instilled in Protestants a spirit similar to that expressed in the republican motto of 'Sinn Fein,' ourselves alone. Previously loyalists found independence from Britain inconceivable; in 1912–14 it was conceived, replete with threats of civil wars and provisional governments, in protest over a matter of central importance to British as well as Irish politics. A series of elections had been contested specifically over home rule, and its passage through parliament represented the very kind of adaptation for which Britain prided itself. Thus in smuggling guns, taunting the government, and encouraging mutiny, Unionists were repudiating the self-same constitution to which they professed loyalty. Given this sort of behavior, it is tempting to conclude that their 'loyalty' is no more than a ruse, an insincere, even hypocritical, subterfuge whose sole purpose is to entrap British complicity. But such an interpretation misses the point. For Protestants, loyalty to Britain is inseparable from loyalty to themselves: British support is the condition of all those traditions that define what it means to be Protestant. It is for this reason that Protestants became so desperate; when their loyalty fell unrequited, they felt dispossessed.

Protestants described the fate to which Britain was abandoning them in 'Ulster's Solemn League and Covenant,' which was signed by virtually every adult Protestant in Ulster. In tone and allusion the Covenant communicated deep forebodings. Speaking of home rule as 'disastrous to . . . [our] material well-being,' 'subversive of . . . freedom,' and 'destructive of citizenship,' Protestants were protesting that they were about to be stripped of everything that made them a community. Prosperity, freedom, citizenship, and tradition would be destroyed, even worse defiled, by the accession to power of their hereditary foe. Hence the religious tone, the reverent references to forefathers, the solemnity: at stake was their communal identity. For by upsetting the political primacy that Protestants had enjoyed for centuries in Ireland, home rule forced them to defy that power – Britain – to which they had habitually professed loyalty. Their tradition of loyalty diverged from that of dominance, dividing Protestants against themselves.

Protestants and Catholics understood that the spirit of home rule was far more radical than its letter. If home rule had been implemented, Catholics would have been in a position to whittle away the privileges enjoyed by Protestants. Not only would the state have presumably ceased sanctioning the systematic advantages that Protestants held in jobs, living standards, and property, but it would have subjected an illiberal society to liberal political institutions. And as the gap elevating Protestants over Catholics closed, Protestants would have lost objective confirmation of their feeling of superiority, their 'cherished position' as they called it in the Covenant. With Catholics as entitled as Protestants, Protestants would cease being 'Protestant.' Their superiority might have dropped to parity, or even inferiority. Thus Unionist apprehension of home rule was not as hysterical as might first seem, for it recognized that to legitimate Catholic majorities was to delegitimate Protestant superiority: the survival of the people they had always been was truly at stake for Protestants.

Because home rule attacked their birthright, Protestants were virtually unanimous in rejecting it. Beckett, for example, writes that unionism was 'supported by all sections of the protestant community: landlords, manufacturers, merchants, professional men, farmers, industrial workers, all displayed the same enthusiasm.'[5] This solidarity is attributed by Beckett to privilege; 'what protestants of all ranks were preparing to fight for, though they might not have admitted it, was the maintenance, in some form, of threatened protestant ascendancy in Ireland.'[6] When Protestants could not remain true to both Britain and their traditions, the contingency of their loyalty surfaced. Once implicit, it became conditional. Certainly Protestants respected British traditions, but they expected that in return Britain would respect theirs.[7] If Britain recognized their primacy in Ireland, then Protestants would remain fervently loyal; but if it curtailed their influence, then Protestants were obliged to defy Britain (partly for its own good, since Britain was betraying its Empire along with Protestants).

The problem for Protestants was that they could not choose one or the other, Britain or themselves; they needed both. The Protestant dilemma is in part that they can maintain their superiority only with the help of Britain, but it is also that loyalty to Britain is essential to the Protestant identity; they call themselves 'loyalists' because such is their self-image. Thus Protestants must depend, nervously, on British governments less sensitive than they to the full gravity of the Catholic menace; and depending on the undependable, Protestant loyalism became contradictory. In the name of loyalty, Protestants acted disloyally; after threatening rebellion, the Covenant ends with the words 'God save the King.' And Protestants meant it. Believing their rebellion staged on behalf of such British values as freedom, prosperity, and Protestantism, Unionists fancied themselves to be acting in the most British of fashions. But be this as it may, the fact remained that the objective import of Protestant behavior in Ireland was the subordination of Catholics; the freedom Protestants demanded was the freedom to dominate Catholics.[8] Their survival as a people required no less.

III

In the previous chapter it was argued that in times of crisis republicanism reverts to the model provided by the Easter insurrection; that this disposes republicanism to snatch failure from success and success from failure; and, therefore, that republicanism neither wins nor loses but instead sustains Northern Ireland's conflict. In this unionism resembles republicanism; as the logic behind the Easter rebellion was imitated by the likes of 'Bloody Friday' and the hunger strikes, so the Protestant general strike of 1974 was portended by the 1912–14 Ulster crisis. But there is one telling difference between the general strike and the Ulster crisis: in opposing home rule Protestants were rationally defending a fundamental threat to their primacy in Ulster; in the general strike Protestants overturned a compromise that would have *secured* their primacy. Whereas the loyalist rebellion of 1912–14 attacked home rule to prevent Catholics from being empowered over Protestants, the 1974 general strike was directed against institutions meant to weaken the IRA and to confirm the 'rights of the majority.' This poses three obvious questions; given that the avowed targets of the strike – the newly established power-sharing government and the Council of Ireland – were designed to undermine the IRA, why did Protestants deliberately destroy them; why did Protestants choose confrontation rather than co-operation with Catholics; and why did Protestants act in a manner that seems so irrational?

The two institutions toppled by the general strike were meant to fill the vacuum opened by the abolition of Stormont in March 1972. Without Stormont, Britain reluctantly assumed direct rule over Northern Ireland, but as this was precisely what both Labour and Conservative governments had wished to avoid,[9] Britain sought to escape the problem by restoring self-government to Northern Ireland. To this end the Conservative government of Edward Heath assigned to Home Secretary William Whitelaw the task of devising a formula acceptable to the Irish Republic as well as to both of Northern

Ireland's communities. In October 1972, Britain announced officially that political power would be returned to Northern Ireland if, and only if, the executive was acceptable to both communities and was willing to discuss with delegates from the Republic matters of joint concern to northern and southern Ireland.[10]

Elections to the proposed assembly were held in June 1973, with the SDLP sweeping the Catholic vote (19 seats), and with the Protestants divided among four parties, Paisley's Democratic Unionist Party (8 seats), the Vanguard Unionist Party (7 seats), the Official Unionist Party (22 seats), and unaffiliated Unionists (11 seats). Minor parties won 9 seats.[11] Over the ensuing six months Britain focused negotiations on Brian Faulkner, leader of the Official Unionist Party, hoping that the prospect of office would entice him to share power with the SDLP despite his campaign promises to the contrary. British efforts succeeded when, in late 1973, Faulkner committed the Unionist Party to an executive that would not only share power with the SDLP (as well as the small, non-sectarian Alliance Party) but would also co-operate with the Republic. Accordingly, the Northern Ireland Assembly assumed official responsibilities on 1 January 1974 and ratified the Sunningdale Agreements (providing for the Council of Ireland) on 14 May 1974. The strike began that night.

To understand the Protestant reaction against power-sharing-cum-Council-of-Ireland, it is useful to describe briefly the two institutions. Power-sharing acknowledged that the lack of representative institutions disposed Catholics, and to a lesser degree Protestants, to turn to 'terrorism' to seek redress for grievances otherwise unredressed. Certainly Britain denied that the lack of effective institutions justified terror, but it had decided that 'terrorists' could be fought better by political than military means. If Catholics supported republicanism for lack of alternatives, then power-sharing, by extending effective representation to previously excluded interests, would create a parliamentary alternative to violence. Britain's plan, then, was to dissolve the military problem in the political solution.

The same strategy of including the excluded led to the formation of the Council of Ireland. The Council would seem to have signified a victory for unionists, since in exchange for recognition of the 'Irish dimension' of Northern Ireland's problems, the Republic agreed first, to co-operate in combating terrorism; secondly, to participate with representatives of the Northern Ireland government on a body with limited and essentially mundane responsibilities;[12] and thirdly, to acknowledge that unification could come only with the consent of

Northern Ireland's majority, that is, only with the consent of the Protestants. Far from eroding partition, the Council thus formalized a position that the Republic had previously left informal, namely, that Northern Ireland, until and unless it decided otherwise, was distinct and separate from the Republic. This was no small step given that the Republic's constitution asserted sovereignty over the six counties. Thus in exchange for token recognition of the Republic's special interest in Northern Ireland, Protestants received what they had always sought: a commitment from the Republic that the fate of Northern Ireland was theirs to decide.

Power-sharing and the Council of Ireland should have secured the position of northern Protestants. The one returned unionists to government, the other recognized partition, and together the two were designed to undermine the IRA. All of this moreover was offered at what appears a modest price: the participation of moderate Catholics as junior partners in unionist governments. It is, therefore, testimony to the contradictions of their position that, despite these protections, Protestants elected two parties opposed to participation with Catholics in government (the Democratic Unionist Party and the Vanguard Unionist Party) and a third party that adopted a position of studied ambiguity on power-sharing (the Unionist Party under Faulkner). When Faulkner reneged on his perceived opposition in order to head the power-sharing government, he was quickly forced to resign from the Unionist Party, leaving him with a group of supporters in the Assembly but no party beyond it. And when, despite Protestant opposition to power-sharing, the executive was installed anyway in January 1974, Protestants took advantage of the February 1974 elections to Westminster to elect 11 unionists pledged against power-sharing (the SDLP won Northern Ireland's twelfth seat). All this, however, was to no avail; the power-sharing executive, notwithstanding consistent rejection by a majority of the electorate, remained in office. Thwarted constitutionally, Protestants in 1974 resorted to the extra-parliamentary defiance of the general strike.

The strike lasted two weeks, beginning on 15 May 1974 and ending with the resignation of the power-sharing Executive on 28 May. For the first day or two Protestant support for the strike was lukewarm, but thereafter grew rapidly. Although the British and Northern Irish governments claimed that Protestant workers were coerced into honoring a strike they opposed, it is clear that officials underestimated the popularity of the strike.[13] Certainly intimidation occurred, but as intimidation is a feature of most general strikes, it hardly explains the success of this one. The strike triumphed because of popular backing, without which the army could easily have arrested the 'ringleaders.' Yet the army scrupulously avoided confrontation with the strikers, refusing to dismantle the barricades or arrest enforcers,[14] and allowing the strikers to tighten their grip on Northern Ireland by issuing work passes for essential services, allocating gasoline, setting the hours in which shops could transact business, and most importantly, reducing the output of energy.[15]

The strike was led by the Ulster Workers Council (UWC), an organization of workers, often with trade union or paramilitary backgrounds,[16] coming together for the specific purpose of destroying the power-sharing government and the Council of Ireland. While honored in every significant Protestant sector of Northern Ireland's economy, agricultural as well as industrial, the UWC had taken particular care to recruit the predominantly Protestant workforce manning Northern Ireland's power stations. During the strike, the UWC ordered a steady reduction in the output of electricity, which had several felicitous effects from the perspective of the UWC. First, it extended the strike by depriving factories of energy. Secondly, it granted the UWC control over such indispensable services as sanitation, communications, and heating. And thirdly, it positioned the UWC to ruin – and not merely disrupt – Northern Ireland's economy in consequence of the fact that Northern Ireland's generators had to operate at a minimal capacity (about 15 per cent); otherwise they would shut off for several weeks before they could be turned back on. This meant that the UWC could – and did – raise the specter of a modern, urban, and industrial society deprived of energy for a prolonged period of time, leaving Northern Ireland unable, among other things, to operate the pumps that prevented Belfast, which is built on land with a low water table, from flooding in its own waste.[17] While inexorably reducing power output to 'the point of no return,' the UWC finally ordered a total work stoppage of 'electricity, gas, water, sewage, telephones, fuel supplies, security guards, firemen, bakeries, food deliveries, even . . . gravedigging.'[18] In the face of the calamity that would inevitably follow such measures, the power-sharing government had no choice but to recognize the strike: it resigned.

The question is: why did the Protestants destroy an arrangement that would have weakened the IRA, secured the Republic's recognition of partition, and restored their political ascendancy? The answer is that,

consciously or unconsciously, Protestants act according to the imperative not merely to prevail over Catholics but to maintain a radical
separation between the two communities. When Catholics entered
previously orange citadels of power, Protestants did not care that this
might broaden support for the established order, but decided that it
necessitated the most extreme counter-measures. As a Protestant
country for a Protestant people, Northern Ireland had, if it was to
remain true to itself, to be governed exclusively by Protestants. To
admit Catholics to power, even in the interests of stabilizing Protestant
hegemony, was to dispense with the indispensable Protestant ex-
clusivity. And though power-sharing would have granted Protestants
the preponderant share of power, this was because of their superior
numbers, not status. Protestants were but another interest, albeit the
largest, to be represented, with the special protections built into
power-sharing designed for Catholics, not Protestants; the minority
could reject the majority's government by refusing to participate in it.
Thus power-sharing may have returned many powers to Protestants,
but by preventing them from using their powers as they saw fit, it
frustrated Protestants: they could no longer be themselves.

Election returns indicated widespread Protestant opposition to
power-sharing, but the strike showed that it upset Protestant workers
most of all: they conducted the strike. This is especially notable since it
reversed the typical pattern of unionist politics; in both the struggle
against home rule and the subsequent history of Northern Ireland,
workers habitually deferred to elite leadership. While groups of
workers from time to time challenged their deference, [19] they never
reversed it. The strike was different, however: Protestant workers
called it, organized it, and, abetted by the advice of some politicians,
led it to victory, which suggests that they felt themselves more
susceptible to Catholic encroachments than did other Protestants. The
problem, as the Protestant working class sensed, was that power-
sharing, by narrowing the discrepancy between the legitimacy of
Protestant interests and the illegitimacy of Catholic ones, would
reduce Protestants to the status of Catholics. This is precisely why
Protestant workers struck at the prospect of co-opting Catholics. Not
only would power-sharing and the Council of Ireland have extended to
Catholics prerogatives, such as effective political representation, that
were traditionally Protestant; but this extension would have blurred
the contrast between what it meant to be Protestant and Catholic. To
treat Catholics as Protestants would have cost Protestants the unique
privileges that historically defined their community.

IV

As the Ulster crisis and the general strike illustrate, Protestants deeply need and distrust Britain. Needing Britain to maintain their position over Catholics, yet worrying that Britain will abandon them to the Republic at the critical moment, Protestants display intense yet conditional loyalty. If such ambivalence is indeed linked to their fate as settlers, then it is to be expected that the politics of other settlers would in some ways parallel that of Ulster Protestants. To explore the possibility that the conflict between Protestants and Catholics in Northern Ireland is rooted in the structures of settler colonialism rather than local peculiarities, this chapter will now turn to the politics of another settler colony, South Africa. The purpose of the comparison is not to argue that Protestants and whites or Catholics and blacks are identical, but rather that the similarity of settlers facing hostile native majorities with uncertain backing from the colonial powers has fashioned comparable, not to say identical, politics in Northern Ireland and South Africa.

The first white settlement in South Africa was established on the Cape of Good Hope by the Dutch East Indies Company in 1652 to provision ships travelling between the East Indies and Europe. As the settlement was intended as a supply station, and as supplies, especially cattle, were acquired through trade with the indigenous Khoikhoi, the Company discouraged territorial expansion lest it provoke war and disrupt trade. But before long former servants and soldiers of the Company had accumulated so much land that they not only took over the cattle trade, but also initiated a significant migration of whites from the Cape to the interior. Neither the Company nor its British successors in 1806 could prevent this 'trekking,' even though Britain, like its Dutch predecessors, sought to limit expansion so as to avoid conflict with natives (by this time the whites had reached the Xhosa). The British, writes George Fredrickson,

> hoped to limit white expansion and regulate contacts with the indigenous people in such a way as to maintain control over the frontiersman and prevent interracial violence. Left to themselves, settlers were prone to engage in aggressive behavior that risked provoking native wars because they assumed that government forces would bail them out and that the resulting peace treaties would open up additional land for their own use. From the point of view of the Colonial Office, territorial gains from one native

war simply provoked another and were part of a never-ending sequence that placed an intolerable burden on the exchequer while bringing no tangible benefits to the British Empire.[20]

British attempts to restrain settler expansion were, however, doubly unsuccessful; they 'bitterly disillusioned' Afrikaners without curbing their treks.[21] Indeed, British interference prompted the largest migration of all; in 1836–8 Afrikaners departed the Cape for the interior in the Great Trek.

The Afrikaners embarked on their trek largely to escape the limitations placed on the exploitation of black labor by Britain. In 1828, Britain freed the Khoikhoi from 'most restrictions on their economic freedom,' making them 'at least on paper . . . virtually equal to the European settlers in their civil rights.'[22] Then, in 1834, Britain emancipated the Cape's slaves, depriving whites of the forced black labor that they had regarded as essential since the earliest days of the Cape Colony.[23] This intrusion into the 'domestic relations' of whites was, from their point of view, intolerable for psychological as well as economic reasons. Whites would lose not only labor but status too, for the import of British intrusion was *gelykstelling*, that is, the equalization of status between blacks and whites. And as Irish Protestants depend on Catholics for definition, so Afrikaners (perhaps more than the wealthier English South Africans) forged a common identity by degrading blacks and privileging themselves.

> Commitment to a labor regime under which non-European slaves did virtually all of the menial and subservient work had the effect of lessening the possibility of class conflict among whites by elevating all of them to a relatively privileged social status. . . . The degradation of non-whites frequently served to bind together the white population, or some segment of it, to create a sense of community or solidarity that could become a way of life, and not simply a cover for economic exploitation.[24]

Thus while Afrikaners certainly objected to losing black labor, they also feared that black equality would undercut their superiority. Blacks, for Afrikaners, had to be distinguished from whites for psychological as well as economic reasons.

Afrikaners were so intent on keeping blacks different from themselves that, despite their deep religious convictions, they discouraged the conversion of blacks to Christianity. In the early years of the colony this was because blacks were enslaved on the basis of their religion, not race, and so conversion would have interfered with slavery; but even after race superseded religion as the mark of slaves, Afrikaners maintained religious distinctions. They wanted, evidently, to contrast blacks to whites as sharply as possible. According to Fredrickson,

> It appears that South African masters remained acutely un-comfortable with slaves or other non-white dependents who practiced the same religion and thus partook of the same cultural heritage as themselves. Indeed, the . . . 'homogeneity' between 'white' and 'Christian' or 'black' and 'heathen' persisted in the discourse of the Afrikaners until late in the nineteenth century. What is more, they made strenuous efforts to see that these linguistic correlations mirrored reality – by neglecting and sometimes vigorously discouraging the propagation of Christ-ianity among their nonwhite dependents. Since they craved a cultural gap as well as a racial one, they preferred to allow color and religion to remain reinforcing aspects of differentness rather than making a clear decision . . . as to which was to have priority.[25]

It was precisely this desire to dichotomize black and white – a desire registered by different religions, special privileges, and, ultimately, separate territories – that *gelykstelling* would thwart; '*gelykstelling* threatened a way of life as well as a system of labor.'[26] In the face of this challenge to their identities as well as interests, Afrikaners responded in much the same way as Irish Protestants responded to a similar specter; they 'in effect demanded *carte blanche* to treat [blacks] in any way that their interests and security seemed to require.'[27] When Britain rejected the Afrikaner demand, the Afrikaners rejected Britain: they moved to where they could treat blacks as they saw fit.

From the 1830s through 1850s Afrikaners escaped British meddling by trekking beyond the Cape Colony to establish independent republics where their constitutions 'gave formal expression to their revulsion against *gelykstelling* and to their determination that no form of racial equality would be countenanced in their own jurisdiction.'[28] These republics imposed various forms of forced labor, though in exchange for British recognition they did shy away from actual slavery.[29] In 1877 Britain annexed one of the republics, only to lose it four years later in the first Boer war. But the discovery of gold in 1886 revived British ambitions, resulting in the seond Boer war from 1899–

1902. The Afrikaners, of course, lost the war but won the peace, as after their defeat they were extended 'a free hand to rule over blacks more or less according to the settlers' own traditions.'[30] Their influence was only increased when Britain conferred effective independence on South Africa in 1910; Afrikaners constituted a majority of the white population, and only whites were enfranchised politically. If united, Afrikaners, despite losing the war, could control the government a mere decade after their defeat.

While Afrikaners certainly resented interference in black–white relations, their conflict with Britain was not really over the role blacks were to play in South Africa, though there were disagreements over the means by which that role could be best be secured. It was not that the British were notably less racist than Afrikaners, for British practices were themselves certainly racist. 'The real differences between liberal reformers and those engaged in face-to-face racial subjugation was not so much over which race should dominate as over the methods by which that supremacy should be maintained.'[31] These differences were less important in politicizing Afrikaners, however, than was their subordination to English South Africans. Growing numbers of Afrikaners demanded parity with, though not yet superiority over, the English population of South Africa.

The conflict between Afrikaner and English was grounded in the cultural and economic inferiority of the one to the other. Culturally, the English regarded Afrikaners as less than fully civilized, and their language as little better than pigeon Dutch. And economically, Afrikaners were consistently poorer than the English, especially after many small farmers were forced from the land and proletarianized in the decades after the Boer wars.[32] Once proletarianized, Afrikaners were exposed to competition from black workers, forcing them to seek political protection for their economic interests. In the meantime, Afrikaner nationalists had formed the National Party in protest of their cultural subordination. Demanding recognition of the linguistic and anti-imperialist traditions of their community, the National Party appealed to the abiding hostility of Afrikaners to English. But as cultural issues alone were insufficient to propel the National Party to power, it endorsed the Afrikaner working-class demands for protection from black workers in the 1920s, thus joining together the cultural and economic grievances of the Afrikaners against English hegemony.

As those benefiting from sectarianism perpetuate it in Northern Ireland, so is racism perpetuated in South Africa. And as in the one case the beneficiaries include workers as well as elites, so is it in the other. Northern Irish Protestants exclude Catholics from jobs that would compete with Protestant workers; South African whites reserve certain jobs exclusively for themselves. This was especially conspicuous for the key industries, shipbuilding and gold mining, in the respective economies. The workforce of each is, and historically has been, dominated by the settler population, with one notable difference. The workforce in Belfast shipyards is overwhelmingly Protestant; although the employers withhold exact figures, most estimates of the composition of the workforce suggest that it is around 90–5 percent Protestant and 5–10 percent Catholic. The situation is somewhat different in South Africa's gold mines; because most jobs are unskilled, and because skilled work is reserved for whites and unskilled for blacks, the great majority of mine workers are black, not white. But the essential point applies to South Africa as well as Northern Ireland; settlers generally monopolize the key skilled working-class jobs.

The imposition of a racially stratified workforce in South Africa's gold mines was of pivotal importance in the development of South Africa's political economy. The particulars of this evolution depended, naturally enough, on the particulars of South Africa's gold-mining industry, specifically that its profitability hinged more on the quantity than the quality of the gold.[33] This posed a problem because the price of gold, unlike most commodities, was fixed internationally, meaning that the additional costs of mining low-grade South African gold could not be passed on to the buyer. Since the costs of capital were also more or less fixed, the mine owners were left little alternative but to minimize labor costs; otherwise the mines would become uneconomic.[34] Accordingly, the companies prevailed on the state to depress the costs of black labor,[35] thereby creating a black proletariat beneath a white aristocracy of labor.

> The labour force of the gold mines thus came to comprise a large sector of unskilled, ultra-cheap, forced (non-white) labour, and a small sector (about one-tenth of the labour force) of skilled, expensive, free (white) labour.[36]

The skilled white working class was largely recruited from Europe, but the semi-skilled – and therefore more vulnerable – white workers were often Afrikaners who had been forced off the land in the previous generation. Although the 1911 Mine and Works Act sanctioned an industrial color bar reserving higher paying skilled and semi-skilled positions for whites, the companies opposed it, for in compelling them to employ higher paid whites for jobs which lower paid blacks could perform, the color bar increased costs, and reduced profits. White workers argued, however, that the companies had themselves created the necessity of the color bar; by underpaying blacks, the companies created the need for white workers to protect themselves from black competition. 'It was the involvement of the employers . . . in racial discrimination which generated the involvement of white workers . . . in racial discrimination.'[37]

In principle, of course, white workers might have protected themselves from black undercutting by helping blacks achieve parity with them. In practice this was infeasible for economic as well as psychological reasons, for if blacks had been paid market wages, the gold mines would have become unprofitable and white workers would have lost their jobs along with their privileges.[38] Thus white workers were trapped; they could not eliminate the black threat to their position without eliminating their position as well. It was therefore only a matter of time before the employers would exploit this vulnerability, especially since costs increased during the First World War as a result of inflation, a shortage of black labor, wage increases for whites, and the extension of the color bar.[39] And in spite of these gains for white workers and setbacks to the companies, the whites remained dissatisfied, for many highly skilled English workers had enlisted in the war and been replaced in the mines not only by less skilled, and thus more vulnerable, Afrikaners, but also by blacks who had acquired the skills to replace whites in general and Afrikaners in particular.

In response, white workers demanded, and the government conceded, an extension of the color bar to exclude blacks from semi-skilled work,[40] thus further inflating costs that could not, for market reasons, be passed on to the buyers. These additional costs prompted a profitability crisis after the war, forcing the companies to cut wages for whites, to substitute black for white labor, and in general to remove many, though not all, of the protections extended to white against black workers. This, in turn, provoked a veritable insurrection of white workers. The rising was suppressed by the state at the cost of several hundred lives, permitting the companies to reduce white wages and weaken, but not eliminate, the color bar.[41] Although these changes inevitably left white workers more insecure, they were far from helpless, for white, unlike black, workers enjoyed political power as part of their colonial birthright. They could, and did, fight against their employers; the result was a major victory for white workers.

White workers were deeply shaken by the failure of the strike, since it showed that employers could and would replace them with black workers. That whites could be replaced was in ways even more unsettling than that the employers would replace them, as it discredited the myth that whites were 'naturally' superior to blacks. If blacks could replace whites, then they were *per force* as good as their 'betters.' Thus deprived of their 'natural' superiority at the very moment employers were diluting their social superiority, white workers realized that they 'could maintain a privileged position [only] by erecting artificial barriers against black advancement,'[42] that is, only by using political power. This they did in conjunction with Afrikaner nationalists who, for their part, were seeking to extend their base by appealing to the class as well as cultural interests of Afrikaner workers. Thus a deal was struck between Afrikaner workers and cultural nationalists whereby the one received protection from black competition, while the other became the dominant political force in South Africa.

English settlers controlled South Africa culturally, economically, and politically from the early nineteenth through early twentieth centuries. But when in 1910 South Africa became a self-governing white dominion, the more numerous Afrikaners were able to exert their powers politically. As the majority of the white electorate, Afrikaners elected their Boer war leaders – Generals Botha, Smuts, and Hertzog – to head South Africa's inaugural government. However, in 1913 Hertzog split from his erstwhile comrades over their policy of fusing Afrikaner and English into one nation, arguing that 'the separate existence and traditions of the Dutch-speaking group' would be overwhelmed by integration with the more culturally, economically, and politically advanced English nationality.[43] Hertzog instead advocated a 'two stream' nationality policy that would maintain separate English and Afrikaner nationalisms within a unified white state. As his separate but equal doctrine conflicted with the government's integrationist policies, Hertzog left the cabinet to form the National Party, whose essential platform was 'the two-stream idea of white South African unity, and the policy of "South Africa [as opposed to the British Empire] first".'[44] These proposals met with lukewarm support until South African backing of Britain in the First World War revived interest in the National Party's policy of 'South Africa first.'

The prospects of the National Party nonetheless remained limited as long as it advocated only the ethnic interests of Afrikaners. Thus in the aftermath of the labor agitation in the gold mines in the early 1920s, the Nationalist allied with the predominantly English Labour Party, promising to protect the class interests of white labor. At the time of the alliance,

> [T]here were many points of contact between their respective policies. On the one hand the Nationalists, associating British imperialism with entrenched money interests in South Africa, tended to be vaguely anti-capitalist in their propaganda if not always in their practice. On the other hand, the Labour Party tended to match the Nationalists in its determination to maintain the colour bar as the only way of maintaining the standards of the white workers.[45]

The resulting 'anti-capitalist and white racist'[46] pact carried the parliamentary elections in 1924, with the National Party emerging as the dominant partner in the coalition government.

The Herzog government pursued three distinctive aims. First, it favored the interests of South Africa over imperial interests, without, however, advocating an independent republic for fear of offending prospective English supporters. Secondly, the Hertzog government sought to elevate Afrikaner culture to the level of English culture by, for example, raising the Afrikaans language to official status. Hertzog's goal was not to 'Afrikanerize' the state, but to preserve the weaker of white South Africa's 'two streams.' And thirdly, the government enacted the 'civilized labor policy,' which provided for whites to replace non-whites in public employment at 'civilized' wages, and the 'Mine and Works Act,' which reserved 'certain categories of skilled and semi-skilled work for Whites alone.'

> The industrial color bar and the 'civilized labor policy' com-pleted the basic pattern of government-supported discrimination in the South African economy. Whites were to be guaranteed jobs, artificially high wages, and exclusive access to skilled work – all at the expense of African aspirations.[47]

Thus what white workers failed to win through strikes they achieved

by forging a fateful alliance with Afrikaner Nationalism – a movement that preserved from its agrarian slave-holding past a firm belief that white men should always have the advantage over 'kaffirs.' Together [white labor and Afrikaner Nationalism] strengthened the pattern of racial segmentation in industry and legitimized the notion that the government had a positive responsibility to establish and maintain a privileged and protected economic status for the entire white community.[48]

These labor, national, and cultural policies of the Hertzog government paid off handsomely when the National Party superseded the Labour Party to win an absolute majority in the 1929 parliamentary elections. For in strengthening the National Party, the pact government weakened the Labour Party, dividing it in a manner reminiscent of the Northern Ireland Labour Party (NILP). As the NILP was paralyzed by partition, reluctant to endorse or reject it for fear of offending one community or the other, so the South African Labour Party (SALP) was unable to support complete discrimination unanimously. The SALP opposed white superiority no more than the NILP opposed partition, but both Labour parties, by hesitating before endorsing total and exclusive settler superiority, sacrificed the support of settlers without gaining that of natives. In hesitating, they reflected the paradoxical position of Labour parties in settler societies. For while, on the one hand, Labour must defend Protestant or white supremacy to maintain its position among working-class settlers, on the other, it thereby endorsed an ultimately self-defeating logic. By accepting the colonial interests of working-class settlers as paramount, both Labour parties strengthened the hand of those parties – the Unionist in one case, the National in the other – that advocated systematic settler hegemony. With the Labour parties thus outflanked on the issue that they themselves identified as decisive, they were ill-positioned to challenge such leaders as Hertzog. But if Labour could not challenge Hertzog, intransigent nationalists demanding Afrikaner, not British, superiority could mount a challenge; settlers threaten the status quo from the right, not the left.

Although Hertzog once led Afrikaner nationalists, his consistent advocacy of parity with, not superiority over, the English eventually alienated militant Afrikaner Nationalists. In response to their pressure, Hertzog broke with the National Party and formed a government with his erstwhile rival, General Smuts, which renounced the 'two-stream' policy for fusion with the English in 'one white nation,'[49] and prompted militant Afrikaners to establish the Purified National Party (the name later reverted to the simple National Party). At first this splinter group was isolated even from most Afrikaners; but as Hertzog's original right wing split forming the National Party in 1914 faced dismal prospects at the outset only to triumph a decade later, so did the reconstituted National Party. The right wing, by preserving the settler identity in the face of British as well as native inroads, preserved that spirit of independence, even of isolation, which is as much a part of the Afrikaner as of the Ulster Protestant tradition.

The National Party has governed South Africa uninterruptedly since 1948. In this period Nationalist policy has been marked by two related thrusts – apartheid and Afrikaner nationalism – that, though deeply rooted in previous South African history, only reached full fruition after 1948. Certainly, for example, residential segregation, economic discrimination and white supremacy were officially as well as unofficially sanctioned long before apartheid. But though apartheid hardly introduced racist practices to South Africa, it did fashion them into an internally coherent, even visionary, system. Similarly, Afrikaner nationalism, while implicit in Afrikaner politics for the previous century and a half, was asserted much more aggressively by the post-1948 Nationalist governments. Using state power to 'Afrikanerize' virtually the entire public as well as much of the private sector,[50] successive Nationalist governments advanced Afrikaner over and against English interests. The contention here is that both Afrikaner nationalism and apartheid represent the interests of settlers, the one against English power, the other against the native population: the politics of the National Party is that of settlers.

Apartheid reflected an irreconcilable contradiction. On the one hand, apartheid manifested the complete, absolute, and unremitting anathema with which whites in general, and Afrikaners in particular, viewed the prospects of integration. Apartheid revealed not simply that Afrikaners as individuals despised integration with blacks, but that they believed that their survival as a people precluded such contact. Integration was not left to individual choice, but banned as the fundamental law of the land. Apartheid did not permit – it mandated – separation.[51] On the other hand, Afrikaners, while denouncing racial interaction of any kind, simultaneously depended on black labor for their growing industries. To offset the implications of the dependence of whites on black workers, blacks are deemed migrant employees temporarily visiting 'white' areas, who as transients, naturally forfeit voting rights and much labor protection. Thus:

[A]partheid can best be understood as the systematic attempt to reverse economic integration as much as possible by legislating social barriers in order to channel the inevitable consequences of African economic advancement in the interests of the privileged whites.[52]

Apartheid rigidly separated white and black lest the contrast between them become grey. By dichotomizing South Africa, Afrikaners use race as the Irish use religion, to distinguish between privileged settlers and dispossessed natives. In the same way as privileges unified Protestants against Catholics, so with Afrikaners:

[T]he enactment of racial laws ... in the first decade of Nationalist rule was as much directed at fostering Afrikaner unity in light of its internal stratification as it aimed at holding the 'black threat' at bay.[53]

The National Party united Afrikaners against not only blacks, but also South Africans of English descent. Prior to the 1948 National government, the English dominated South Africa culturally and economically. The Nationalist victory, however, changed all this; culturally, the government invested unprecedented status in the Afrikaner language and religion; and economically, the government fortified the Afrikaner bourgeoisie as well as working class against English capital. But perhaps most of all, apartheid extended to Afrikaners the 'tangible psychological rewards of belonging.'[54]

In the [apartheid] legislation two considerations were inextricably linked: without a privileged position the Afrikaners could not survive as a separate people; without safeguarding the racial separateness of the people, a privileged position could not be maintained.[55]

Thus by privileging Afrikaners, apartheid maintained their identity against both blacks and English.

The Afrikaner identity is, like that of many settlers, less than fully secular. Like Ulster Protestants, Afrikaners claim not only that God takes a special interest in them but that their history proves them to be His chosen people. For Afrikaners this was best illustrated by the Great Trek; in their minds Britain was undercutting, even humiliating, them on behalf of blacks,[56] forcing the Afrikaners to wander the desert in search of the promised land, beset, all the while, by black massacres of the God-fearing trekkers. The treachery of the British and the savagery of the natives (Afrikaners had now reached the Zulus), were, however, merely God's way of testing the faith of Afrikaners; and by persevering in the Calvinism of their fathers, they passed the test.[57]

Religion reinforced as well as reflected the hostile material conditions encountered by Afrikaners. For material as well as psychological reasons, Afrikaners opposed integration as an erosion of their privileges. Religion, by obligating them to exclude those cursed with God's disfavor, sanctified this. As Moodie writes, 'because of the divine election of Afrikanerdom, anything threatening Afrikaner separateness became demonic.'[58] Thus the colonial imperative to separate natives from settlers was disguised as divine obligation; apartheid ceased to be a matter of choice and became a sacred duty. And Afrikaners must remain privileged over, as well as separate from, those not favored by Him. After all, if Afrikaners were not better than other groups He would not have favored them, and if they were not better to begin with, certainly His favor made them better. Thus God's calling implies Afrikaner superiority over the English as well as blacks.[59] It is for this reason that Afrikanerdom is described as a 'civil religion'; the material implications of their religion are integral to the emotional identity of ordinary Afrikaners, reminding 'them of their sacred separation from English and black African.'[60] It is God's will that they stand alone.

V

This sketch suggests similarities as well as differences between South Africa and Northern Ireland. Some similarities are obvious: in South Africa as in Northern Ireland settlers are systematically privileged over natives, with race rather than religion serving to distinguish the privileged from the deprived. In one as in the other, settler privileges are mutually reinforcing, creating two different and conflicting sets of interests and identities. And in both, settlers oppose integration, assimilation, inclusion, in short, anything threatening to bridge the Manichean divide elevating them psychologically as well as materially over natives.[61]

But as similarities between Northern Ireland and South Africa are obvious, so are differences. First, Afrikaners have historically preferred republicanism to unionism, that is, independence from, instead of association with, Britain. Secondly, Afrikaners constitute a minority of the population, a fact disposing them to formalize privileges that Protestants could leave largely informal once Northern Ireland was established. Finally, Afrikaners depend much more directly than do Ulster Protestants on native labor. Yet in spite of these dissimilar settings, the two peoples are subject to a similar logic; the differences between them express differences in their situations rather than motivations.

The difference between the dependence of Afrikaners on, and the independence of Ulster Protestants from, native labor is obvious and consequential. For the fear that power might accrue to blacks as a result of their indispensability to the productive process motivated much of apartheid. Because blacks were essential to South African industry, they were positioned to assert political power, to erode the distinction between work 'appropriate' to whites and blacks, to reduce segregation, to undermine, in short, the very bases of settler colonialism. To prevent this potential from being realized, Afrikaners developed apartheid to monopolize political power and to maintain their cultural separation despite their economic dependence. In Northern Ireland, however, the lack of economic integration pre-cluded the need for such elaborate structures as apartheid. *De facto* superiority was sufficient to the task at hand; nothing as exotic as apartheid was really required.

Because they constitute a small minority of the population, Afrikaners depend on black labor and overt repression. Ulster Protest-ants, in contrast, could dispense with Catholic labor and a massive secret police apparatus. Certainly Protestants employed repression when challenged, but until 1969 the Protestant majority not only could do without flagrant repression, but could practice majority rule. But again, the difference conceals an underlying similarity. Despite their rhetoric, the Ulster crisis and the general strike show that Ulster Protestants too reject liberal standards when their interests require. Partition generally allowed Ulster Protestants to present a cleaner appearance than Afrikaners could, but when necessary, they resorted to the more direct methods at their disposal.

The republicanism of Afrikaners and the unionism of Ulster Protestants likewise represent similar responses to different circum-stances. To Afrikaners Britain appeared as a constant threat to freedom; to Protestants the British threat is only occasional. Thus Afrikaners openly renounced 'imperialism,' while Protestants confer a conditional loyalty on the colonial power. Both sought, however, a free hand over internal affairs; British interference with Afrikaners provoked treks and with Protestants crises and strikes. And both groups of settlers rebelled when Britain threatened their superiority, but with a difference: Afrikaners gloried in the independence that Protestants resisted until loyalty to 'Ulster' overwhelmed that to Britain.

Because the hegemony of Afrikaners does not rest on British support, they had less incentive to instill disloyalty among blacks. But having fostered it anyway, the more marginal Afrikaners discovered that it enhanced their position. As white elites need at least a modicum of support to maintain their position, and as this has come from other whites, black disloyalty is functional for the Afrikaner working class. By allowing Afrikaner workers to command privileges at black expense, and by enhancing their leverage over white elites, Afrikaner, like Protestant, workers developed a vested interest in opposing concessions that might reduce their leverage as well as privileges. In the same way as Protestant workers defended colonial privileges in the home rule crisis and general strike, so Afrikaner workers defended their privileges through labor agitation and apartheid. And as Protestant workers actually benefit from the Catholic opposition aroused by their intransigence, so Afrikaner workers benefit from the political importance they derive from the racist measures they themselves demand. Given these benefits as a consequence of native disloyalty, settler workers are inclined to insist on their privileges even when elites would prefer to trade working-class privileges for political stability.

The concessions most disturbing to both Protestants and Afrikaners have been those that reduced the distinction between natives and themselves. This is partly, of course, because material gains for natives generally entail losses for settlers. But as the Ulster crisis and general strike show for Protestants, and the Trek and apartheid for Afrikaners, both peoples are concerned with status and prestige as well as material standing. Thus concessions to Catholics or blacks, even if they elevated natives without reducing settlers, nonetheless threatened settlers with the loss of the privileged status that defined them. And if the mere threat of compromise prompted bitter protest, the prospect of compromising political power provoked rebellion. For lacking 'natural' superiority, settlers, and especially working-class settlers, ultimately relied on political power to preserve their colonial birthrights. It is for this reason that settlers oppose extending political influence to natives: even the co-optation of natives into colonial structures implied the legitimacy of some native, and thus the illegitimacy of conflicting settler, interests. In the face of such fundamentally subversive implications, settlers have fought desperately to restrict political power to themselves. With a free hand over their internal affairs, Ulster Protestants and Afrikaners rested secure; without it both were vulnerable to external betrayal and internal subversion.

Both Ulster Protestants and Afrikaners fate themselves to insecurity. By insisting on privileges, both material and psychological, they foster enduring and irreconcilable contradictions with their subordinates. Materially, Ulster Protestants (and Afrikaners) maintain political hegemony by excluding Catholics (and blacks) from political representation, and economic hegemony by relegating Catholics (and especially blacks) to underemployment, and often actual unemployment. Psychologically, Ulster Protestants (and Afrikaners) believe themselves to belong to the better, more prestigious community. As these material and psychological superiorities imply the permanent subordination of Catholics (or blacks), Protestants, particularly those feeling themselves vulnerable to Catholic encroachments, insist on separation from Catholics. And as Protestants can maintain their collective privileges only as long as united, the intransigence of some obliges all to intransigence, since to alienate privileges regarded as inalienable by working-class Protestants is to commit the unpardonable sin of dividing a community that must remain undivided. Thus as compromising privileges divides settlers, and as dividing settlers is unacceptable politically, intransigents hold the veto among both Protestants and Afrikaners.[62] 'Realists' – whether Smuts and Botha in the 1910s, Hertzog in the 1930s, O'Neill in the 1960s, or Faulkner in the 1970s – may propose compromise in pursuit of stability, but are all ultimately overwhelmed by right-wing appeals to settler unity in defending their privileges from betrayal. Thus settlers repudiate the very reforms designed to stabilize their position. Privilege counts for more than security: hence their wrath.

7

Conclusion

'Anyone who thinks he knows the answer to Northern Ireland is ill-informed.'

A Northern Ireland politician

I

Sixty-five years after Northern Ireland was created and 17 years after it erupted in violence, British policy remains much the same as always: it maintains Protestant hegemony militarily, politically, and economically. But whereas for the first 50 years of Northern Ireland's existence Britain managed to support Protestant hegemony from a distance, it is now engaged actively and directly in Northern Ireland's politics. British officials often talk as if this course is followed for lack of responsible alternatives, but maintaining a status quo biased in favor of Protestants is only one of three broad policies available to Britain, the other two being protecting the union in exchange for fundamental reforms and consenting to the unification of Ireland. Until the still ambiguous 'Agreements' with the Republic of Ireland, however, Britain shied away from the other options for fear of offending Protestants. It continued direct rule, entertained but rarely implemented reforms, and paid as little attention to the violence as possible. While this approach is unlikely to resolve Northern Ireland's conflict, it does allow Britain to retreat from the immediate consequences of its policy, even if it increases economic, political, and human costs in the future. Britain, in other words, is servicing but not repaying its debt in Northern Ireland.

The political deadlock in Northern Ireland has been too peripheral and too intractable for any British government to bother investing the political capital necessary to pursue a breakthrough. From the mid-1970s through the mid-1980s, successive British governments instead made a series of half-hearted efforts to conceal conflict and contain damage. Britain's initial response to the collapse of the Sunningdale government was to pretend that nothing had happened; it called for devolved government under conditions that effectively restated the case for power-sharing. When the unionist coalition that carried the ensuing election rebuffed British conditions, Britain decided to wait for Northern Ireland's politicians to come to their senses. In the meantime Britain 'filled' the 'political vacuum' by decreeing that the violence was really criminal, not political, in nature, and as such was to be dealt with by the (overwhelmingly Protestant) police and militia, not the army. While this had from Britain's perspective the happy consequence of justifying a reduction in the number of soldiers stationed in Northern Ireland, 'criminalization' hardly represented a serious reading of the situation. It denied that the violence was political, delayed a real solution, and prepared for the hunger strikes that revived the Provisionals.

When criminalization raised more problems than it deferred, Britain decided to supplement it with devolution. Plans for an Assembly were announced, elections were held, and Britain let it be known that powers would be devolved as the Assembly gained cross-community support. The idea was that the carrot of devolution would induce unionists to share power with moderate Catholics, although Britain did not make power-sharing an explicit condition for fear of antagonizing unionists. British concern for unionist sensitivities backfired, however, when the SDLP boycotted the Assembly, leaving it a debating chamber for unionists to which Britain dared not devolve power. Meanwhile Britain pays the bills, focuses on more malleable problems, and waits for the Northern Irish to accept 'reason'. The wait, however, is likely to be a long one, not as some are wont to believe because the Northern Irish are congenitally irrational, but because they are acting according to the structures and incentives that Britain itself has established.

For centuries Britain rewarded Protestants for their 'loyalty' in the face of Catholic disloyalty, conferring political power, higher socio-economic status, and prestige on Protestants. These benefits in hand, Protestants saw little reason to compromise with Catholics unless they stood to lose the union and with it everything they valued. Yet this is precisely the threat that British governments refuse to brandish, instead letting Protestants have their cake and eat it too, permitting them to remain in but not of the United Kingdom, and allowing them to use Britain to uphold their domination over Catholics – all in the belief that 'guarantees' would make Protestants more amenable to compromise. The effect, however, is quite the opposite. By guaranteeing the essential demands of Protestants, Britain rewards their intransigence and reduces incentive for them to accede to British requests. Thus British 'policy' consists of encouraging what it means to discourage, and then complaining that Protestants do not behave differently.

By allowing Protestants to block reforms, Britain undermines moderate Catholics, forges constituencies for the republicans, and then vows never to submit to 'terrorism.' Republicans have learned, however, that Britain yields to nothing else; violence has succeeded in achieving independence in the south and bringing down Stormont in the north and non-violence has failed in achieving home rule, civil rights, and power-sharing. Thus the implicit hypocrisy of British criticisms of republican violence: by ignoring peaceful protests and underpinning Protestant hegemony, Britain elicits the violence it deplores. This raises the obvious question of why Britain invests lives, money, and reputation in what seems a futile endeavor. The explanation is certainly not economic, not with Britain spending more 'protecting its investment each year than it has invested in total.'[1] These costs in conjunction with the human and diplomatic ones would seem to make Northern Ireland a problem with which Britain would gladly dispense. Such, certainly, is the consensus of British public opinion, with polls showing that only a minority of the electorate wants Britain to remain in Northern Ireland. Why, then, does Britain not sneak away like a thief into the night?

Part of the answer is that four centuries of British rule have changed much in Ireland, but not the facts of geography. As Britain conquered Ireland to protect its western flank, so it remains interested in the loyalties of its neighbor. Britain need not fear that Ireland might become 'another Cuba' to want to keep its fingers in what it regards as its sphere of influence. But Britain does not want its fingers burned, and this disposes it to upset matters as little as possible, while at the same time shaping the basic institutional parameters of Irish politics. Not only would withdrawal from Ireland after centuries of involvement be extremely difficult for a British government, but the government embarking on this course would necessarily make the 'Irish question' its highest priority. The tendency, therefore, is for British governments to avoid those costs by postponing the hard decisions. Britain stays not because it covets Northern Ireland but because it cannot figure out how to leave.

Thus Britain holds Northern Ireland as inexpensively and

unobtrusively as possible, attempting 'Ulsterization' and distancing itself from the 'troubles.' But while the short-term effect of such indifference is to cushion Britain from the worst costs of Northern Ireland, the long-term effect is to maintain Protestant hegemony and confirm the republican view that Britain will withdraw when confronted with higher and inescapable costs. Consequently, British policy turns against itself, inviting republicans to apply more pressure in the conviction that Britain will eventually carry its contempt for Ireland to the logical conclusion of withdrawal.

II

If Britain ranks Northern Ireland as a low priority, the Republic regards it as an increasingly important one. The Republic worries that instability in the north might converge with long-term developments in the south to disrupt the southern state. The fear is not unfounded, for Ireland combines the highest birthrate in Europe with the lowest growth rate among OECD countries,[2] meaning that its already high unemployment rate is likely to become chronic once the 50 percent of the population which is younger than 25 and the 33 percent younger than 14 enter the job market. This conjunction appears still more combustible in light of the inability of successive Irish governments to manage the worsening economy. Thus far the Republic's two main political formations – the Fianna Fail Party and the Fine Gael–Labour coalition – have been able to survive the strains resulting from mounting economic problems, but the last five years of uncharacteristically fragile governments suggest that Ireland's party system is weakening. Disturbed by these trends, Ireland's political elite has recently stressed the need to resolve the crisis in the north to prevent it from spreading south.

The Republic has argued since the early 1980s that the political deadlock in Northern Ireland can be broken only by expanding the context of a solution beyond Northern Ireland to include the Republic as well. The Republic further argues that Britain must involve it formally in the governing of Northern Ireland; otherwise Northern Ireland's Catholic minority will remain estranged from the state and receptive to republicans. This position was developed most fully in the *Report* of the New Ireland Forum, a commission representing the SDLP and the Republic's three main parties and through them over 90 percent of the island's Catholics.[3] The Forum's proposals were originally rejected out of hand by Britain as well as by unionists, although Britain subsequently accepted an extremely limited version of the third proposal. The important point, however, concerns not the small successes of the Forum but the broader inability of mainstream Irish nationalism to come to grips conceptually and politically with what it sees as a worsening problem.

The Forum contended that Northern Ireland's conflict had reached 'critical proportions,' and jeopardized 'democratic principles' south as well as north of the border. It went on to claim that:

> The situation is daily growing more dangerous. Constitutional politics are on trial and unless there is action soon to create a framework in which constitutional politics can work, the drift into more extensive civil conflict is in danger of becoming irreversible. . . . The consequence for the people of Northern Ireland would be horrific and it is inconceivable that the South and Britain could escape the serious threats to stability that would arise.[4]

With the southern parties believing their interests at stake in Northern Ireland, the Forum advanced three specific proposals for a 'new' Ireland: a unitary state; a federal state; and joint sovereignty of the Republic and Britain over the north. Naturally none of these appealed to Ulster Protestants, but the Forum maintained that each would allow for the expression of their distinctive traditions. Thus the unitary state, which looked suspiciously like a united Ireland, would guarantee religious liberties, separate Church and state, assure Protestants representation in an upper legislative chamber, and broaden the definition of what it meant to be Irish to include Protestants. The federal–confederal state would invest substantial powers in two regional assemblies, one of which would have substantial unionist representation, and would permit Protestants to retain symbolic connections with Britain. And joint British and Irish sovereignty, by conferring 'equal responsibility for all aspects of government' on London and Dublin, would express both the 'Britishness' of unionists and the 'Irishness' of nationalists.[5]

Each proposal, it will be noted, tries to institutionalize both the role of the Dublin government and the legitimacy of unionist as well as nationalist traditions, with the latter point constituting what the Forum saw as its most constructive contribution to co-operation in Northern Ireland: recognition of the distinctive traditions and identities of unionists. The Forum insisted that Ireland consists of two traditions and that to exclude either was to foster conflict. Hence it spoke of 'an honoured place' for all traditions, of 'two sets of legitimate rights' and of the 'mutual recognition and acceptance of both' unionist and nationalist ways of life in a new Ireland.[6] And hence it weighed various arrangements for dual citizenship, joint sovereignty, and British as well as Irish symbols. It hoped to entice Protestants into dropping their habitual aversion to Irish unity by acknowledging the integrity of unionist traditions explicitly and implicitly. But however laudable its ecumenicalism, the Forum ignored two problems: that the question of sovereignty could not be fudged and that unionists rejected equal rights and mutual recognition along with the rest of the Forum's recommendations.

The Forum finessed the issue of sovereignty, aspiring to make both the Republic and Britain sovereign over Northern Ireland, which not only ignored the vast discrepancy between British and Irish power, but also misunderstood the nature of sovereignty. Sovereignty is, by definition, what arbitrates disputes authoritatively and conclusively; to divide it between sovereign governments would both divide the indivisible and undermine the very authorities that the Forum meant to uphold. Northern Ireland could be part of the United Kingdom or of the Republic (or conceivably of neither), but not of both without creating administrative, constitutional, and political havoc. Who, if both were sovereign, would adjudicate disagreements between Dublin and London?

The obstacles to dividing sovereignty would likely be insurmountable in the best of circumstances, but the particular nature of unionism redoubles them. The Forum ignored the general problem, however, and minimized the particular one; by accepting unionist rhetoric about religious liberty and British allegiances, the Forum convinced itself that retaining substantive and symbolic attachments to Britain and guaranteeing religious liberties would allay Protestant opposition to its proposals. From this followed the Forum's concern with institutional structures and constitutional protections. But in responding to the expressed objections of Protestants, the Forum took unionist commitments to Britain and religious liberty too seriously and domination over Catholics too lightly. The Forum was aware that '[u]nionists seek to prevent . . . loss of their dominant position consequent upon giving effective recognition to the nationalist identity and aspiration,'[7] but did not explain how to incorporate unionism and nationalism into the new Ireland when the content of unionism is the exclusion of nationalism. Hence the derision with which unionists greeted the *Report* exposed its essential fallacy: unionists are not pluralists interested in consensus but settlers committed to the vestiges of their hegemony.

If the Forum expected unionists to denounce the *Report*, it hoped that Britain would discuss the proposals in the spirit in which they were ventured and press Protestants for significant concessions. To this end Garret FitzGerald, Ireland's prime minister and driving force behind the Forum, met with Thatcher to discuss the *Report*. After two days of what he thought were productive conferences, Thatcher informed a press conference (televised live in Ireland) that 'I have made it quite clear that a united Ireland was one solution that is out. A second solution was a confederation of two states. That is out. A third solution was joint authority. That is out – that is a derogation of sovereignty.'[8]

Thatcher's response traumatized 'responsible' southern opinion in general as well as the Forum in particular, for both agreed that the Forum had established its credibility with Britain by offering constructive suggestions, denouncing republicans, and affirming the common struggle against 'terrorist' violence. The irony of this strategy, however, is that it failed because it succeeded; by convincing Britain of its good faith, close friendship, and general dependability, the Republic deprived itself of leverage over British policy. For with the Republic conceding what Britain wanted, Britain had scant incentive to offer the Republic something of substance. Unionists, on the other hand, avoided this trap; by kicking and screaming whenever Britain hinted that concessions might be appropriate, they forced Britain to make their fears the axis of its policy. Thus the moderation which constitutional nationalists believe to be pragmatic may constitute an impractical response to an immoderate problem.

III

If Britain lacks the incentive and the Republic the capacity to reconcile Northern Ireland's two communities, Protestants would seem the one actor with both the motive and opportunity to make a serious effort at restoring stability to Northern Ireland. Their stated commitment is to the British connection, which is not only compatible with, but also would be strengthened by, a power-sharing government. In one stroke Protestants would secure British approval, protect their stake in the union, satisfy Catholic demands for representation, and isolate the IRA – all in exchange for unionists recognizing the right of

Catholics to meaningful participation in institutions that would
actively reaffirm the British connection. Neither Britain, the Republic,
nor Catholics has a workable solution within such ready reach, yet
Protestants consistently reject it.

Protestants reject power-sharing because they refuse to trade part of
their heritage to secure the rest. As settlers, they still define themselves
in contrast to Catholics, and thus depend on – and cannot dispense
with – their superiority over Catholics. Both their interests and
identities are inherent in the discrepancy in status between Protestants
and Catholics. Thus to accord Catholics equal status is to subvert
what it means to be Protestant, with secure as well as marginal
Protestants depending on the superiority. For the middle and upper
classes, even if not benefiting directly from privileges, do benefit from
the union with Britain, the union presupposes the solidarity of all
Protestants, and solidarity is achieved by privileging Protestants at the
expense of Catholics. Hence the logic of their position prevents
Protestants from taking those measures that would secure themselves:
they opt for domination over stability.

If Protestants exclude Catholics as a condition of their unity, they
persist in this behavior because Britain indemnifies them from the
worst economic and political costs. Britain has convinced itself that
unionists reject power-sharing for fear of unification and that once
persuaded of their unconditional right to maintain the union, they will
mend their ways and share power with moderate Catholics. But the
fallacy of British logic is exposed by the failure of each and every
British effort to win Protestant consent for Catholic power; by ruling
out unification Britain surrenders leverage over Protestants. Thus
when Protestants sabotage its proposals, Britain is left short of
sanctions, having previously assured Protestants that they can
exercise their veto without fear of unification. Needless to say, this
provides scant incentive for unionists to accommodate Britain: they
get what they want already.

Unionist strategy succeeds in maintaining British support for
Protestant hegemony, but at a very high psychological cost. They live
in dread of the day that Britain reverses course and betrays them to
the fate that haunts them always. Fear, though, does not soften their
position. The more bitter the Catholic challenges and the more desperate
their dependence on fickle British governments, the more tenaciously
do Protestants fight to keep what is 'rightfully theirs.' Republican
outrages and British vacillations serve only to remind loyalists of the
need for vigilance. Thus they care not that in rebuffing compromises

they try British patience and vindicate republican violence. But they should care, for their ultimate undoing will be that Britain does not require their services and need not continue accepting crisis as a norm. In staving off small concessions, Protestants have hastened the day that Britain will dump them onto the Republic: they converted a strong position into a weak one.

IV

For the bulk of the 1970s unionists were shielded from the most damaging consequences of their intransigence by the political ineptitude of republicans. The Provisionals were content to play out the flip side of unionist logic, apparently more interested in sustaining than winning their struggle. Recently, however, the Provisionals have embraced politics as essential to military success, and accordingly, have upgraded the status of Sinn Fein. Once merely the 'political wing' of the far more important IRA, Sinn Fein has now achieved something approaching co-equal status, as reflected in the Provisionals' slogan of achieving liberation with a ballot in one hand and an Armalite rifle in the other. While the specific connection between the IRA and Sinn Fein is secret, it appears that a core group, which stresses that political and armed struggle are equally important, has assumed effective control over both. But whatever the precise relation between them, the traditional republican commitment to violence for its own sake has been replaced by a more sophisticated and imaginative understanding of republicanism. The Provisionals have taken to politics with a relish.

A decade ago the Provisionals were caught in a vicious cycle; having defined republicanism in terms of physical force, they staked all on an armed campaign that confirmed the resolve of their more powerful enemies. Thus even their successes gave rise to failures; they maintained the ideal of a united Ireland but were thwarted by the way they pursued it. Catholic support for the hunger strikes, however, showed the Provisionals the desirability of broadening their appeal and diversifying their methods. Since then the Provisionals have scaled down the bombings and shootings that used to comprise the whole of their struggle and have calibrated their violence according to the political situation. If, for example, Sinn Fein's fortunes are served by renewed polarization, the IRA can arrange it; if, however, Sinn Fein needs a more moderate image, the IRA can curtail its activities. All the while, of course, Sinn Fein offers uncritical blessing to the IRA, but in addition now fields candidates in both north and south, now champions community issues peripheral to the 'national struggle,' and now talks of subjects (such as trade unions and women's issues) that it once ignored.

These changes in the Provisionals were inaugurated by a new generation of political and military leaders. The preceding generation had been deeply suspicious of politics, socially conservative, typically from the south, generally *petit-bourgeois* in background and consciousness, and committed to a 32-county Gaelic republic. Although occasionally voicing socialist sentiments, these were less important to them than setting bombs and staging 'ambushes.' In contrast, the current generation of republican leaders matured in the conflict of the 1970s, understands the centrality of politics, takes socialism as part and parcel of the republican ideal, identifies itself as working class, and is distinctly northern in life experience. Collectively these changes in leadership have convinced the Provisionals to press on social as well as national demands and to conceptualize the struggle for a republic as inextricably linked to working-class needs for jobs, housing, and the like. The Provisionals, in other words, are beginning to adapt republicanism to the immediate concerns of their community.

The emergence of the generation now in its mid-to-late thirties was facilitated by the dead-end reached by the Provisionals in the mid-1970s. While able to continue detonating bombs with numbing regularity, the Provisionals were after a decade of incessant violence no closer to – and perhaps further from – their objective in the late 1970s than they had been at the outset of their campaign. The constitutional connection to Britain remained fixed, loyalists were as determined as ever, Catholics were demoralized, and the quality of recruits had declined to the point that republican 'hooliganism' was a greater concern in the Catholic ghettoes than in the lobbies of parliament. These obstacles, which were clearly insuperable to the older generation, prepared for the ascension of more political republicans anxious to clean up, broaden, and diversify their movement. In five years they have converted the Provisionals from a tired and fruitless organization into one able to strike in new and different as well as tried and tested ways.

If the flagging fortunes of the Provisionals encouraged a change of strategy, the vulnerability of the SDLP rewarded it. The Provisionals were in a position to consolidate the gains won through the hunger strikes because of the weakness of the SDLP. To be sure, the SDLP still outpolled Sinn Fein, but given Britain's failure to force unionists to share power with it, the SDLP was stranded in the awkward position of recognizing parties that refused to recognize it. This problem was compounded by the SDLP's knowledge that it received British patronage because of the threat posed by republican violence, without which Britain would not bother with well-meaning but ineffectual Catholic moderates. Thus depending on the Provisionals for its credibility, the SDLP was hard pressed to resist Provisional attempts to recapture the political initiative among Catholics and to cast themselves as bright and vibrant in contrast to the tiresome familiarity of the SDLP.

The new popularity of the Provisionals was attested by their improved performances in elections. The Provisionals have risen from a desultory percentage to average about one third of the Catholic vote in a series of elections beginning with the hunger strikes. Sinn Fein remains, of course, a minority of a minority, but the seats it has recently won in local government position it to push issues that force the SDLP to choose between two bad options, either to back Sinn Fein proposals (and thus implicitly acknowledge republican leadership) or to side with unionists against its 'own kind.' Either way, the SDLP loses and the Provisionals gain. The Provisionals have, of course, been in a strong position before only to squander it. The question now is whether, having escaped their usual pitfalls, they have materially improved their prospects of victory or merely set about discovering new ones.

The immediate danger to the more political Provisionals may issue from the IRA itself. While the new leadership apparently sets the political and military agenda, its emphases on living conditions and participation in local government councils are inconsistent with some of the most hallowed republican icons. Already it is being accused of diverting attention from the national question and sanctioning partitionist institutions, which were, it may be recalled, the same accusations levelled against the Official IRA when traditionalists split to form the Provisionals. To refute the objections of traditionalists, the new leadership must broaden its political base, challenge the SDLP for pre-eminence among Catholics, and destroy Britain's hope of an internal solution without, however, becoming captive to their increasing popularity. The balance is extremely delicate. For if the Provisionals pursue 'armed struggle' against the wishes of prospective supporters, they undermine their new political strategies (and thus themselves); but if they sacrificed armed to political struggle, they vindicate the criticisms of the traditionalists and risk the fate of the Officials.

The new leadership faces potential challenges from those younger as well as older than itself. Here again the experience of the Officials may be instructive; when the Officials renounced violence in the mid-1970s, they suffered a second split, with much of the younger membership seeking action through the Irish Republican Socialist Party. Certainly the Provisionals would never even hint that they might renounce 'armed struggle,' but in de-emphasizing it in favor of political methods, they have frustrated some 'volunteers' who desire more 'action' than is politic. In this context it is worth noting two possibilities; first, a higher proportion of Provisional violence is now staged in the rural and more conservative border areas, where republicans are more inclined to see partition as the sole issue and traditional armed struggle as the only solution. This suggests the possibility that the Provisional leadership, which is drawn primarily from Belfast and Derry, may not have established itself as securely in rural as urban areas. Secondly, British intelligence reportedly saw the bombing of the Conservative Party convention at Brighton as an attempt by dissident Provisionals to undercut the new political direction of the leadership. Whatever the validity of this interpretation, it does point to ways that older traditionalists and younger rebels can combine to undermine the agenda of the leadership. And even if the leadership can consolidate itself, it must still juggle violent and non-violent strategies simultaneously. Thus, while the Provisionals' dual political and military strategies create opportunities, they also pose separate, and sometimes conflicting, imperatives: it is still unknown whether this will prove invigorating or debilitating.

The Provisionals may encounter problems from their constituencies as well as members, for their very ascendancy may lead Catholics to expect them to deliver some goods. But it is unclear what they can deliver, for combined British and unionist opposition is likely to limit their achievements. In the short term, this may not hurt much, since unionist denunciations confirm Sinn Fein's credentials among Catholics. In the longer run, however, unionists might turn Sinn Fein's electoral strategies against it. By devoting substantial efforts to replacing the SDLP as the predominant electoral representative of the Catholic population, the Provisionals commit themselves to achieving more than the SDLP. Yet inevitably this entangles republicans in the very difficulties that have undone nationalists: to operate as a minority in ostensibly democratic institutions is to risk futility. Certainly the danger is not as stark for the Provisionals as the SDLP, since they do have other ways of making their points, but these tend to vindicate those among their number who reject politics on principle. Thus the same forces that create constituencies for both constitutional and extra-constitutional politics also work against one organization pursuing both: the Provisionals must work in the same institutions that they denounce verbally and attack physically.

The Provisionals' greatest problem in 'going political' is not, however, the delicacy of their task but the non-negotiability of their defining commitment. For no matter how the Provisionals broaden their methods and concerns, they still demand a unified republic for the whole of Ireland. This, in turn, triggers familiar problems, since whatever their internal changes, the Provisionals not only face a hostile British–unionist alliance, but are disinclined to compromise: a republic must be sovereign; sovereignty is indivisible; and to compromise is, therefore, to lose. Thus, whether reformed or unreformed, the Provisionals oblige themselves to wage a struggle they are not likely to win soon.

V

With the Provisionals committed to continuous struggle, the unionists to domination, the Republic to dividing the indivisible, and Britain to avoiding the whole mess, the probability of a mutually acceptable resolution of Northern Ireland's conflict is low. The reasons for this have been developed already; these do not, however, make the unification of Ireland either likely or promising. Unification remains unlikely until Britain decides that the short-term costs of withdrawal are worth the long-term savings, which would presume Northern Ireland to be important enough to command the attention of a British government but unimportant enough to dispense with. And unification is unpromising unless Protestants and Catholics, and especially their warring working classes, reach some sort of *rapprochement*; otherwise the Provisionals' talk of socialism is no more than pleasing rhetoric, holding out ideals that can have no basis in reality.

Socialism represents the antithesis of Northern Ireland's colonial order; the one proclaims freedom, justice, and equality, the other reproduces oppression, injustice, and inequality. To bring socialism to Northern Ireland would, however, entail the unification of the very working classes still polarized by the vestiges of colonial privilege. For as long as the Protestant and Catholic working classes remain split in two, with differences in status and allegiance reinforcing each other, the class that is expected to serve as the agent of progressive change is unable to extricate itself from the problem. That catches leftists in a quandary, with even avowed socialist movements playing into, and strengthening, the dichotomy they mean to overturn. Thus the tragedy of Northern Ireland is more than 'gunmen' holding whole communities captive, more than violence superseding politics: the tragedy is that four centuries of colonialism have created the need, though not the conditions, for genuinely radical change. Meaningful progress is improbable without an alliance of Protestant and Catholic workers, but the most intimate interests and identities of Protestant workers obstruct one.

Radicalism, then, would have little chance of success in Northern Ireland were it not for the fact that reform has even less. But the same forces that limit the likelihood of radical change nearly extinguish that of moderate reform. Both radicals and moderates confront a social order unreceptive to change, and the latter then renounce the only means that have made inroads into the inequality at the heart of Northern Ireland. Thus moderates, by dooming themselves to futility, discredit themselves as an effective alternative to republicanism. And Britain, by protecting the forces that doom moderate reform, makes violence inevitable.

8

Afterword

'Ulster says: NO!'

Loyalist slogan

In November 1985, the British and Irish governments announced the 'Anglo-Irish Agreements.' In these Britain adopted the reasoning, but not the prescriptions, elaborated by the Forum. Deciding that it had deferred long enough to Protestant fears and hoping to protect the SDLP from the encroachments of the Provisionals, the British government accepted the claim that the Irish government could play a productive role in Northern Irish affairs. Accordingly, the Agreements affirmed British sovereignty but guaranteed to bring ministers and officials of the Republic into formal consultations on Northern Ireland's political, security, and legal affairs. Britain's hope is that this 'Conference,' by giving institutional expression to the 'nationalist identity' of northern Catholics, will strengthen the SDLP and weaken the Provisionals.

The Republic embraced the Agreements whole-heartedly, partly to salvage something from the Forum's *Report* and mostly to achieve British recognition of its role in Northern Ireland's politics. With its dreams of respectability realized, the Irish government happily repeated its vows to respect partition and threw into the bargain the promise to co-ordinate its police force with that of Northern Ireland. It then set about preparing responsible proposals that, by representing nationalist identities and traditions, would make Catholics feel more welcome in Northern Ireland. However, these endeavors are not without risk to the Republic. Participation in the official affairs of Northern Ireland not only makes the Republic an inviting target for Protestant paramilitaries, but also gives the Republic responsibility without power. The Republic believes that the Agreements are historic, which is true. It is also true that the British and Irish governments have been discussing matters of joint concern for years. Discussions might be more productive now that they are institutionalized, but they will not necessarily alter the policies that Britain ends up implementing. The hullabaloo surrounding the Agreements notwithstanding, Britain will still make decisions according to its assessment of the situation. The danger to the Republic, therefore, is that it may be blamed for policies that it cannot decide. The threat, in view of Britain's habitual ineptitude in Ireland, is not to be minimized: the Irish government could find itself defending policies which are indefensible according to its electorate.

The Republic believes that these risks are justified by its ability to temper and legitimate British rule in the eyes of northern Catholics. But as southern Catholics may be disappointed by the Republic's lack of effective powers, so might northern Catholics. When they question the efficacy of the Conference, as they inevitably will, northern Catholics must be reassured that the Republic is providing them with valuable representation. Otherwise they will dismiss the Conference as a cloak to disguise essentially unchanged policies. The problem for the Republic is that northern Catholics may have legitimate grounds for their doubts, for the Conference may intimate more than it can deliver. The claim made by the advocates of the Conference is that the Irish government can now offer Britain advice – but it could always do that. The only real difference is that the advice is now presented in the 'Conference.' The risk, therefore, is that the Conference may be repeating one of Britain's classic mistakes. It may not produce enough substantive changes to impress Catholics, but it certainly implies enough to mobilize Protestants. Thus Britain is again threatening Protestants where they feel most vulnerable, but Catholic support is not necessarily consolidated.

The Conference faces two opponents, the Provisionals and the unionists. So far the Provisionals are playing their cards close to their vest, contesting elections while continuing violence, and obviously hoping to implicate the southern government in untenable British policies, thus discrediting it among Catholics north and south of the border. In this strategy the Provisionals are likely to be helped considerably by their unspoken alliance with outraged unionists, who have denounced the Conference as a sop to terrorists and a step toward a united Ireland. The Republic, unionists point out, was included in both the Conference and the negotiations leading up to the Agreements, but unionists were excluded. The Agreements do offer a carrot, however. If unionists agree to share power with the SDLP, the

Conference would be dismantled and power vested in a devolved government. Thus unionists are trapped between the two unsatisfactory options of the Conference and power-sharing, but are given an incentive to opt for the latter. If unionists reject power-sharing, the Conference will continue without their presence, but if they accept power-sharing, unionists would include themselves and exclude the Republic.

The initial reaction of Protestants has been predictable. Their entire delegation to Westminster resigned in protest against the Conference, then stood for re-election on an anti-Conference platform, with all but one being returned to parliament. So far Britain is ignoring the united opposition of Protestants, letting them deny themselves the voice that Catholics have achieved. The problem with this strategy is that if Protestants could tolerate British policy before the Conference, they are likely to survive it after. For what has changed is not the author of decisions but the process that goes into making them. Now as before Britain will make the decisions, presumably according to its own lights. If, however, the Conference results in significantly different policies, Britain would further mobilize Protestants, which would, on the one hand, encourage Britain to compensate by assuaging Protestant fears and, on the other, motivate loyalist paramilitaries to take direct action against Catholics. Either development would draw the Provisionals back into the picture. Thus the Conference, though meant to weaken the Provisionals and the unionists, may unite them against the center.

The Conference, then, means different things to different audiences. To Britain, it is a way of building the SDLP by involving the Republic in consultations, without compromising its sovereignty over Northern Ireland. Britain can pick and choose among Irish suggestions, secure in the knowledge that the current Irish government is completely committed to the Conference. To the Republic, the Conference promises the official status that it has long craved, though perhaps at the cost of defending British policies publicly that it bemoans privately. To the SDLP, the Conference reverses many of its losses to the Provisionals, as was indicated by its gains in the elections called after the unionists resigned from parliament. But the SDLP still does not control its own fate; it depends on the Republic to convince Britain to act on its behalf. And, like the Republic, the SDLP is vulnerable to the possibility that Britain, now that it has implicated nationalists in its decisions, will continue the same policies as before. These dangers, however, are in the future; for now Britain, the Republic, and the

SDLP have taken the political offensive in Northern Ireland for the first time since the hunger strike: they must use it to their advantage.

This will not be easy. Having joined forces, the three must now overcome the 77 percent of the electorate which voted against the Agreements and *do* something: it is well and good to talk, but they must also act. In acting they are likely to discover that they are trying to accommodate contradictory interests, seeking both to combine British sovereignty with Irish participation and to promote Catholic interests without damaging those of Protestants. The Conference must, if it is to make good on its commitment to represent nationalist traditions, provide tangible benefits to ordinary Catholics. But previous moves in this direction have antagonized unionists. Thus the Conference depends on a delicate blend of illusion and reality: Britain must convince the Republic that its advice counts, Protestants that their essential interests are secure, and Catholics that genuine changes are contemplated – and all this while refusing to derogate its sovereignty. This shell game of confusing appearance and reality may succeed, but it is more likely that Britain will frighten one side without mollifying the other. Northern Ireland's scars, it should be clear by now, are too deep to be covered by cosmetics.

Notes

1 The Luck of the Irish

1. The New Ireland Forum, *The Cost of Violence arising from Northern Ireland since 1969*, Dublin, The Stationery Office, 1984, pp. 3–4.
2. Samuel Huntington is a good representative of this view. In *Political Order in Changing Societies*, Huntington argues against the thesis that backwardness generates instability, contending rather that it 'is not the absence of modernity, but the efforts to achieve it which produce political disorder.' (p. 41) He accepts, however, that modernization, once achieved, does bring stability; 'modernity means stability.' (p. 43) While this may very well be true as a general principle, Northern Ireland would seem to present a stark counter-case. Not only is Northern Ireland a highly industrialized, albeit depressed, society governed by parliamentary democracy, but Northern Ireland also ranks very high on the kinds of socio-economic indices of modernity that Huntington endorses, such as literacy. Northern Ireland is, in Huntington's terms, modern, not modernizing; if 'modernity' does indeed 'breed stability' (p. 41), one would reasonably expect Northern Ireland to display slightly more. Samuel P. Huntington, *Political Order in Changing Societies*, New Haven, Yale University Press, 1968.
3. A note on terminology. There is no completely neutral way to refer to the six counties of Northern Ireland. Protestants like to refer to them as 'Ulster.' Catholics, on the other hand, object that 'Ulster' really consists of nine, not six, counties. They tend to refer to them as the 'six counties' or the 'north,' terms that Protestants dislike because they imply some connection with the 26 counties to the south. The least objectionable term is probably the area's official name: Northern Ireland. 'Northern Ireland' will generally be used henceforth, although 'Ulster' will sometimes be used to refer to the geographical as opposed to political entity.
4. This point was demonstrated by the Protestant general strike of 1974 that overturned a coalition government of Protestant and Catholic political parties. For a description of the strike, see Robert Fisk, *Point of No Return*, London, André Deutsch, 1975.

5. It is for this reason that the Northern Irish are so unconcerned with the religion of foreigners. In a year I was asked my religion only twice.

6. Catholics generally deny that they mean to exclude Protestants from the Irish nation, but as Conor Cruise O'Brien points out, 'By "the Irish race" is meant, as far as Ireland is concerned: Primarily, people of native Irish stock, descended from Gaelic speakers, professing the Catholic religion, and holding some form of the general political opinions held by most people of this origin and religion; secondarily, people of settler stock in Ireland, and Protestant religion: to the extent that these cast in their lot with the people of the first category, culturally or politically, or preferably both.' Conor Cruise O'Brien, *States of Ireland*, New York, Vintage Press, p. 51. This book was also published by Hutchinson in London.

7. It is worth noting that Irish Protestants come in various denominations. About half are Presbyterian, 40 percent are Anglican (or Church of Ireland, as they are called in Ireland), and the remaining 10 percent are mostly Methodist (Denis P. Barrit and Charles F. Carter, *The Northern Ireland Problem*, London, Oxford University Press, 1972, p. 19). Thus 'Protestantism' is a composite of various religions, several of which have serious theological differences.

8. Richard Rose, *Governing Without Consensus*, Boston, Beacon Press, 1971, p. 477.

9. Ibid., p. 274.

10. Ibid., pp. 256 and 264. Rose does find, however, that there is a stronger correlation between religious fervor and political involvement for Protestants than for Catholics.

11. Ibid., p. 208. A similar point is made by David Miller, *The Queen's Rebels: Ulster Loyalism in Historical Perspective*, Dublin, Gill and MacMillan, 1978, p. 5.

12. Rose, *Governing Without Consensus*, p. 274.

13. O'Brien, *States of Ireland*, p.12.

14. Ibid., p. 38

15. Ibid., p. 35

16. Ibid., p. 307.

17. They are murky for two reasons. First, the profits that Britain does remove from Northern Ireland could also be removed were Northern Ireland to unite with the Republic of Ireland. Not only does Britain now invest in the Republic, but the Common Market assures its right to invest in Ireland, united or partitioned. Secondly, the British government spends over a billion pounds a year in Northern Ireland, a considerable sum for an economy as weak as that of Britain. Put differently, 'by the 1970s the *annual* subvention to Northern Ireland easily exceeded the total amount of modern industrial capital.' See Paul Bew, Peter Gibbon, and Henry Patterson, *The State in Northern Ireland: Political Forces and Social Classes*, Manchester, Manchester University Press, 1979, p. 175.

18. Liam de Paor, *Divided Ulster*, Harmondsworth, Penguin, 1973, pp. 60–1.

19. Michael Farrell, *The Orange State*, London, Pluto Press, 1976, p. 11.
20. Socialist republicans emphasize the exceptions that prove the rule. In the 1870s there were unsuccessful efforts to ally the Protestant and Catholic peasantries. In 1932 there were several riots of the Protestant and Catholic unemployed against the lack of benefits during the depression. From these two examples socialist republicans argue that Protestant and Catholic workers are disposed to unity, not division. See, for example, Farrell, *The Orange State*, pp. 121–132.
21. de Paor, *Divided Ulster*, pp. xix–xx.
22. This point is made more generally by Edna Bonacich, 'A Theory of Ethnic Antagonism: The Split Labor Market,' *American Sociological Review*, 1972, vol. 37 (October), pp. 547–59.
23. Bew et al., *The State in Northern Ireland*, p. 144.
24. Ibid., p. 38.
25. Ibid., p. 62.
26. Ibid., p. 89.
27. Bew et al., 'Some Aspects of Nationalism and Socialism in Northern Ireland,' in Austen Morgan and Bob Purdie (eds), *Ireland: Divided Nation, Divided Class*, London, Ink Links, 1980, pp. 154–5.
28. Martin Kilson, 'British Colonialism and Transformation of Traditional Elites: Case of Sierra Leone,' from Wilfred Cartey and Martin Kilson (eds), *The Africa Reader*, New York, Vintage Press, 1970, pp. 115–22.
29. Martin Kilson, 'Modes of Adaptation,' in ibid., p. 74.
30. Elizabeth Colson, 'African Society at the Time of the Scramble,' in L. H. Gann and Peter Duignan, *Colonialism in Africa 1870–1960*, volume I, Cambridge, Cambridge University Press, 1981, p. 53.
31. Robert Delavignette, 'Colonial Government through Direct Rule: The French Model,' Cartey and Kilson (eds), *The Africa Reader*, p. 78.
32. Quoted by John E. Flint, 'Nigeria: The Colonial Experience,' Gann and Duignan, *Colonialism in Africa*, p. 246.
33. J. F. A. Ajayi, 'Colonialism: An Episode,' ibid., p. 505.
34. Flint, 'Nigeria', p. 228.
35. Albert Memmi, *The Colonizer and the Colonized*, Boston, Beacon Press, 1960, p. xii.
36. H. H. Gerth and C. Wright Mills, *From Max Weber*, New York, Oxford University Press, 1970, p. 296.
37. Ibid.
38. Ibid.
39. Richard Lowenthal, 'Government in the Developing Countries: Its Functions and Its Form,' in Henry W. Ehrmann (ed.), *Democracy in a Changing Society*, New York, Praeger, 1964, p. 187.
40. Rose, *Governing Without Consensus*, p. 93.
41. As cited in ibid., p. 92.
42. Rosemary Harris, *Prejudice and Tolerance in Ulster*, Manchester, Manchester University Press, 1972, pp. ix–x.

43. Ibid., p. 222.

44. Ibid., pp. x–xi.

45. Ibid., p. 143. I remember meeting in Belfast a man who had married a woman from the other side. They were living apart during their vacation from the Middle East, where they were working, and while in Belfast he was evidently seeking out foreign company to avoid trouble. I have rarely met anyone as frightened of discovery.

46. Denis P. Barrit and Charles F. Carter, *The Northern Ireland Problem*, London, Oxford University Press, 1972, p. 53. There is now what is euphemistically called a 'peace line' dividing the Protestant and Catholic areas of west Belfast. While it may not have quite accomplished that purpose, it does discourage residents of one community from entering the other. Not that such discouragement is really necessary – the threat of assassination does the trick quite nicely.

47. Ibid., p. 56.

48. Ibid., p. 54.

49. Harris, *Prejudice and Tolerance*, p. 140. 'I was perfectly clear that . . . individuals felt that they ought to support shopkeepers of their own side rather than the other.'

50. Rose, *Governing Without Consensus*, pp. 280–1.

51. Edmund A. Aunger, 'Religion and Occupational Class in Northern Ireland,' *Economic and Social Review*, vol. 7, No. 1, October 1975, p. 4. It is unclear exactly what the impact of the past decade of economic decline has been on class stratification, but it can safely be said that unemployment has risen markedly for both Protestants and Catholics.

52. Discrimination in Northern Ireland was admitted in a series of official reports shortly after the violence erupted in 1969, most notably *Disturbances in Northern Ireland: Report of the Commission appointed by the Governor of Northern Ireland* (Cameron Report), Belfast, HMSO, September 1969, Cmd. 532.

53. Protestants demonstrated their loyalty most impressively in the First World War. The UVF joined the British army and made an attack on German lines in the Battle of the Somme. The attack was predicated on protection on both flanks, but the British units retreated; outflanked, the UVF pushed into German lines anyway and were slaughtered; 5,500 died in a day and a half. See Stewart, *The Ulster Crisis*, pp. 237–45.

54. The two most conspicuous examples are the 'Ulster rebellion' of 1912–14 and the general strike of 1974. Both are discussed in chapter 6.

55. Only one bill introduced by a Catholic was ever enacted into law by Stormont. The bill protected wild birds.

56. As, for example, in the Easter rebellion of 1916 and the recent hunger strikes, which are discussed in chapter 5.

57. Prime Minister O'Neill made a similar point in his resignation speech. He claimed that if Protestants treated Catholics like Protestants, the Catholics would behave accordingly. What O'Neill did not realize was,

first, that this was precisely the loyalist criticism of him and, secondly, that Catholics were insulted by the suggestion that they ought to behave like 'Protestants.' 'It is,' complained O'Neill 'frightfully hard to explain to Protestants that if you give Roman Catholics a good job and a good house they will live like Protestants, because they will see neighbours with cars and television sets. They will refuse to have eighteen children, but if a Roman Catholic is jobless and lives in the most ghastly hovel, he will rear eighteen children on National Assistance. ... If you treat Roman Catholics with due consideration and kindness, they will live like Protestants, in spite of the authoritative nature of their Church.' As quoted in Farrell, *The Orange State*, p. 256.

58. In this sense the Protestant working class occupies a position comparable with that of the Afrikaner working class in South Africa and the Sephardic Jews in Israel. In all three cases, the working classes are more hostile to the dilution of colonial privileges than are elites. The point is picked up in chapter 6.

2 The White Man's Burden

1. W. E. H. Lecky, (ed. L. P. Curtis), *A History of Ireland in the Eighteenth Century*, Chicago, University of Chicago Press, 1972, p. 4.
2. J. C. Beckett, *The Anglo-Irish Tradition*, London, Faber and Faber, 1976, p. 23.
3. These policies are discussed by Ian Lustick, 'State–Building Failure in British Ireland and French Algeria,' 1985, Institute of International Studies, University of California, Berkeley, p. 18. Lustick draws skillfully and extensively from Sir John Davies, *Discovery of the True Causes of Why Ireland was Never Entirely Subdued* in Alexander Gross (ed.), *Works of Sir John Davies*, Lancashire, 1876. Davies writes, for example, that the Normans or Old English 'did feare, that if the Irish were receiued into the King's for protection, and made Liege-men and Free-subiectes, the state of England woulde establish them in the possessions by Graunts from the Crowne; reduce their Countries into Counties, ennoble some of them; and enfranchise all, and make them amesueable to the Lawe, which woulde haue abridged and cut off a great part of that greatnesse which they had promised vnto themselues; they perswaded the King of England, that it was vnfit to Communicate the Lawes of England vnto them; that it was the best pollicie to holde them as Aliens and Enemies. . . .' As cited by Lustick on p. 18.
4. Nicholas P. Canny, *The Elizabethan Conquest: A Pattern Established, 1565–76*, New York, Barnes and Noble, 1976, pp. 1–28. It is also published by Redwood Burn, Ltd, Trowbridge, Wiltshire.
5. The point was made in 1560 by the earl of Sussex, then the lord-lieutenant of Ireland: 'I am forced by duty to give advice . . . not so much for the care I have of Ireland, which I have often wished to be sunk in the sea, as for

that if the French should set foot therein, they should not have such an entry into Scotland as her majesty could not resist, but also by the commodity of the havens here and Calais now in their possession, they should take utterly from England all kind of peaceable traffic by sea, whereby would ensue such a ruin to England, as I am feared to think on.' As cited by Canny, *The Elizabethan Conquest*, p. 30.

6. Ibid., pp. 66–92.
7. The quote is from Mountjoy and is cited by David Beers Quinn, *The Elizabethans and the Irish*, Ithaca, New York, Cornell University Press, 1966, p. 139.
8. Lecky, *History of Ireland*, p. 7. See also pp. 5–13. On p. 6 Lecky describes the war as 'literally a war of extermination. The slaughter of Irishmen was looked upon as literally the slaughter of wild beasts. Not only the men, but even the women and children who fell into the hands of the English, were deliberately and systematically butchered. Bands of soldiers traversed great tracts of country, slaying every living thing they met. The sword was not found sufficiently expeditious, but another method proved much more efficacious. Year after year, over a great part of Ireland, all means of human subsistence were destroyed, no quarter was given to prisoners who surrendered, and the whole population was skilfully and steadily starved to death. The pictures of the condition of Ireland at this time are as terrible as anything in human history. Thus Spenser, describing what he had seen in Munster, tells how, "out of every corner of the woods and glens, they came creeping forth upon their hands for their legs could not bear them. They looked like anatomies of death; they spoke like ghosts crying out of their graves; they did eat the dead carrion, happy when they could find them; yea, and one another soon after, inasmuch as the very carcasses they spared not to scrape out of their graves."
9. The point was made by Mountjoy: 'Because the Irish and English–Irish [that is, Normans] were obstinate in Popish superstition, great care was thought fit to be taken that these new colonies should consist of such men as were most unlike to fall to the barbarous customs of the irish, or the Popish superstition of Irish and English–Irish, so as no less cautions were to be observed for uniting them and keeping them from mixing with other than if these new colonies were to be led to inhabit among the barbarous Indians.' Cited by de Paor, *Divided Ulster*, p. 6.
10. Lustick, 'State Building,' pp. 21–6.
11. Lecky, *History of Ireland*, p. 31.
12. Lustick, 'State Building,' p. 29.
13. Lord Macaulay (ed. Hugh-Trevor Roper), *The History of England*, Harmondsworth, Penguin, 1968, pp. 243–8.
14. Lecky, *History of Ireland*, p. 46.
15. It is worth noting here that the Pope backed William of Orange in Ireland.

16. Lecky, *History of Ireland*, p. 47.
17. Ibid., p. 42. The parallels between the Penal Laws and apartheid are telling. Both were imposed by settler minorities to secure an otherwise insecure hegemony; both extended beyond political to include social, cultural, and economic oppression; and both were designed to prevent the possibility of challenge to the dominant settler minority.
18. Beckett, *The Making of Modern Ireland*, p. 156; L. M. Cullen, *An Economic History of Ireland since 1660*, New York, Harper and Row, 1972, pp. 26–49. For the Protestant response see Johnathan Swift's *Drapier's Letters*, in, for example, *The Portable Swift* (ed. Carl Van Duren), New York, Viking Press, 1973.
19. Beckett, *The Making of Modern Ireland*, p. 171.
20. As David Miller points out, 'the Protestant tenantry were accustomed to being arrayed in arms under their landlords' leadership to maintain order whenever the French/Spanish/Catholic/Jacobite threat with the pre-sumed native threat accompanying it, reared its ugly head.' David W. Miller, *The Queen's Rebels: Ulster Loyalism in Historical Perspective*, Dublin, Gill and Macmillan, 1978, p. 25.
21. Beckett, *The Making of Modern Ireland*, p. 214.
22. Miller, *The Queen's Rebels*, p. 50.
23. Beckett, *The Making of Modern Ireland*, p. 179.
24. This point derives from the argument made by Eric R. Wolf, *Peasant Wars of the Twentieth Century*, Harper and Row, New York, 1973, pp. 276 and 302. Wolf does not consider the case of Ireland, but it would seem to fit with his argument. Peter Gibbon makes a different point, arguing that small-scale Protestant farmers were inclined to radicalism, but counter-posed to them was a class of journeymen cottiers. (p. 27) The journeymen, according to Gibbon, made a bargain with their former landlords. 'In compensation for his proletarianization the weaver could become once more a 'citizen,' that is, partake in the rights and obligations of the honest settler of the plantation. The chief of the rights involved in this bargain . . . was the confirmation and maintenance of the differential status of Catholic and Protestants tenants. With the displacement of Protestant weavers to the bottom of society, this took on a special significance.' (p. 33) Gibbon is unknowingly describing the imperative of Protestant settlers to contrast their privileges to the deprivations of Catholics. It is ironic that Gibbon makes this point about 'differential statuses' several times, for he continually denounces those who talk of 'timeless contradictions between colons and natives.' (p. 22) Thus on the one hand, Gibbon describes Protestants acting according to colonial imperatives, while on the other he disassociates this from colonialism and attributes it to a 'definite set of social conditions.' (p. 22) Gibbon's confusion stems from his assumption that the two are opposite, that an explanation must focus on colonialism or specific conditions. But the two are not opposites; specific conditions develop in the context of –and are

based on – the enduring contradiction of Protestants to Catholics. Peter Gibbon, *The Origins of Ulster Unionism*, Manchester, Manchester University Press, 1975.

25. Beckett, *The Making of Modern Ireland*, p. 253.
26. Hereward Senior, 'The Early Orange Order: 1795–1870,' in T. Desmond Williams (ed.), *Secret Societies in Ireland*, Dublin, Gill and Macmillan, 1973, pp. 36–45.
27. Robert Kee, *The Green Flag*, New York, Delacorte Press, 1972, pp. 97–107. Also published in London by Weidenfeld and Nicolson.
28. Ibid., pp. 108–21.
29. Beckett, *The Making of Modern Ireland*, p. 263.
30. Ibid., p. 278.
31. Ibid., p. 286.
32. In the words of a late eighteenth-century Protestant spokesman: 'The connection between England and Ireland rests absolutely on Protestant ascendancy. Abolish distinctions, and you create a Catholic superiority . . . It may be sayd, What is it to England whether Protestants or Catholics have the pre-eminence in Ireland? It is of as much consequence as the connection between the two countries, for on that it depends. While you maintain the Protestant ascendancy the ruling powers in Ireland look to England as the foundation of their authority. A Catholic Government could maintain itself without the aid of England, and must inevitably . . . be followed by a separation of the countries.' Quoted by Patrick O'Farrell, *Ireland's English Question: Anglo-Irish Relations, 1534–1970*, New York, Schocken, 1972, p. 130.
33. Beckett, *The Making of Modern Ireland*, p. 287. See also Beckett's *The Anglo-Irish Tradition*, pp. 87–8.
34. Samuel Clark, *Social Origins of the Irish Land War*, Princeton, Princeton University Press, 1979, pp. 82–90.
35. One Protestant critic of Emancipation insisted that if Catholics 'had all been Protestants for fifty generations back, I would not consent to the overwhelming of the Constitution by such a torrent . . . a copious adulteration of rabble. . . . I do not now desire you to consider them as differing from you in religion, but merely their poverty, their numbers, their ignorance, their barbarous ignorance, many of them not being able even to speak our language, and then think whether giving them the franchise will not be a most pernicious vitiation of the Constitution.' As cited in O'Farrell, *Ireland's English Question*, p. 64.
36. 'A tenant having incorporated his capital, in one form or another, in the land, and having thus effected an improvement of the soil, either directly by irrigation, drainage, manure, or indirectly by construction of buildings for agricultural purposes, in steps the landlord with a demand for increased rent. If the tenant concede, he has to pay the interest for his own money to the landlord. If he resist, he will be very unceremoniously ejected, and supplanted by a new tenant, the latter being enabled to pay a

higher rent by the very expenses incurred by his predecessors, until he also, in his turn has become an improver of the land, and is replaced in the same way, or put on worse terms. In this easy way a class of absentee landlords has been enabled to pocket, not merely the labour, but also the capital, of whole generations, each generation of Irish peasants sinking a grade lower in the social scale, exactly in proportion to the exertions and sacrifices made for the raising of their condition and that of their families. If the tenant was industrious and enterprising, he became taxed in consequence of his very industry and enterprise. If, on the contrary, he grew inert and negligent, he was reproached with the "aboriginal faults of the Celtic race." ' Karl Marx, 'The Indian Question – Irish Tenant Right,' from *Ireland and the Irish Question, A Collection of Writings by Karl Marx and Frederick Engels* (ed. R. Dixon), New York, International Publishers, 1972, pp. 59–60.

37. The Irish land system was 'so complex that it was not unknown for two people to be both landlord and tenant to one another.' Clark, *Social Origins of the Irish Land War*, p. 36. Clark is certainly the best source on the Irish land system and agrarian agitation, but as he focuses on the west of Ireland, much of his argument is inapplicable to Ulster.

38. O'Farrell, *Ireland's English Question*, p. 107. Perhaps the government was heeding the advice of Thomas Carlyle: 'Ireland is like a half-starved rat, that crosses the path of an elephant. What must the elephant do? Squelch it – by heavens – squelch it.' Quoted by O'Farrell, p. 112.

39. F. S. L. Lyons, *Ireland Since the Famine*, Glasgow, Fontana, 1976, pp. 41–6.

40. Clark, *Social Origins of the Irish Land War*, passim, especially p. 291.

41. Ibid., p. 3.

42. As quoted by Conor Cruise O'Brien, *Parnell and His Party*, London, Oxford University Press, 1957, p. 69.

43. Ibid., p. 231.

44. Kee, *The Green Flag*, p. 386.

45. For an analysis of the composition of the leadership of the home rule party, see O'Brien, *Parnell and His Party*, pp. 129–33, and the tables on p. 152.

46. For the development of Ulster's economy, see the collection of essays edited by J. C. Beckett and R. E. Glasscock, *Belfast: Origin and Growth of an Industrial City*, London, BBC Publications, 1967.

47. As the Earl of Westmoreland, a British administrator in Ireland, had written somewhat earlier, 'The fears and jealousies that universally affect the Protestant mind are not confined to Parliament, but affect almost every individual and every public body. The steadiest friends of British government apprehend that indulgence will give the Catholics strength to press for admission to the State. In this they see the ruin of political power to Protestants, and . . . a total change of the property of the country. The final consequence will be a confederacy of the Protestants, with very few exceptions, to resist every concession. They will resolve to support their

own situation by their own power. You will lose for the Catholics the very
indulgence which you desire to procure.' As quoted by Patrick O'Farrell,
Ireland's English Question, p. 129.

48. A. T. Q. Stewart, *The Ulster Crisis*, London, Faber and Faber, 1967, as
cited on p. 22.

49. Kee, *The Green Flag*, as cited on p. 469. It is worth remembering that
Ulster's delegation to Westminster actually supported home rule by a 17
to 16 majority.

50. Aiken McClelland, 'The Later Orange Order in Ireland,' in Desmond
Williams (ed.), *Secret Societies in Ireland*, Dublin, Gill and Macmillan, 1973,
pp. 126–37.

51. It is worth noting that the mutiny caused remarkably little disturbance
among British leaders. Indeed Winston Churchill was the only leader of
real stature who seemed to have been truly bothered by the rebellion. The
leader of the rebellion even ended up as chief of the British general staff
during the First World War.

52. This syndrome is discussed in chapter 5.

53. The Black and Tans were mostly former British soldiers who had not
reintegrated into British society after the First World War; some were
recruited into the army from British prisons. They arrived in Ireland in
1919 and soon distinguished themselves with their indiscipline.

54. For a good account of the atmosphere among the participants in the civil
war, see Frank O'Connor, 'After Aughrim's Great Disaster' in *An Only
Child*, London, Pan Press, 1970, pp. 145–219. For another literary and
more political expression of the conflict, see Sean O'Casey's 'Shadow of a
Gunman' and 'Juno and the Paycock' in *Three Plays*, London, Macmillan,
1972.

3 The Gerrymandered State

1. Eamonn McCann, *War and an Irish Town*, Harmondsworth, Penguin,
1974, pp. 18–9. This discussion is not included in the Pluto Press edition
of the book.

2. Peter Gibbon, *The Origins of Ulster Unionism*, Manchester, Manchester
University Press, 1975, p. 20.

3. Ibid., p. 20.

4. Bew et al., *The State in Northern Ireland*, pp. 46–50.

5. Farrell, *The Orange State*, pp. 104–5.

6. Ibid., p. 16.

7. For example, James Craig, then a minister in the British government and
a year later the first premier of Northern Ireland, addressed the shipyard
workers after the expulsions. Asked whether he approved of the recent
expulsions Craig responded, 'Yes.' The response, while presumably
embarrassing to the government, met with no rebuke: it expressed British
as well as Unionist policy. Ibid., p. 34.

8. Ibid., p. 27.
9. Ibid., p. 30.
10. The Specials were divided into three branches (A, B, and C), with recruitment based on the UVF. All branches were entirely Protestant, highly undisciplined, and detested by the Catholic community. Some, including the British commander-in-chief for Ireland, thought them so undisciplined as to be counter-productive. Their excesses, however, proved most useful in intimidating the Catholic population, though at the expense of confirming Catholic antagonism to the new state that was to be represented by the Specials. Ibid., pp. 95–7.
11. Ibid., p. 58.
12. Ibid., p. 62.
13. R. H. S. Crossman, *The Diaries of a Cabinet Minister, Volume III, 1968–70*, London, 1977, p. 187, as cited in Patrick Buckland, *A History of Northern Ireland*, Dublin, Gill and Macmillan, 1981, p. 187. While Crossman's point refers to the late 1960s, it is more broadly true of the whole period from 1921–69.
14. Bew et al., *The State in Northern Ireland*, p. 51.
15. Ibid., p. 53.
16. Ibid., p. 57.
17. Ibid., p. 62.
18. Ibid., p. 76.
19. This is drawn from Appendix A, John F. Harbinson, *The Ulster Unionist Party 1882–1973*, Belfast, Blackstaff Press, 1974, pp. 178–80.
20. de Paor, *Divided Ulster*, p. 105.
21. Ibid., p. 106.
22. Farrell, *The Orange State*, p. 256.
23. Patrick Buckland, *Ulster Unionism and the Origins of Northern Ireland 1882–1922*, Dublin, Gill and Macmillan, 1973, p. 124.
24. de Paor, *Divided Ulster*, p. 105.
25. Buckland, *Ulster Unionism*, p. 142.
26. Harbinson, *The Ulster Unionist Party*, p. 76.
27. Sunday Times Insight Team, *Ulster*, Harmondsworth, Penguin, 1972, p. 115.
28. Harbinson, *The Ulster Unionist Party*, p. 93.
29. Ibid., p. 79.
30. Belinda Probert, *Beyond Orange and Green, The Political Economy of the Northern Ireland Crisis*, Dublin, The Academy Press, 1978, p. 63.
31. Ibid., pp. 8 and 16. For a discussion of the history of the Orange Order, see Paul Bew et al., *The State in Northern Ireland*, pp. 9 and 46. Rosemary Harris also discusses the role of the Orange Order in integrating Protestants.
32. Buckland, *Ulster Unionism*, p. 23.
33. Harbinson, *The Ulster Unionist Party*, p. 52.
34. Ibid., pp. 111 and 38.

35. As J. L. McCracken put it, 'there is no floating vote on the constitutional issue.' As cited by Richard Rose, *Northern Ireland: A Time of Choice*, London, Macmillan Press, 1976, p. 71.

36. Farrell, *The Orange State*, p. 184.

37. Ibid., p. 145.

38. The Stormont government paid the bulk, though never more than 80 percent, of the construction costs of Catholic schools. This had, from the point of view of the Unionist Party, the felicitous effect of keeping Catholic school children separate from Protestant children.

39. Buckland, *A History of Northern Ireland*, p. 66.

40. McCann, *War and an Irish Town*, p. 12–13.

41. The shipbuilding, repairing, and marine engineering industries, for example, lost 40 percent of the jobs from 1960–4. Buckland, *A History of Northern Ireland*.

42. For elaboration of this argument, see McCann, *War and an Irish Town*, Penguin edition, pp. 207–17; Farrell, *The Orange State*, pp. 227–38; and Anders Boserup, 'Who is the Principal Enemy?' London, 1972, pp. 12–21. For a different view, see Paul Bew et al., *The State in Northern Ireland*, pp. 129–61.

43. This argument is best made by Eric Hobsbawm, *Industry and Empire*, Harmondsworth, Penguin, 1975, passim.

44. This argument is put in Keynesian terms by Michael Stewart, *Politics and Economic Policy in the United Kingdom since 1964*, Oxford, Pergamon, 1978, passim.

45. John Sayers, 'The Political Parties and the Social Background,' and K. S. Isles and N. Cuthbert, 'Economic Policy,' from Thomas Wilson (ed.), *Ulster under Home Rule*, London, Oxford University Press, 1955, pp. 67–8 and 151. For a good discussion of Northern Ireland's economic problems during this period, see Probert, *Beyond Orange and Green*, pp. 65–78.

46. Probert, *Beyond Orange and Green*, p. 68.

47. Ibid., pp. 67–8.

48. Terence O'Neill, *The Autobiography of Terence O'Neill*, London, Hart-Davis, 1972, p. 42.

49. Farrell, *The Orange State*, p. 225.

50. F. H. Newark, 'The Law and the Constitution,' in Wilson (ed.), *Ulster under Home Rule*, p. 37.

51. O'Neill, *Autobiography*, p. 40.

52. Brian Faulkner (ed. John Houston), *Memoirs of a Statesman*, London, Weidenfeld and Nicolson, 1978, p. 28.

53. Probert, *Beyond Orange and Green*, p. 52.

54. To this end the government proposed to combine two industrial towns outside Belfast, Lurgan and Portadown, into a single industrial center named Craigavon, after James Craig. Both towns, incidentally, are heavily Protestant.

55. O'Neill, *Autobiography*, p. 109.

56. Terence O'Neill, *Ulster at the Crossroads*, London, Faber and Faber, 1969, pp. 58 and 116.

4 The Troubles

1. O'Brien, *States of Ireland*, p. 161; Sunday Times Insight Team, *Ulster*, p. 49; *Disturbances in Northern Ireland, Report of the Commission appointed by the Governor of Northern Ireland* (Cameron Report), paragraphs 185–93; de Paor, *Divided Ulster*, p. 171; and Max Hastings, *Barricades in Belfast: The Fight for Civil Rights in Northern Ireland*, New York, Tapling Press, 1970, pp. 132–50.
2. For descriptions of the civil rights movement, see de Paor, *Divided Ulster*, pp. 151–90; Cameron Report, passim; Sunday Times Insight Team, *Ulster*, pp. 40–79; O'Brien, *States of Ireland*, pp. 152–86; Farrell, *The Orange State*, pp. 245–89; Hastings, *Barricades in Belfast*, pp. 41–94; and McCann, *War and an Irish Town*, pp. 27–56.
3. Cameron Report, paragraph 189.
4. McCann, *War and an Irish Town*, pp. 35–45.
5. Farrell, *The Orange State*, p. 248.
6. O'Neill, *Ulster at the Crossroads*, p. 69.
7. Hastings, *Barricades in Belfast*, pp. 95–102, and McCann, *War and an Irish Town*, pp. 55–7.
8. As McCann, *War and an Irish Town*, p. 24, writes, 'There was one sense in which the civil rights movement was "anti-Protestant." The movement was demanding an end to discrimination . . . In a situation in which Protestant workers had more than their fair share of jobs, houses and voting power the demand for an end to discrimination was a demand that Catholics should get more jobs, housing and voting power than they had at present – *and Protestants less.* This simple calculation seemed to occur to very few civil rights "moderates," but five minutes talk with a Paisleyite counter-demonstrator in 1968 or 1969 would have left one in no doubt that it was not missed by the Protestant working class.' This point escapes, for example, the Sunday Times Insight Team, p. 27: 'The beginning of the subsequent story of Ulster is a fatal error by the ruling Protestants. It was to mistake the Civil Rights movement of the sixties for an attack on the State of Ulster itself. Thus, by choice of the ruling elite, the energy of the reformist impulse has been made to shake the foundations of society.'
9. Bew et al., *The State in Northern Ireland*, p. 195.
10. Sunday Times Insight Team, *Ulster*, pp. 101–2.
11. *Report of the Advisory Committee on Police in Northern Ireland* (Hunt Report), Belfast, HMSO, 1969, Cmd. 535.
12. Callaghan, *A House Divided*, London, Collins, 1973, p. 15. For a discussion of British objectives during the period, see also Bew et al., *The State in Northern Ireland*, pp. 174–86.

13. Callaghan, *A House Divided*, p. 21.

14. Ibid., p. 24.

15. Ibid., p. 65.

16. McCann, *War and an Irish Town*, p. 70.

17. Callaghan, *A House Divided*, p. 54.

18. Ibid., p. 125.

19. Ibid., p. 72. Italics added. To prevent any misunderstanding, Callaghan had Protestant anxieties very much in mind while forming British policy.

20. McCann, *War and an Irish Town*, pp. 73–4.

21. Sunday Times Insight Team, *Ulster*, p. 162.

22. Ibid., pp. 208–12. As the authors point out, these riots were important for two reasons. First, the provocative Orange parades were permitted despite their obvious dangers in hope of protecting 'moderate' unionists from right-wing critics; and secondly, the Provisionals made their debut in defense of a Catholic Church that the army was too busy to protect. This symbolism, needless to say, was not lost on the Catholics.

23. Ibid., p. 220; see pp. 212–21 for the background and description of this event. It is worth noting that Tories reduced civilian control of the army, ibid., p. 232. Also see Simon Winchester, *In Holy Terror*, London, Faber and Faber, 1974, pp. 68–75.

24. Sunday Times Insight Team, *Ulster*, pp. 227–8, and McCann, *War and an Irish Town*, p. 89.

25. J. Bowyer Bell, *The Secret Army: A History of the IRA*, Cambridge, Mass., MIT Press, 1979, pp. 397–415, for a discussion of this period. This book is also published by Sphere Books, Ltd. London.

26. Ibid., p. 363.

27. The Sunday Times Insight Team, *Ulster*, p. 177.

28. McCann, *War and an Irish Town*, p. 83.

29. Winchester, *In Holy Terror*, p. 109.

30. See, for example, ibid., pp. 150–2.

31. McCann, *War and an Irish Town*, p. 79, cites one such incident: the rioters 'were the sons and daughters of the area, and however much their activities may have been regretted or condemned there could be no question of any section of the [Catholic] people backing the army *against* them. "Hooligans you can call them, Father," asserted a woman to the priest in the grounds of the Cathedral after mass one Sunday, "and hooligans some of them certainly are; but they are our hooligans!" '

32. A similar process was occurring in Protestant areas with the Protestant paramilitary organizations.

33. Britain indemnifies the destruction of property by 'terrorists.' By 1980 it had paid out £22m. It also paid out £865m in 1979 alone to subsidize Northern Ireland's economy. Paul Wilkinson (ed.), *British Perspectives on Terrorism*, London, George Allen and Unwin, 1981, pp. 4 and 6.

34. Henry Kelly, *How Stormont Fell*, Dublin, Gill and Macmillan, 1972, p. 6.

35. Faulkner had been a dominant figure in Unionist politics for the better

part of 20 years. During his career he developed a reputation for what his admirers thought shrewdness and his detractors called treachery. In his early career he depended heavily on support from the Orange Order, and made his reputation with sectarian attacks on Catholics. Within a couple of years, however, he had proved himself to be an unusually able administrator; as Minister of Commerce he received much of the credit for Northern Ireland's economic growth in the late 1950s and early 1960s. His successes encouraged his ambition to become prime minister. Thus developed a prolonged power struggle between Faulkner and O'Neill, with Faulkner ultimately using his considerable influence among the unionists against O'Neill and his policy of reform. When the reforms were inaugurated, however, Faulkner was responsible for implementing them, which he proceeded to do energetically.

36. Winchester, *In Holy Terror*, pp. 149–53.
37. Callaghan, *A House Divided*, p. 164.
38. Ibid., p. 163 in particular, and pp. 162–73 in general. Sunday Times Insight Team, *Ulster*, pp. 260–79.
39. McCann, *War and an Irish Town*, pp. 91–5.
40. Winchester, *In Holy Terror*, pp. 186–211.
41. Under direct rule, Northern Ireland was governed by a Secretary of State for Northern Ireland; the first minister was William Whitelaw.
42. A UDA statement from this period reads in part: 'We are betrayed, maligned and our families live in constant fear and misery. We are a nuisance to our so-called allies and have no friends anywhere. Once more in the history of our people we have our backs to the wall, facing extinction by one way or another. This is the moment to beware, for Ulstermen in this position fight mercilessly till they or their enemies are dead.' As cited in Martin Dillon and Denis Lehane, *Political Murder in Northern Ireland*, Harmondsworth, Penguin, 1973, p. 282.
43. Ibid., pp. 72–4 and 24–8.
44. Ibid., p. 87.
45. For the text of the 'Sunningdale Agreement,' see Richard Deutsch and Vivien Magowan, *Northern Ireland 1968–73: A Chronology of Events, Volume II*, Belfast, Blackstaff, 1974, Appendix 7, pp. 376–8.
46. It was this issue that was at stake in the 1981 hunger strikes. Britain claimed that the republican prisoners were common criminals convicted by normal judicial processes, while republicans insisted that they were political prisoners. Given that republicans were denied the right to trial by jury, one wonders about Thatcher's sense of the normal judicial processes. For a list of Northern Ireland's special judicial procedures, see Merlyn Rees, 'Terror in Ireland – and Britain's Response,' in Wilkinson (ed.), *British Perspectives on Terrorism*, p.84.
47. This was the immediate stimulus for the 'peace women' who received so much attention from the media in 1976. A car driven by two Provisionals ran into an army roadblock; the army opened fire, killing one and

wounding the other; and the car veered out of control onto the sidewalk, killing three children.

48. As quoted from Cardinal O Fiaich, the primate of Ireland, in *The Economist*, 12 December 1981, p. 14.

5   Rebellion as a Cause

1. Arend Lijphart, 'Consociational Democracy,' in Robert J. Jackson and Michael B. Stein, (eds.), *Issues in Comparative Politics*, New York, St. Martin's Press, 1971, pp. 227–8. In a subsequent book Lijphart addresses Northern Ireland directly, arguing that it 'exemplifies the least favorable balance of power situation: a dual division without equilibrium and with one segment capable of exercising hegemonic power.' *Democracy in Plural Societies: A Comparative Exploration*, New Haven, Yale University Press, 1977, p. 137.

2. It is worth emphasizing that Protestants demand the exclusion of Catholics from political power, not political institutions. Thus as long as they monopolized cabinet posts, Protestants had few complaints about Catholic membership in Stormont.

3. The reason Catholic parliamentarians found British allies is quite simple. The British regarded them in the 1860s–80s as in the 1970s as the most effective way of isolating republicans. As Patrick O'Farrell writes in *Ireland's English Question* (p. 143), Gladstone's support of disestablishment and the 1870 Land Act were attributable to republican violence in the 1860s. 'Had the English government made no response whatever, by way of reform, to the Irish violence of the 1860s, a constitutional movement to press for further reform would have been an absurdity, and the result would have been that all elements in Irish life would have been pushed, probably with some rapidity, towards a common revolutionary extremism.' The reasoning behind Britain's advocacy of power-sharing in 1976 was similar. As unreformed Stormont and direct rule had failed to establish order, Britain sought through power-sharing to strengthen Catholic parliamentarians in order to weaken Catholic republicans. The point, then, is that Catholic parliamentarians depend for a hearing on republican extra-parliamentarians; they are ignored until and unless Britain decides that they are the lesser of two evils, and this occurs only when republicans are strong enough to present themselves as a serious evil.

4. In this vein it might be remembered that Jonathan Swift, an Irish Protestant, asked in the early eighteenth century, 'Were not the people of Ireland born as free as those of England? How have they forfeited their freedom? Is not their Parliament as fair a representative of the people as that of England? . . . Am I a freeman in England, and do I become a slave in six hours by crossing the channel?' Jonathan Swift, *The Portable Swift* (ed. Carl Van Doren), New York, Viking Press, 1948, p. 29.

5. Quoted by Sean Cronin, *The Revolutionaries*, Dublin, Republican Publications, 1971, p. 10.

6. Ibid., p. 23.

7. For a description of the rebellion, see Kee, *The Green Flag*, pp. 108–21; for a more complete treatment, see Thomas Pakenham, *The Year of Liberty*, London, Panther Press, 1972; or for a wonderful novel on the subject see Thomas Flanagan, *The Year of the French*, New York, Pocket Books, 1979.

8. Sean Cronin and Richard Roche, *Freedom The Wolfe Tone Way*, Tralee, Ireland, Anvil Books, 1973, p. 73.

9. Ibid., p. 18.

10. William Butler Yeats, *The Collected Plays of W. B. Yeats* (ed. Norman Jeffares), New York, Macmillan, 1971, pp. 49–57. Copyright 1934, 1952 by Macmillan Publishing Company. Copyrights renewed 1962 by Bertha Georgia Yeats, and 1980 by Anne Yeats. A. P. Watts Ltd. and Macmillan Publishing Company have kindly extended permission to quote from Yeats.

11. Ibid., p. 56.

12. Ibid., p. 56.

13. Ibid., p. 57.

14. The influence of Yeats and other writers on republicanism is discussed at length by William Irwin Thompson, *The Imagination of an Insurrection*, New York, Harper and Row, 1972. Yeats himself, however, developed deep misgivings over his role in encouraging the insurrection.

15. It ought not to be thought that those who thwarted the plot were paragons of practicality. The plot was uncovered by Michael (The) O'Rahilly who, after revealing it to his superiors, promptly joined the rebels whose rebellion he had just doomed to failure. Thomas M. Coffey, *Agony at Easter*, Baltimore, Pelican, 1971, pp. 13–7. The background as well as the events of the insurrection is the subject of a collection of essays edited by Kevin B. Nowlan, *The Making of 1916*, Dublin, Stationary Office, 1969.

16. Padraic H. Pearse, 'Ghosts,' *Political Writings and Speeches*, Dublin, Talbot Press Ltd., 1962, p. 230.

17. Ibid., 'Oration on Robert Emmet,' p. 65.

18. Ibid., 'Oration on Wolfe Tone,' p. 58.

19. Ibid., 'Oration on Robert Emmet,' p. 66.

20. Ibid., p. 69. Robert Emmet led the remnants of the United Irishmen in a 'rebellion' in July 1803. Several dozen men assembled to seize Dublin Castle, the center of British administration in Ireland, but they dissolved on their way to their destination. Realizing that his plan had failed, Emmet fled Dublin, eventually joining his fiancée, where he was captured. At his trial, however, he delivered a stirring speech, thus guaranteeing his reputation as a republican.

21. Ibid., 'Oration on Robert Emmet,' p. 71.

22. Ibid., 'O'Donovan Rossa – Graveside Oration,' pp. 136–7.

23. Ibid., 'Psychology of a Volunteer,' pp. 104–5.

24. Ibid., 'The Coming Revolution,' p. 98, and 'From a Hermitage,' p. 185.
25. Ibid., 'Peace and the Gael,' p. 217.
26. Ibid., 'The Coming Revolution,' p. 98. The similarities of this view to that of Frantz Fanon are striking. 'At the level of individuals, violence is a cleansing force. It frees the native from his inferiority complex and from his despair and inaction; it make him fearless and restores his self-respect.' Frantz Fanon, *Wretched of the Earth*, New York, Grove Press, 1968, p. 94.
27. For a good summary of the negotiations, see George Dangerfield, *The Damnable Question: A Study in Anglo–Irish Relations*, Boston, Little, Brown and Co., 1976, pp. 305–50.
28. In the event, the British did not convene the border commission because the Northern Ireland government refused to send a delegate.
29. For a funny and insightful description of the civil war, see O'Connor, *An Only Child*, pp. 165–219.
30. Ireland revoked the bases in the 1930s and withdrew from the commonwealth in the 1940s.
31. See J. Bowyer Bell, *The Secret Army, The IRA 1916–74*, Cambridge, Mass. MIT, 1979, pp. 99–147 for a full discussion of this period.
32. For a thorough discussion of the 1956–62 campaign, see Bell, *The Secret Army*, pp. 289–336. It is worth mentioning that during these years the IRA avoided Belfast for fear of Protestant retaliation.
33. The London Sunday Times Insight Team makes the point: 'For if the IRA, instead of refusing as in the past to recognize the existence of Ulster [sic], was now encouraging people to claim their full rights as citizens of it, only one conclusion – a correct one – could be drawn: the new-look IRA was prepared *de facto* to recognize partition and the separate existence of Northern Ireland.' Sunday Times Insight Team, *Ulster*, p. 49.
34. Hence when the name IRA is used, the Provisionals are meant.
35. The Provisionals' bombs may destroy property but they are more destructive to jobs. Britain indemnifies the loss of property due to 'terrorist' violence; it does not, however, indemnify the loss of income resulting from the destruction of the employees' workplace.
36. See Sunday Times Insight Team, *Ulster*, pp. 269–70 and 273; McCann, *War and an Irish Town*, and Winchester, *In Holy Terror*, pp. 173–5.
37. Wilson's speech was made on 25 November 1971. For a Protestant reaction to the political initiative of which the speech was a part, see Brian Faulkner (ed. John Houston), *Memoir of a Statesman*, London, Weidenfeld and Nicolson, 1978, pp. 133–4 and 150–1.
38. Winchester, *In Holy Terror*, p. 228; Sean Mac Stiofain (then head of the Provisionals), *Revolutionary in Ireland*, Edinburgh, Gordon Cremonesi, 1975, p. 258. It should be noted that Catholic pressure for the truce was condoned, even orchestrated, by the most influential authority among Catholics: the Church. McCann, *War and an Irish Town*, pp. 108–9.
39. Mac Stiofain., p. 268. 'There was only one way to smash the notion that

the [republican] resistance had been reduced to weakness and to make sure that the units went into the truce with their morale high. . . . I decided to go out with a bang.'
40. The truce collapsed after a perfectly common and predictable incident. The housing authority had awarded to Catholics some houses on the edge of a Catholic housing estate in Belfast. Since the houses had previously been vacated by Protestants as a result of intimidation, Protestant paramilitary organizations opposed, and the local army commander vetoed, the move. When Catholics, with Provisional support, began to move in anyway, the army fired tear gas to disperse the crowd, leading the Provisionals to terminate the truce summarily. Winchester, *In Holy Terror*, pp. 250–1.
41. It is important to keep in mind that Catholics often supported the Provisionals more for their militant community defense than their specific ideology. But if Provisional ideology is not what wins the Provisionals popularity, it does structure Catholic outrage. Thus British repression confers on republican ideology an influence greater than it would otherwise wield. Catholics might not have agreed with Mac Stiofain that 'the sacrifices and suffering of revolutionary war can never be justified by mere reform' (p. 258), but the logic of the situation was such that Catholics sometimes supported him anyway.
42. The sense of this point was conveyed in Mary Holland, 'John Hume looks for allies,' *New Statesman*, Vol. 98, 30 November 1979, No. 2541.
43. McCann, *War and an Irish Town*, p. 119.

6 Unrequited Loyalty

1. George Dangerfield, *The Strange Death of Liberal England*, New York, Perigee, 1961, pp. 18–68.
2. Ibid., pp. 84–5. For a full treatment of the opposition of Ulster Protestants to home rule, see Stewart, *The Ulster Crisis*, passim. Also see Dangerfield, *The Damnable Question: A Study in Anglo–Irish Relations*, pp. 45–90.
3. For example, Bonar Law, then leader of the Conservative Party, announced: 'I can imagine no length of resistance to which Ulster will go which I shall not be ready to support.' As quoted by Beckett, *The Making of Modern Ireland*, p. 426.
4. The full text of the Covenant reads: 'Being convinced in our consciences that Home Rule would be disastrous to the material well-being of Ulster as well as the whole of Ireland, subversive of our civil and religious freedom, destructive of our citizenship, and perilous to the unity of the Empire, we, whose names are underwritten, men of Ulster, loyal subjects of His Gracious Majesty King George V, humbly relying on the God whom our fathers in days of stress and trial confidently trusted, do hereby pledge ourselves in solemn Covenant throughout this our time of

threatened calamity to stand by one another in defending for ourselves and our children our cherished position of equal citizenship in the United Kingdom, and in using all means which may be found necessary to defeat the present conspiracy to set up a Home Rule Parliament in Ireland. And in the event of such a Parliament being forced upon us we further solemnly and mutually pledge ourselves to refuse to recognize its authority. In sure confidence that God will defend the right we hereto subscribe our names. And further, we individually declare that we have not already signed this Covenant. God save the King.' Women signed a slightly different version. As quoted by Stewart, *The Ulster Crisis*, p. 62.

5. Beckett, *The Making of Modern Ireland*, p. 428.
6. Ibid.
7. As the Reverend Martin Smyth, current Grand Master of the Orange Order, puts it: 'while the loyalty of Orangemen to the Queen was conditional it was nonetheless wholehearted.' As cited by Miller, *The Queen's Rebels*, p. 3.
8. David Miller argues that Ulster's conditional loyalty is not as self-interested as it seems, that it is in fact based on the social contract tradition, particularly Whig and Scottish contractualism. Miller's point is that Ulster Protestants regard political obligation as essentially similar to private ethics, that 'one ought to be loyal to the king for the same reason that one should keep ordinary bargains. If the ruler defaults on his side of [However] the proper course for subjects whose king violates his bargain . . . is not to repudiate his regime, but to refuse compliance with his laws and try to coerce him into keeping . . . the bargain.' (ibid., p. 5) Loyalty, therefore, becomes a personal rather than a political relationship (p. 119), involving the integrity of a people's word, not crass considerations of power and advantage. While this argument makes considerable sense, it strips 'loyalty' of its political substance, namely, Protestant domination. In Miller's view, Protestants demand honor and integrity irrespective of the policies that are honored. It stretches credibility, however, to argue that Protestants want simply to uphold agreements quite apart from the fact that these benefit them at the expense of Catholics. It is the substance of the matter – and not, as Miller suggests, only the procedure – that counts.
9. Sunday Times Insight Team, *Ulster*, p. 103.
10. Richard Deutsch and Vivien Magowan, *Northern Ireland 1968–73: A Chronology of Events, Volume II*, Belfast, Blackstaff, 1974, p. 234A.
11. Ibid., pp. 374–5.
12. The co-operation of the Republic in combating terrorism was to take the form of trying republicans in the south for crimes they committed in the north (article 10), which had not been done previously. The Council's responsibilities concerned natural resources and the environment; agriculture, forestry, and fisheries; trade and industry; electricity generation; tourism; roads and transport; public health; and sport, culture, and the

arts (article 8). The Sunningdale Agreement is reprinted in ibid., Appendix 7, pp. 376–8.

13. The British Secretary of State for Northern Ireland, Merlyn Rees, originally urged stern measures against the strikers, but several months later admitted that 'The Protestant backlash . . . showed itself through industrial action amongst the Protestant working class and it could not have been put down by military action.' Cited by Robert Fisk, *Point of No Return*, London, André Deutsch, 1975, p. 220.

14. Ibid., pp. 47–8, 87, 91–3, and 104. As Lieutenant-General Sir Frank King, then General Officer Commanding Northern Ireland, said: 'If you get a very large section of the population which is bent on a particular course, then it is a difficult thing to stop them from taking that course . . . you can't go round shooting people because they want to do a certain thing.' At least not Protestants. As cited in ibid., p. 152.

15. Ibid., pp. 63 and 160.

16. See, for example, ibid., pp. 33–5. It should, however, be emphasized that while the leaders of the strike were often shop stewards, the strike was staunchly opposed by union leaders.

17. Ibid., p. 219.

18. Ibid., p. 215.

19. For a description of several of these challenges, see Farrell, *The Orange State*, pp. 104–7, 121–39, and 227–8.

20. George Fredrickson, *White Supremacy: A Comparative Study in American and South African History*, New York, Oxford University Press, 1981, pp. 42–3.

21. Ibid., p. 48. It should be noted that for purposes of clarity the term 'Afrikaner' is used for the people then called 'Boer.'

22. Ibid., p. 165.

23. Ibid., pp. 55, 65–8.

24. Ibid., pp. 69–70.

25. Ibid., pp. 84–5.

26. Ibid., p. 167.

27. Ibid., p. 169.

28. Ibid., p. 177.

29. Ibid., p. 180.

30. Ibid., p. 139.

31. Ibid., p. 187.

32. Ibid., p. 230.

33. Frederick A. Johnstone, *Class, Race and Gold*, London, Routledge and Kegan Paul, 1976, p. 17.

34. Ibid., p. 40.

35. Ibid., pp. 16, 23, 36, and 44. For example, black workers were subject to penal sanctions for breach of contract and the contracts forbade blacks to seek other employment for a minimum of six months.

36. Ibid., p. 25.

37. Ibid., p. 75.

38. Ibid., p. 87.
39. Ibid., p. 96.
40. Ibid., p. 109.
41. Ibid., p. 149.
42. Fredrickson, *White Supremacy*, p. 211.
43. T. Dunbar Moodie, *The Rise of Afrikanerdom*, Berkeley, University of California Press, 1975, p. 74.
44. Ibid., p. 178.
45. Brian Bunting, *The Rise of the South African Reich*, Harmondsworth, Penguin, 1964, p. 34.
46. Moodie, *The Rise of Afrikanerdom*, p. 91.
47. Fredrickson, *White Supremacy*, p. 233.
48. Ibid., p. 237.
49. Bunting, *The Rise of the South African Reich*, p. 44.
50. Heribert Adam, *Modernizing Racial Domination*, Berkeley, University of California Press, 1971, p. 170, and Heribert Adam and Hermann Giliomee, *Ethnic Power Mobilized: Can South Africa Change?*, New Haven, Yale University Press, 1979, pp. 163–76.
51. For a list of specific measures, see Bunting, *The Rise of the South African Reich*, pp. 142–59.
52. Adam, *Modernizing Racial Domination*, p. 8.
53. Adam and Giliomee, *Ethnic Power Mobilized*, p. 41.
54. Ibid., p. 52.
55. Ibid., p. 117.
56. Moodie, *The Rise of Afrikanerdom*, p. 3.
57. Ibid., pp. 5 and 11. As some Afrikaners, like some Israelis and Irish Protestants, invoke divine favor to justify settler supremacy, it is worth considering why the Old Testament plays such a prominent role in settler colonies. The reason, perhaps, lies in the harshness of the settler experience. In South Africa, for example, the Afrikaners trekking into the wilderness to escape British rule encountered a rough pioneer life. The land itself was inhospitable, especially for those accustomed to the comforts of the Cape Colony, and the hardships of nature were not the only difficulties confronting Afrikaners. Behind them lay the constant danger that Britain would expand into the new-found republics as soon as it served the purposes of the Empire. And ahead of them were the Zulus, ever threatening to reclaim the lands they thought rightfully theirs. As a result of these insecurities, Afrikaners needed faith that, as the chosen people, they would be tested severely but would ultimately overcome their many enemies. Thus their insecurity in relation to both Africans and Britain provided Afrikaners with a powerful incentive to believe in a particular kind of religion. Besides, the Old Testament does not preach mercy.
58. Ibid., p. 15.
59. Ibid., p. 164.

60. Ibid., p. 21.
61. The similarities even include such details as the devotion of both to the color orange (the Orange Order, the Orange Free State, etc.).
62. This is obviously the issue currently dividing Afrikaners, with the government proposing more or less substantive reforms and the rightwing rejecting them on the grounds that superiority is indivisible. To concede part of their heritage, they argue, is to undermine all of it.

7   Conclusion

1. Bew et al., *The State in Northern Ireland*, p. 175.
2. Padriag O'Malley, *The Uncivil Wars: Ireland Today*, Boston, Houghton Mifflin Co., 1983, pp. 87–8.
3. New Ireland Forum, *Report*, Dublin, The Stationery Office, 1984, p. 1.
4. Ibid., pp. 5 and 22.
5. Ibid., p. 37.
6. Ibid., pp. 1 and 23.
7. Ibid., p. 20.
8. *New York Times*, 20 November 1984.

Index